POLITICS OF
KNOWLEDGE

POLITICS OF
KNOW

ALSO BY RICHARD OHMANN

Shaw: The Style and the Man

English in America: A Radical View of the Profession

Politics of Letters

Selling Culture: Magazines, Markets, and Class
at the Turn of the Century

EDGE

THE COMMERCIALIZATION OF THE
UNIVERSITY, THE PROFESSIONS, AND
PRINT CULTURE

◆

RICHARD OHMANN

Foreword by Janice Radway

Wesleyan University Press   Middletown, Connecticut

Published by
Wesleyan University Press, Middletown, CT 06459
© 2003 by Richard Ohmann
All rights reserved
Printed in the United States of America
Designed by Richard Hendel
Set in Minion and Mantinia by
B. Williams & Associates

5 4 3 2 1

Library of Congress Cataloging-in-Publication Data
Ohmann, Richard M. (Richard Malin), 1931–
Politics of knowledge : the commercialization of the
university, the professions, and print culture /
Richard Ohmann ; foreword by Janice Radway.
p.   cm.
Includes bibliographical references (p.) and index.
ISBN 0–8195–6589–x (cloth : alk. paper)
ISBN 0–8195–6590–3 (pbk. : alk. paper)
1. Education, Higher–Political aspects–United States.
2. Universities and colleges–United States–Sociological
aspects.   I. Title.
LA228.O38   2003
378.73–dc21   2003050085

Most of the essays and interviews in the present work
have appeared in slightly different versions elsewhere.
A list of these prior publications, with credits and
acknowledgments, appears toward the end of the book.

CONTENTS

FOREWORD

As Richard Ohmann himself makes clear at the end of his introduction to *Politics of Knowledge*, what he offers here are diverse essays on the state of the university, the professions, and print culture. They are essays in the very best sense. Which is to say, they are *essais*—speculative yet analytical offerings—experimental meditations seeking to make sense of a fractious present through a searching inquiry into the complex particulars of an unruly past. Each essay, furthermore, is occasional in nature. Each responds thoughtfully to the specifics of the present moment at which Ohmann writes about the institution and the professional labor that has absorbed him so deeply over the years. The essays are united not only by their shared focus on the state of the university and intellectual work at the beginning of the twenty-first century, however, but also by Richard Ohmann's particular *way* of responding to the specifics of the present moment. Indeed what threads its way throughout all of these remarkable essays is Ohmann's deep conviction that responsible social and political practice can only follow from an actively constructed and *engaged* historical understanding.

I evoke the concept of engagement deliberately here because it foregrounds the notion of involvement as a kind of complex entanglement. At the same time, however, the etymology of the word "engagement" evokes the action of actively binding or promising, usually through some sort of contract; hence, the connotations that engagement carries as a form of serious commitment. Richard Ohmann's form of engagement in *The Politics of Knowledge*, it seems to me, has this rich, multilayered sense. On the one hand, he actively tries to acknowledge and understand his embeddedness or entanglement in the details and concrete particulars of the present moment within which he speaks, writes, and acts. He does so, however, not simply by looking around him with attention and critical acuity but also by actively trying to link the present with an equally complex past, which he just as actively undertakes to investigate and comprehend. His work deliberately engages the present *with* the past, then; it carefully construes the past as a way of coming to terms with all that structures and limits the present and yet still endows it with certain unrealized possibilities. Ohmann's engagement is also itself a kind of promise, therefore, a promise to attend to those unrealized possibilities. This is to be done not simply by criticizing the past but by actively remembering what it closed off and curtailed as a result of certain specific actions and events. Ohmann's most profound engagement, then, is with the nature of the present as a *link* between past and future. His writing nearly always contains a double promise; it promises to remember the past and its effects in the present even as it also promises to use that knowledge to fashion a desirable future.

Taken together, these essays present the thoughts of one of our most committed and passionate of intellectual citizens about the fate of the university and the intellectual work it once sheltered in a world vastly changed since the moment of the university's first flourishing in the United States early in the twentieth century. Indeed, Ohmann writes with both anger and sadness about the privatization of education and the increasing corporatism of colleges and universities. He shrewdly analyzes the nature of the crisis in the academic job market, especially within the humanities, and documents its connection to the growing reliance on poorly paid, temporary, part-time, and graduate student labor. Similarly, he tracks the origins of efforts by state legislatures to hold faculties accountable even as he wonders what all this has to do with the growing movements to teach technical writing in English departments and to demand that ever more research demonstrate practical application.

What all this amounts to, Ohmann suggests, is something more than a personal job crisis for an unfortunate few. It is even more consequential, he argues, than a simple transformation in the basic organization and funding of higher education. These problems, Ohmann, maintains, are symptoms and warning signals of far more consequential realignments, that is, of potentially substantial changes to the fundamental class structure of contemporary society brought about by the transformation of Fordist, industrial capitalism into a regime of flexible accumulation. What we may be witnessing, he suggests, is nothing less than the disintegration of the professional-managerial class, that complex cadre of intellectual laborers brought into being along with the suburb, the mass media, and the university around the turn of the twentieth century in order to manage a corporate and consumer economy and to educate subjects appropriate to its various sectors.

Building on the accounts of flexible accumulation ventured by Michael Aglietta and the "regulation school" of economics as well by David Harvey and others, Ohmann argues vigorously in the essays collected here that even as flexible accumulation strategies have transformed the nature of the corporation and the structure of the world economy, so, too, have they insinuated themselves into the university context. He maintains in fact that the much lamented features of the academic job crisis are only the local version of now widespread labor practices like outsourcing, subcontracting, job sharing, temp work, part-time work, piece work, home work, maquiladora schemes, and prison labor. These forms of labor have evolved as part of a vast corporate effort to address widespread problems like increasing debt, declining profits, and a turn in the U.S. trade balance. In fact, Ohmann argues, the financial crisis that is transforming colleges and universities has arisen because these larger economic problems have caused a significant decline in the portion of the social surplus going into higher education via state appropriation and private philanthropy. Cash-strapped universities respond to the situation by passing an ever greater proportion of the costs of education on to their students and by cutting costs through reorganization guided by evaluation and assessment schemes borrowed directly from the corporate sector.

Increasingly, universities rank their internal colleges and departments on the basis of productivity schemes designed to measure activities that generate revenue even as they produce new knowledge. This move has been augmented and legitimized by new legislation that has enabled universities to patent and commercialize discoveries made through research for which the federal government has paid. Ohmann astringently and ominously suggests that when this happens the logic of capital has thoroughly infiltrated the processes of inquiry, research, and knowledge production. More to the point, perhaps, this process is taking place not only in traditional institutions like Columbia where the vice provost has enthusiastically proclaimed that the university uses "knowledge as a form of venture capital"; it is also taking place, and perhaps even more insistently, in the for-profit schemes of new, proprietary colleges and universities like the University of Phoenix and in universities run by corporations for their own employees. The upshot of all this of course is that changes like these fundamentally challenge the relative autonomy of the academic disciplines to determine what is worth investigating and why. They also ultimately wrest control of the curriculum from the faculty by placing it within a market where demand is directly or indirectly created by business.

Richard Ohmann's thoughtful and clear-eyed consideration of these issues is especially chilling because *The Politics of Knowledge* is in no way a simple, nostalgic lament for the university we once knew. In fact, Ohmann understands well that the American university has *always* been tied to corporations, just as it has been bound up in the business of social reproduction. As a consequence, it has tended to enforce class distinctions and to concentrate knowledge production in ways that are conducive to state and economic interests. At the same time, however, Richard Ohmann is also a veteran of movements that sought to make the humanities curriculum more diverse, more critical, and more aware of the university's implicit politics. He knows first hand, therefore, that some PMC people—professors, doctors, and lawyers, among them—have managed to use the autonomy they enjoy as members of valorized professional guilds to ask troubling questions, to pursue inquiry wherever it may lead, and ultimately to critique the very institution that seeks to discipline knowledge on behalf of the social formation it serves. Ohmann's speculations about the consequences of the emerging situation are profoundly troubling, then, because his historical arguments so compellingly establish that what we recognize as curiosity and open-ended inquiry in fact depends upon certain social and material conditions of possibility—professional autonomy among them. And these conditions, he warns us, may well be eroding under the relentless pressure to commodify all knowledge and to subordinate its pursuit to the demand that it produce profit for a lucky, powerful few.

What is to be done? Richard Ohmann is modest enough to admit that he isn't sure. Organize on behalf of the professional-managerial class? To what end? Why argue that professors, doctors, lawyers, editors, publishers, and others ought to retain their power and prestige and their professional autonomy? Is that what we need? A politics under a banner proclaiming, "Exempt People with Advanced Degrees from the Perils of the Market," as Ohmann puts it? In fact, Ohmann is not foolish enough to believe that PMC people represent the revolutionary vanguard. On the other hand, he recognizes that a relentless process has been initiated that threatens to appropriate all human knowledge for profit. If this takes place, his book suggests, the space for ethical and political critique will have diminished considerably and the intellectual commons and public goods will themselves have suffered enclosure as thoroughly and undeniably as once did the public lands. That, clearly, would be a disturbing prospect, a future that Ohmann's bracing foray into the history of the university and the professions seeks to foreclose.

Although he admits that there isn't cause for any easy hope, Richard Ohmann does remind us that the economic forces that are fundamentally reorganizing businesses and universities alike may actually be creating conditions of possibility for the forging of new social alliances. He suggests, in fact, that as agile capital relentlessly constrains and deskills professional knowledge workers such as professors, teachers, and doctors in the very same way it did laborers, foremen, and technicians earlier in the century, it may in fact be redrawing social fault lines. This could enable those who once were divided from each other by education, income, and prestige to find common cause enough to organize in opposition to the further depredations that will almost certainly be caused by the further privatization and accumulation of all human resources in the service of the fortunate and powerful few. While this might seem like a long shot, Ohmann's profoundly responsible book makes it very clear that there is little time for delay in attempting to make it happen. Social alliances across traditional class and cultural lines simply must be forged and, while there is still time and the freedom to do so, progressive knowledge workers must find a way to contribute to this process. Richard Ohmann certainly has done his part.

Janice Radway

ACKNOWLEDGMENTS

Many of the thirteen essays that follow began as talks or invited articles. I thank all those who gave me platforms, but in particular I want to thank those who invited, urged, or wheedled me to write about topics I might not otherwise have taken up. Andre Schiffrin of the New Press overcame my reluctance to write about English and the cold war and helped me shape my thoughts. Maria-Regina Kecht organized the conference and the book of which "Teaching Historically" was a part. Brian Huot, Mary Rosner, and others at the University of Louisville asked me to take part in the first Thomas R. Watson conference, on the professionalization of composition; essay 6 is the result. My former student Mark Frankel brought me out of a funk to talk with graduate students at Buffalo on the university and the professional-managerial class; many talks and writing forays later, that effort appears here as essay 7. My first try at publishing in cyberspace, "Teaching Literacy for Citizenship," owed to Mark Bousquet and Leo Parascandola, who put together an issue of *Workplace* on composition in the managed university. Ellen Schrecker, then editor of *Academe,* persuaded me to write about accountability for her excellent journal. I am grateful to Janice Radway and Carl Kaestle, who invited me to write a chapter on books and magazines for volume 4 of a large, collaborative history of the book in the United States, who organized a fine conference for us contributors, and who gave me invaluable editorial advice; Janice Radway also generously wrote a foreword for this book. David Bleich charmed or coerced me into writing "The Personal as History." My interrogators in the two interviews that end this book—John Trimbur and Jeffrey Williams—elicited many reflections and half-baked thoughts from me that fed later writing. Finally, I give credit to Louis Kampf: for letting me praise him at his retirement symposium (see essay 3) and for thirty-five years of friendship and collaboration.

I leave out dozens of friends and fellow scholars who have helped me in ways too numerous to mention and conclude with two other kinds of help. Tom Radko and Suzanna Tamminen of the Wesleyan University Press have been precise, thoughtful, and *patient* editors.

And family: Elizabeth Powell, Nicole Polier, and Sarah Ohmann gave heart, encouragement, stimulation, and political debate. Sarah also took on the endless and almost insuperable challenge of teaching me to use the computer. William Roseberry was intellectual companion, trusted advisor, peerless commentator, learned friend, and more. I dedicate this effort to his memory.

INTRODUCTION

Many pundits, officials, and ordinary people said the attacks of September 2001 changed the world forever, propelling us into a new stage of American history, if not of human history. After the initial horror let go of my throat, I had a similar response: That's it! Thirty-five years of work for peace and justice, against what Eisenhower called the "industrial military complex," down the tubes, kaput, finito. In an hour's daredevilry the fanatics gave our leaders carte blanche to put an unthinkably powerful military apparatus into use anywhere and at any time, while voiding the Bill of Rights and wrapping themselves in the flag.

The official announcement of a new historical chapter was one of those speech acts that can help bring about what they describe. And events have in part confirmed my own dystopian fears. Yet history does not pivot on single acts. Even the murder of Archduke Ferdinand and the German invasion of Poland sprung forces already assembled and coiled. The world a year after September 11, 2001, looks a lot like the world just before that date. Hard cheese for poor countries: still another U.S.-imposed regime in Afghanistan; a neighboring military government our newest best friend (unless it makes war on India); direr and more brazen threats to dispatch the government of Iraq; the politics of oil; continued American disdain for measures to preserve the planet. And at home, those big tax cuts for rich people holding up in spite of a new fiscal crisis of the state; consumers heroically borrowing money to fight recession in the spending of it; corporate greed exposed again; another brutal education act by another Education President promising to heal the schools with discredited medications; leading liberals (Ted Kennedy, no less) collaborating with conservatives in this—as in the war on Afghanistan, the destruction of Palestine, and the rebuilding of a national security state.

At the same time, dissenters begin to perk up, declare the emperor to be seminaked, scout around for new paths of resistance. History doesn't change course in a day, nor in response to decisions made at an al-Qaeda summit in Malaysia. But societies and world systems do change, gradually if noisily, until quantity tips into quality, until analysts scan the horizon and say, "Look, globalization!" or "Look, flexible capitalism!" I'm one of those analysts. This book is about history's movement in our time, with some backward looks at the time before. My proposed moments of transition are one starting about 1970 and an earlier pivotal moment around 1900—that one a matter of wide agreement. As my subtitle indicates, I locate transition most revealingly in surges of commercialization: focusing on the production and uses of knowledge, especially in education, the academic profession, and publishing, and tying change to broader shifts in American and world capitalism.

I offer these essays, then, as a series of attempts to understand some present situations historically and some recent events as incorporated within larger historical processes. The situations and events that served as my starting points or provocations—the occasions of these talks and articles and chapters—are close in to my working and political life. A personal turn in scholarly writing; the progress and condition of literary studies; the way writing instruction has become a professional field; the use and abuse of part-time and temporary academic labor; pressures on the university to run on business principles more than in the past; the related movement to make educators accountable; hard times for the academic profession; changing dimensions of academic freedom; Louis Kampf's retirement. Two essays come out of my scholarly interest in books and magazines. These are the kinds of topic on which people invite me to speak or write, or that I choose when given the choice. Either way, I try to put my topic—an issue, problem, or crisis—in historical context. This I do out of long habit and intellectual conviction: "Always historicize," say I, with Fredric Jameson and many others. I believe that historicizing a difficulty or concern makes its dimensions clearer than they would otherwise be, and hence grounds more sensible action. That's justification enough for these essays, if they are perspicuous— and I invite the reader who agrees with me on that point to skip the remainder of this introduction for now and return to it after reading the essays, should they have stimulated in him or her a more abstract interest in what the author thinks about history and agency.

For "always historicize" is not a recipe, just a place to begin. That's because history is no ready-made set of compartments or shared story of how things happened. It is an infinitely large pile of data that historicizers can measure into a cauldron of competing hypotheses and narratives—and even data won't hold still; they depend on principles of selection and (gulp) on interpretation itself. Poststructuralism did not create this abyss of meanings; it's how things are. It's also no cause for despair. We can go right on piecing together historical episodes and connections and theories, knowing that we have no unshakable foundation on which to build truth, but knowing also that conversation and debate and testing and fresh evidence will narrow interpretive choices and make some ways of telling history's tale more compelling than others, for this or that purpose and in this or that time.

Enough of philosophical doubt for now. Indeed, although it is not my aim to refute skepticism by pointing to real history, in the way that Dr. Johnson refuted Bishop Berkeley by kicking a stone, readers of the essays and interviews gathered here will find me speaking often in confident tones about what happened and why. The war on "political correctness"? A counterattack on 1960s movements, planned with some care in conservative think tanks, and gradually endowed with respectability in Republican and neoliberal circles. The crusade for accountability? Generated at roughly the same time, in response to the same democratic movements, to Great Society educational projects and to the economic troubles that brought ample state funding of education into question. The shift from tenured and benefited to casual and ill-paid academic labor? Not a job "crisis," as often supposed, but a thirty-year-long campaign to downsize and privatize the university. The obvious weakening of our profession, along with medicine and accounting and others? A less direct consequence of privatization, which has emerged as a fairly encompassing tendency since 1970. In many of the essays I try to explain local discomforts or conflicts by setting them in broader and longer stories, with agents as strong and as familiar as capitalists and workers.

In so doing, and in the more recent of these essays, I turn again and again to the idea that American society entered a time of crisis and structural change around 1970, issuing by now in an organization of economic and social life more different from that of 1960 than 1960 was from 1920. I began testing this idea, as a speculative instrument, after reading a relatively full statement of it in David Harvey's *The Condition of Postmodernity* (Aglietta and the "regulation school" provided the underpinnings of his analysis). Harvey—and others who have proposed similar chapter breaks in the story of the twentieth century—have looked hard at the shape of the corporation, its strategies of production and marketing, its use of computer technologies, its employment practices, its international activities; at indices of economic health across the United States such as productivity, public and private debt, real wages, the rate of profit, and the balance of trade; and at global rivalries. I have put the scheme to work more locally—on changes in the university, the professions, the generation and sale of knowledge, and the making of commercial culture. In this way I try to illuminate the situations and concerns that launched my writing.

I do not intend a mechanical application of an already validated hypothesis; rather, I mean to elaborate and extend the hypothesis in different terrain and, in that process, test its reach and explanatory power. So I offer this book, second, as a contribution to a broad effort, pursued by many in addition to myself, to understand where we all are in the history of capitalism, and where we might be heading. What might solidify or even confirm the hypothesis that around 1970, the era of the large, stable corporation ("Fordism," as I will abbreviate it) gave way to an era of "flexible accumulation," with attendant transformations in university education and much else? And what could we do with that understanding, if we felt pretty sure about it?

In response to the first question, about what might confirm that an era of flexible accumulation followed Fordism, I offer a four-part answer:

1. Lots of instances, drawn from various quarters of social life (I mentioned a few in the last two paragraphs): The vertically integrated corporations that came to dominate our society in the early years of the twentieth century, blocked by strong competition from European and Japanese rivals and stagnating in domestic operations, turned to agile production and shape changing—in a wave of takeovers, bankruptcies, and spin-offs comparable only to the mergers of 1898–1900 that organized monopoly capital (Fordism) in the first place. See essay 12, "Epochal Change," for an attempt to locate book publishing and the agile media conglomerate in this framework. With monopoly capital came the modern research university that flourished through the boom years after World War II, but then began to change into something else—more market-oriented, more like a for-profit company, more agile—as described at length in essay 13, "What's Happening to the University . . . ?" Apart from examples put forward here and by scholars like Harvey, others abound that confirm the idea of major transformations around 1900 and again around 1970. At the earlier date, for instance mass media (magazines, then broadcasting) came forward, selling the audience's attention to advertisers—a development critical to marketing by and for the giant corporation. Structurally comparable, I think, was the elaboration of

computer technologies after 1970 that facilitated agile business practices of all kinds, including the fragmentation of Fordism's mass audience into niche markets. Or, in a seemingly remote area of life, think of the emergence around 1900 of a campaign for progressive education, in the context of the Progressive movement as a whole; and a similar campaign to transform education at all levels that accompanied the civil rights, feminist, antiwar, and student uprisings in the 1960s and after.

2. A coherent picture: Obviously, a collection of examples like these, no matter how long, would have no more interest than a list of events confirming the prophecies of Nostradamus, without some idea of how the changes came together to form social orders—Fordism, then flexible capitalism.

3. An account of agency: Of which groups acted powerfully, in conflict with some and with the support of others, to transform society. My account stresses the agency of American capitalists, but at both pivotal moments under intense pressure: in the 1890s, from militant workers and from conditions of intolerable risk created by capitalists' own failure to regulate their conduct; in the 1970s and after, from a similar failure to rein in postwar extravagance and from Japanese and European capitalists. At both these junctures, as always, many other groups sought advantage, contended for power, allied themselves with capitalist reformers, and so on. But at both junctures, also, the urgencies of big capital were decisive.

4. More explanatory power than rival hypotheses: Did major changes in university education since 1970 result from the Vietnam War and the reaction it stirred against "golden age" arrangements, including public funding of research for cold war purposes, as Louis Menand argues?[1] Did the marketizing of higher education result from an accumulation of administrative responses to the recessions that have come along at ten-year intervals since the early 1970s, as David W. Breneman argues?[2] I found both these suggestions (upon which I happened as I prepared to write this introduction) helpful and in part compatible with my hypothesis, but not so broad in their reach. It is not for me to decide; and in any case, this is no place to array my ideas in battle formation against other contenders, especially those like Menand and Breneman, whom I imagine as like-minded colleagues working through the same puzzle. My point is that the testing of historical overviews always involves such competitive comparison and negotiation.

So, while I neither set out to argue for a particular story of capitalism nor claim to have made a tight case for it, I hope this book will be of some help to others who think the world has changed more than incrementally in recent decades.

On to the second question: how might we act upon this belief, if we had it? Well, to put the worst apprehension of a compulsive historicizer up front, people of the Left might sensibly grab a beer from the fridge and relax, having concluded that historical pressures will always grind down the good efforts of peace activists, environmentalists, and egalitarians of all kinds, not to mention those of educational workers. If whenever we look at problem—the exploitation of adjuncts, the imposition of high-stakes tests, and so on—we see behind it only the faceless engine of history, that knowledge can paralyze rather than empower. What point in organizing graduate students if their administrative antagonists are little more than foot soldiers in the march of flexible capitalism? The story of traditional unions during that march is grimly instructive. They won battles against one company and another, but the advantages held by capital as a whole—flexible labor practices, global mobility—are gradually pushing the unions out of manufacturing and manufacturing out of the United States. Furthermore, the horses of history are driven, visibly enough, by the hand of the corporation at the reins of politics, bringing on (as I think Gore Vidal has quipped) the rule of our country by a single political party with two right wings, and the regime of international trade agreements and agencies that level the playing field for capital by shooing the other teams right off it.

Does anyone want more reasons to skip tonight's political meeting and get on with private life? Think then about the commodification of leisure, knowledge, education, desire, even anger; commodification whispering that there's nothing but private life, that people can heal any grief with a purchase, that they are consumers before they are citizens, or citizens only by acting as consumers. Think of the ad man, shouting that you can fix the conflicts and abrasions of city life by bounding up a remote canyon in your SUV. Contemplate the wall of ideology put up to separate Americans from political and historical understanding. Think about who owns the media that keep that wall in repair—not because Time Warner and News Corporation and the rest have a contract with General Electric and Microsoft to put out corporate propaganda but because the media conglomerates are corporations too, which must make a profit and must hail us as a passive audience of consumers in order to do that. See how compliantly those media help our leaders build on fear and hijack patriotism to cement world domination.

There's nothing new in most of this: the history makers have had such weapons for a long time. Yet domination is never permanent, never secure. Popular movements joined with capital's own incompetence to shake the hegemonic arrangements of the 1920s and create an American version of the welfare state, many of whose premises hold today in spite of vigorous challenges from the right. The social movements of the 1960s added democratic inclusiveness along new dimensions. Again, those gains are under challenge, but the premise of equality has far wider assent now than fifty years ago: even most enemies of affirmative action claim to be friends of racial and sexual equality, and must so claim, at least publicly, or lose their standing in political discussion. Thus an account of historical pressures that makes them sound or feel like iron law would blind us to the real and effective agency of dissidents even in the recent past. And to represent the present, emerging social order, however powerful its advocates, as heralding the end of history would be crazy as well as dangerous. Agile capitalism is no more solid than other hegemonic arrangements. In fact almost surely less so, because change at breakneck speed will bring more surprises and collisions than will gradual change. Capitalism's destructive force could for the first time split off from and outrun its creative genius. Deep wounds to the natural world are but the most obvious example.

But let's draw back from imagining the convulsions in social life that environmental catastrophe (or nuclear war) would bring on. Short of such desperate days, there could be a day for popular forces to band together and reassert agency, to take history back from the international hotshots and oilmen and casino capitalists and grafters who made the 1990s hum, but who now fall into convulsions they brought upon themselves and, perhaps by the time this book sees print, experience a palpable decline in their own clarity of purpose, their own agency. Stirring words, a bracing challenge. But to do what? Should the balance of agency indeed shift, to what end might we direct our efforts? And remember that, barring a brilliant success on the talk show circuit, I here address these thoughts not to the millions and not to the leadership of al-Qaeda or to some unimaginable band of domestic Che Guevaras, but to you, my friends: teachers and graduate students and knowledge workers (I hope) of various stripes, facing economic and professional hardships. How might the maxim of local action and global vision apply? The immediate task will be organizing as teaching assistants, saving the XYZ program and its full-time instructors, trying to recapture science for the people and not for profit, fighting school voucher programs, and the like. How to relate such conflicts to the modulation of Fordism into turbocapitalism?

A specific difficulty, in this effort, is that the local campaigns most often erupt in response to worsening conditions; "they" are taking something away from "us." We fight to keep them from succeeding or to restore what we have lost. Generalize a particular defensive maneuver, and it becomes (e.g.) a struggle to save tenure, to keep research findings and "courseware" in the faculty's charge, to regain control over curriculum from legislatures and trustees, and so on. Generalize one level higher, and all these fights are about winning back rights and privileges that the academic profession enjoyed forty years ago, or defending what remains of professionalism now. More than understandable. But if the historical narrative sketched in some of the following essays is a roughly accurate picture of what's happening, the profession's autonomy and market power in 1965 were specific to an earlier phase in the development of American universities, of the professions, and of the Fordist economic and social order itself.

Can an element of that order—say tenure and academic freedom (see essay 10)—be rescued and made new apart from the rest, like a 1964 Mustang from the junkyard? I doubt it. Perhaps faculty members and students at Southwestern State can rally to stop the administration from abolishing the geography department and firing its tenured members. This may be a worthy cause as well as a decent one, especially if the geographers are a critical and prickly bunch whose departure would save the administration trouble as well as money. What defenders of tenure should not suppose is that one victory after another in such crises would in time restore the tenure system itself to the role it played in 1965. (They also should not suppose that groups they count on as allies, such as adjunct instructors, will share the tenured faculty's fondness for this particular form of job security; but that's another story.) You can't go home again if it's somebody else's home now.

And if the whole town has been bypassed and abandoned, or gentrified out of your price range. . . .Well, without riding that metaphor out to the end of the line, it should be obvious that nostalgia for a lost time is little help as a political guide and may easily stand as a barrier. There's no chance of reconstituting Fordism, and without that, no chance of rebuilding the public service megaversity that University of California president Clark Kerr described in the 1960s, with the liberal arts at its imaginary center. Departments and programs and even whole (wealthy) colleges may keep a residual academic culture alive. There is of course a still-powerful ideology of classical education, great books, Mark Hopkins at one end of a log and his student at the other, even Plato's academy, upon which to draw in anathematizing universities that sell Western Civilization short: fifteen years ago, Stanford; as I write this introduction, Chicago. The American Council of Trustees and Alumni attributed the university's deficiency in patriotism after September 11 to its having given up on core courses in U.S. history and Western civilization. But to imagine that even such factions, aligned with Lynne and Dick Cheney, think possible and desirable a return to the system of postsecondary education that prevailed in 1960 is absurd. The more so, for people of the democratic Left with some sense of history to hope and work for such an outcome. History will not stall out in this stage of capitalist development, but neither can the Left rewind it to a golden moment of our choosing, any more than the Right can rewind it to a time when capitalism ran on prayer and family values.

In any case, to organize for the return to lost privilege of English, or the academic profession, or the university, or the professional-managerial class, would set us—any such us—against multitudes who had less privilege than we in the old order and have themselves lost ground since 1970. How will the former steelworker now at Dairy Queen and the mom shoved off welfare with no job training or decent child care respond to bumper stickers bearing the slogan I imagine in one of these essays: "Exempt People with Advanced Degrees from the Perils of the Market"? Such an objection will carry no weight with the National Association of Scholars, but progressive academics will want to take it seriously, not because we want the working class to like us but because we need allies in similar historical positions.

The depressing yet hopeful truth, here, is that flexible capitalism has put in similar positions all sorts of people who were previously divided by lines of guild, union, education, gender, class, and political commitment. The welfare mother and the former steelworker share with the teaching assistant in rhetoric a likely future of insecure, ill-paid, part-time jobs. Programmers in Silicon Valley, maquiladora workers along the Rio Grande, and organizers for environmental justice in the Pacific Northwest have in common a vulnerability to the stateless agility of global capital and its increasing power to override mere national protections for labor and the natural world. From such observations to global alliances that build on them is a huge step, surely as daunting a task as moving from "You have nothing to lose but your chains" to a unity of the world's industrial workers before and during Fordism. I mentioned two particular commonalties of disparate groups, above, because they have in fact served as the basis for incipient political groupings. TAs have affiliated with traditional unions, and sometimes with other campus workers; could they be on a front line in building solidarity across groups that do casual labor? Protest against globalization is unsteady so far and dependent on groups that could evanesce tomorrow, but it has brought together coalitions of unionists, environmentalists, students, anarchists, and others whose unity and zeal in a loosely anticapitalist cause would have been hard to imagine before the demonstrations that took place in Seattle in 1999 against various organizations of world trade and finance.

It's easy to think of other commonalties. Higher education and public school systems encounter different but deeply related forces of privatization (e.g., the need to turn faculty research into revenue; voucher schemes). Primary through secondary school teachers must conform to state-mandated curricula and high-stakes testing; college faculties face different but (again) connected demands for "accountability." Contrasting work regimes, professional structures, and degrees of privilege have long kept relations tender between these two groups. Maybe the campaign to push both into the universal market will open the way to new alliances. Those could widen to include other hard-pressed service workers and professions. People in health care are an obvious example, as their work comes increasingly under the management of nonprofessionals and is tailored to urgencies of the balance sheet. Or, at another former boundary, professors might connect with technicians and other knowledge workers, in and out of the university, over use of the Internet for public good rather than private gain, and, more generally, over questions of intellectual property.

It's not my purpose here to set down an agenda for organizing. Who am I to do that anyhow? The point is just that agile capital has erased some old social fault lines. Professors and managers can be downsized along with line workers. The imperative to outsource high-paid work is as potent in the university now as in industry. Privatizers look as calculatingly at higher education and at the public schools as they did at health care twenty-five years ago. Corporations can take advantage of the low cost of educating engineers and programmers in other countries, as they do of low wages for girls in Asian Nike factories. Some of these likenesses may make new alliances possible. All such likenesses invite those wanting to resist the degradation of academic labor and do so in the context of inclusive and democratic movements to think critically about old political habits, and imagine new strategies for the economic world we now inhabit.

No matter how ingenious, an academic labor movement or an alliance against high-stakes testing will not derail turbocapitalism, but it may help define its vulnerable spots while winning a few small victories. Beyond that, no political work around the topics I explore in this book will trouble the apparent resolve of our leaders to run the world as a police state, ignore the aspirations of its peoples, burn oil until it's gone or we roast or both, and line the pockets of the rich at whatever cost. I see hard times ahead, brought on in part by our leaders' ignorance and gross disregard of, well, history. Their master narrative comes out of Apocalypse by way of Main Street verities, and its erasure of history is evident in their use of "evil" as an analytic category. As I write, the system over which they preside is bumping into its home-made historical contradictions. September 11 did not change everything, but may have hastened along the instability of the loony system at which the loony terrorists lashed out. I wish I understood the world better than I do. This book is an *essai* in that direction.

ENGLISH AND THE COLD WAR

◆

I wrote almost all the essays in this book after the Soviet Union had broken apart, and a number of them reflect a need to understand how the world changed for us academics at the end of the 1980s, partly by trying to understand how we lived and were shaped by the history of the cold war period itself. Although this essay appeared in 1997 after several of the others, I lead with it because it includes my fullest treatment of the latter topic.

When the lines of the cold war firmed up, English was a pastoral retreat within the university.[1] Its practitioners celebrated verbal art and Anglo-American high culture. Little disturbed their tranquility beyond a dispute as to whether textual analysis or historical and philological scholarship was to ground their claims to disciplinarity. Few outside the field and almost none outside university cared, so long as English took care of the familiar classics and taught "frosh" to write passable themes.

When the lines of the cold war crumbled, many outside the university cared a good deal about what English was up to. The political Right was noisily attacking it and the rest of the humanities for abdicating curatorship of the great books, abandoning traditional values, and subverting the social order. Mainstream media transmitted and amplified the exposé of multiculturalism and political correctness. Unsettling as this hostile publicity was, it could not be written off as gratuitous. English had indeed charged out of its quiet retreat, turned a critical eye on the social order, challenged many core beliefs and values, and sharply revised its cultural mission. No such defection is ever unanimous; the culture wars go on intramurally, too. Yet, in the forty years of the cold war, the field's center shifted left (for want of a better word). Its leaders are guilty as charged of multiculturalism—of what

the Right sees as cultural treason. Its new recruits are inducted into practices and perspectives that would have seemed scandalous to the generation
that shaped it in the postwar period. Almost no one saw English as "political" then. Now, the politics of literary culture are inescapable and, to many,
welcome.

How did such a change come about? The obvious explanations—Vietnam,
civil rights, feminism, other movements, the subsequent conservative restoration—are right but incomplete, because they do not explain why other
fields have not taken a parallel course to that of English and its neighbors.
So let us consider how English was specially located in the postwar university and the consensus of the early cold war.

I note with some bemusement that an argument can be made—*has* been
ingeniously made, by William H. Epstein—that the Yale English Department
in particular was there before the outset, laying foundations of cold war intelligence work and cold war ideology.[2] Epstein's argument places Yale criticism and scholarship at the origins and near the 1950s center of cold war
thought and method. He does not suggest that people in the field, other perhaps than a very few knowing ones, pursued their academic work in full
awareness of these relations or in service to a Central Intelligence Agency
formulation of the national interest. Rather, the milieu of English at Yale was
one in which tropes of textual analysis and ways of organizing knowledge
that had funded cold war intelligence at the outset retained their allure and
urgency.

But if English helped launch the cold war, it reaped few tangible rewards.
To think of basic and applied science in U.S. universities, powerfully shaped
throughout the period by lavish government and especially military funding
is instantly and obviously to see literary studies as a poor relation, an indirect beneficiary, at most, of scraps of "overhead" redistributed by administrations to the shabbier precincts. Or think of area studies, wrestled into existence and prosperity by the State Department, the CIA, Office of Strategic
Services (OSS) alumni, the Ford Foundation, and so on; nourished by cold
war contracts, prestigious consultancies, the traffic back and forth to Washington; profoundly changing the shape of graduate education and research
in the postwar university.

These two interventions alone substantially remade universities along the
lines of a cold war blueprint. There are many lesser instances: anthropology
mobilized for knowledge and control of subaltern peoples and sometimes

recruited into secret counterinsurgency efforts; linguistics backed in its years of major development by the military and by various arms of the foreign service (not always with the intended results); political science funded in some places (including the American Political Science Association itself) by the CIA and other cold war sources; free market and "developmental" economics the same; and in these last two fields the seductions of prestige and influence, of direct and indirect participation in the making of national policy. The list could go on through less vital symbioses between the cold war state and psychology, foreign-language instruction, even history, with its abundance of prominent OSS alumni,[3] and doubtless other fields.

Whatever ties existed between English and the OSS during the war, whatever reinforcement English offered to cold war thought and feeling afterward, whatever fields of force brought English into conformity with national purpose, meager indeed were the tangible inducements to serve it, in comparison to those visibly and persuasively offered to many other disciplines. Were there *secret* inducements of weight and consequence? Imprudent to dismiss the idea, given later revelations about CIA cultural politics: its funding of the Congress for Cultural Freedom, the money channeled to journals and publishers, the dummy foundations, secret funding of and intervention in the National Student Association, and so on—all this activity directed, incidentally, by agent Thomas W. Braden, formerly of the English Department at Dartmouth. The established foundations supported the cold war rhetoric. In the case of the Guggenheim Foundation, its president, Henry Allen Moe, thundered in his biennial reports on behalf of freedom and against those who would restrain it, proclaimed loyalty to the nation our highest duty, held that scholarship led to a strong United States, and promised that no member of the Communist Party would receive Guggenheim funding.[4]

But when one thinks, again, of patronage in other fields, and of the fact that far and away the largest amount of support for literary research in the 1950s came from the sabbatical programs of individual colleges and universities, all these suppositions and hunches about funding seem a distraction. Literary practitioners did not live close to the corridors of power, as did people in many other fields. I never wondered why my own teachers and other important people in literary studies stayed home, why they did not serve on blue ribbon commissions, why no one sought their advice on the Cuban missile crisis. English was not producing action intellectuals; as a body of knowledge it had nothing to offer (in post-OSS days) to the managers of global affairs.

By the 1950s, too, secrecy seemed an inevitable condition of world politics, of special knowledge in science and beyond. Others were in charge of those matters; we lacked not only their expertise but also the right to know how they were deploying it and the right to voice encouragement or criticism, except for an occasional scandal such as the U-2 incident that lifted the veil of secrecy. Real history was someone else's business. Literary studies went along on history's margin, with little cold war money and excluded from policy circles.

No one invited us to play the great game. We also *chose* our comfortable distance, with who knows what mixture of sour grapes and righteousness.[5] Not for us the battle against international communism. Our spokesmen, Modern Language Association presidents and the like, might put on the rhetoric of freedom and democracy at ceremonial moments, but, dwelling in our house of Culture, we disdained crass patriotism, reviled McCarthy and lesser anticommunists as know-nothings, looked down our noses at the bland pragmatism of the Eisenhower administration. At the core of our ethos was an antagonism toward business, commerce, and commodity culture. Eagerly though we acquired stereos, books, eventually cars and houses, we managed to define ourselves as dropouts from the acquisitive society. A hundred years after Matthew Arnold, we adhered with just a bit of uneasiness to his critique of the philistines, often seen in 1950s America as all but indistinguishable from the aspiring populace. We lived the ideology—well analyzed by Raymond Williams in *Culture and Society* of Culture as somehow apart from society and offering to redeem it, however deaf the ears into which we whispered the offer.

In short, English and its neighbors struck an ambivalent posture of disengagement from and antagonism toward the postwar project of untrammeled capitalist development and U.S. dominance in the world. Literary theory and its attendant practices underwrote the disengagement. New Criticism, in this time of its hegemony, took on the task through its insistence on the autonomy of the literary work. Leading theorists such as I. A. Richards, Cleanth Brooks, W. K. Wimsatt, John Crowe Ransom, Alan Tate, and their gray eminence, T. S. Eliot, differed on some points, but their ideas fused into a catechism of denials: the "intentional fallacy": to equate a work's meaning with its author's intention, and so connect it with his or her actual life; the "affective fallacy": to locate the work in its impact on readers; the "heresy of paraphrase": to associate it with any propositional content. By such maneuvers the New Critics severed poetry from historical process, distinguished it from other practical uses of language, and defined the experience of it as a peculiarly intransitive state of consciousness.

Less explicit but crucial was their separation of that experience from action: "Poetry makes nothing happen," wrote Auden in his poem "In Memory of W. B. Yeats," and the New Critics seconded the motion.

Instead, poetry achieves a reordering and unification of experience, as is clear in the reasons given by New Critics for setting such extraordinary value as they do on irony, ambiguity, tension, and paradox, in critical practice: these devices are important for their "resolution of apparently antithetical attitudes" [157] which both daily life and science leave in dissonance. This idea has its origin, for New Criticism, in Richards's *Principles of Literary Criticism*, where a "balanced poise" [247] of the attitudes plays a central and almost therapeutic role. Richards supposes that our cultural sickness is an imbalance of attitudes and impulses and that poetry can set us right by helping us achieve a state of equilibrium. The more discordant elements drawn into this unity, the more effective the poetry—for this reason Richards praises tragedy as "perhaps the most general, all accepting, all ordering experience known" [247]. And Brooks says that the good poems manage a "unification of attitudes into a hierarchy subordinated to a total and governing attitude. In a unified poem the poet has 'come to terms' with his experience." Now, putting together these suggestions with Eliot's famous diagnosis of a "dissociation of sensibility" in the modern world, I see a sequence of this sort: The world is complex, discordant, dazzling. We want desperately to know it as unified and meaningful, but action out in the world fails to reveal or bring about a satisfying order. The order we need is available in literature.[6]

Thus:

The value of poetry transcends the values of individual poems and poets and lies not in urging one or another moral view but in embracing ('coming to terms with') ethical complexities. A proper reading of poetry neutralizes and flattens out not only impulses toward action but perhaps even those toward moral judgment. Poetry, capital P, can prefer no one value system or course of action but accepts and comprehends all values, all actions, and in fact everything that makes up reality.[7]

We can "come to terms" with dissonance in social life by "containing it, by striking balanced attitudes, as a successful poet does." Through this set of ideas, New Criticism made its own small contribution to the "end of ideology," much celebrated in the postwar period, and to the eclipse of history and politics. Needless to say, literary theory in this vein also answered well to the need for validation of our claims to professional standing by setting off the object of our knowledge from the subjects of other disciplines and authorizing an equally distinct method of study and teaching.

New Criticism was not of course the only contender for dominance in literary studies, but other, contending schools produced similar ideologies. Chicago critics called for a "pluralistic" criticism that would take systems of thought as premises for inquiry rather than as competing doctrines and reduce values to methodological preferences. Northrop Frye's influential *Anatomy of Criticism* allied literature and our work with the vision of a society "free, classless, and urbane," very different, surely, from the society we actually inhabited. Many in literary studies embraced an existentialism stripped away from the politics of its European origins and taken to represent us as lone individuals in company with our acts and our death.[8] Americanists began to theorize our history around hero myths, and invited us to split off the United States from Europe, class conflict, empire. Race, when not simply ignored, became a trope or a matter of original sin. In general, we reached for timeless universals in our understanding of texts: love, death, art, suffering, apart from the squalid mess of history.

Though rather smugly aloof from the trials and triumphs of U.S. capital, we were of course also beneficiaries of both, as universities expanded rapidly to meet its needs, including (especially in the post-Sputnik period) the perceived need to compete economically, as well as militarily, with the Soviet Union. The rising tide lifted English along with engineering, math, and science, largely because composition and introductory literature courses were embedded in the structure of university requirements, but also because in those flush times many undergraduates felt at economic liberty to concentrate in the impractical humanities. Departments grew and jobs proliferated even beyond the ability of old and new Ph.D. programs to meet the demand. Salaries rose from their rather austere postwar levels to levels that almost matched our sense of professional dignity. (Friends marketing themselves at the end of my first year in graduate school, 1953, accepted salaries of around $3,000; when I took an assistant professorship in 1961, it paid $6,400, if memory serves—more than my father had made in his last year as full professor and department head at the downtown college of Western Reserve University in 1945, before leaving for industry in despair of raising a family on an academic salary.)

In materially improving circumstances we brought into the ideology of the professional-managerial class, even as we abstained from the more public and explicit ideology of the cold war system that supported it. We were for the advancement of knowledge, trust in expertise, professional autonomy, cultivation of the individual, advancement through merit, and so on; these attitudes put us at ease in the liberal universities that employed us, grumble though we might about the ascendancy of science, law, and business. More, we held that our work for Culture was in the *real* interest of American society. If only it would pay attention, we could help raise it out of the commercial crassness and jingoist anti-intellectualism that somehow kept diverting it from a nobler historical mission.

So I propose locating English, through the 1950s and early 1960s, in a safe eddy of postwar development, and also in a latent contradiction with respect to the main current. With close to 9 percent of gross national product going into military production on average and about 25 percent to total government spending, the cold war "solved" U.S. capitalism's problem of lagging demand and stimulated the economy to hectic expansion. It carried higher education and the professional-managerial class along with it. Literary studies were an integral if minor part of the military-industrial-government-university complex and claimed a residual share in its spoils. But unlike many other fields, English was not recruited to fight the cold war, not given special inducements, not directly shaped by cold war imperatives. Sidelined thus, people in the humanities were relatively free to cultivate their own interests, in both senses, and to regard the cold war from the standpoint of outsiders. On the whole, we went along unthinkingly with the ideology of the free world, though with no racing of the blood—after all, the Soviets were no threat to our freedom. We condemned, when we did not simply ignore, their harsh regime and those contiguous with it from Berlin to North Korea. But we dissented from the militarization of U.S. society, abhorred the bomb and "brinksmanship," disavowed alliances with dictatorships, had little use for "intelligence," and dissociated ourselves from much of what others thought an incomparable, American way of life, as well as from the project of American business that produced our comfort.

We also (to repeat) were repelled by official anticommunism, not to mention the McCarthy version. A memory: afternoons watching the army-McCarthy hearings over a beer, at Cronin's in Harvard Square; transcendent vulgarity, the senator's main offense to our cultural amour propre; Harold Ickes, I think, referred to his work as a "scabious putrescence"; and that pretty well summed it up for us. Danger? Hardly, for what did we humanists have to do with the Communist Party, and besides, had the Harvard Corporation not made our university safe for anticommunism by (ambivalently) defending Wendell Furry's Fifth Amendment stand against the House Committee on Un-American Activities? The witch-hunters carried on their shameful crusade at a vast distance from "us," posing no threat to the civilizing mission or the professional aggrandizement of academic humanists—so, many of us thought.

We matched up narrow self-interest to ideological dreams and felt pretty safe. But of course the witch-hunts did *not* bypass all of "us." Among people fired for refusing to testify or for taking the Fifth Amendment, usually for the honorable purpose of protecting former comrades, were a number of mainly tenured, academic humanists: Edwin Berry Burgum (English, New York University), Lyman Bradley (German, New York University; for many years treasurer of the MLA), Joseph Butterworth (English, University of Washington), Herbert Phillips (philosophy, Reed), Harry Slochower (German, Brooklyn College), M. I. Finley (classics, Rutgers), Barrows Dunham (philosophy, Temple). Others left before they could be fired (Margaret Schlauch (English, New York University), Saul Maloff (English, Indiana). Many were in effect blacklisted, including Kenneth Burke, turned away from a temporary job at the University of Washington in its time of purges and paranoia.

This roster, carefully assembled by Ellen Schrecker in *No Ivory Tower*,[9] bespeaks no protected enclave for humanists. How did those of us entering the profession in the McCarthy moment register the news? I began graduate study in 1952, and can recall nothing: no bulletins about the latest atrocities, no huddles of fearful or angry teaching assistants, no warnings from our elders, no petitions or meetings in support of persecuted scholars, nothing—except that generalized contempt for McCarthyism and assurance that it had no bearing on the conditions of our own study and employment. Did we think the firings had no lesson or warning for us, because the purged were a different species, some of them weird enough actually to have joined the

Communist Party? By intention or not, the repression encouraged such a distancing, along with the latent idea that it was one thing to derogate business and consumer society from the airy vantage point of Culture but quite another—and less savory—thing to join an organization dedicated to their overthrow.

The purged were not the only ones caught up in these events, some prominent humanists enlisted, reluctantly or righteously, in the anticommunist crusade. Those who preached its gospel or named names or both included the prominent critic Robert Gorham Davis, historian (later librarian of Congress) Daniel Boorstin, historian of ideas Arthur O. Lovejoy (his *Great Chain of Being* a required text for aspirants in English), and philosophers Sidney Hook and James Burnham. Lesser complicity was common, as with Lionel Trilling, who helped draft Columbia's instructions for faculty testimony before the House Committee on Un-American Activities (HUAC), and Robert Heilman, head of English at the University of Washington, who conceded in a memo to its president that his department had in the past harbored too many leftists, and promised to avoid that error in the future.[10] Such interventions, like the firings, are more striking when retrospectively lumped together than they were at that time, when they occurred sporadically and when some were unknown or only locally noted. Still, there were messages for those of us on the sidelines, in our leaders' acts and failures to act.

The disdain toward witch-hunting achieved little organizational form or activist power. Major academic institutions evaded issues, sought compromises, remained silent. Universities let HUAC and anticommunist trustees set the agenda: they advised faculty members to come clean; they accepted and used FBI information; they set up their own inquisitions. Few indeed were those, such as the University of Buffalo, that flat out refused the hysteria. (Harvard, for all its self-commendation over the Furry case, was not of that honorable company.) Few were willing to hire the purged—even those, such as M. I. Finley, with superb credentials. Their guild organization, the American Association of Universities, publicly stated that administrations and faculty members had a duty to cooperate with investigators, and that faculty members who declined were probably not fit to teach.[11] The American Association of University Professors ducked appeals for help from faculty fired or under fire, and, through a combination of ineptness and fear, remained silent on the witch-hunts until 1956, when they were over. Even the

American Civil Liberties Union, internally divided on these questions, held back comment until that time.[12] As I noted earlier, the Guggenheim Foundation announced a blanket exclusion of Communists from its beneficence. The MLA championed foreign-language instruction as serving the national interest[13] and held its tongue about purged members. Nor did our professional leadership find other ways to fight specific repressions, as opposed to lamenting the general phenomenon.

What, then, did we learn from the cold war battles actually fought on our turf, especially those of us apprenticing in the early 1950s? We learned that the state could pry into and severely punish our affiliations and politics, with the cooperation of our employers, dedicated as they supposedly were to freedom of thought; that, in fact, we were *less* free than other workers to challenge power, because of the special obligations we took on with our special privilege;[14] that the stigmatized could expect little if any help from our professional and scholarly organizations, and not much from ad hoc groups of colleagues. All this was plain enough.

Slightly more oblique instruction was available on some other points of conduct. We could freely teach and do research within reasonably broad limits, but activism was risky, and membership in at least one political organization—perhaps, then, others—was suicidal. By extension, to be a professional was to be nonpartisan, to abstain from historical agency. Practitioners of literary studies, like those in all fields, should stay within their own areas of expertise. Not only professional interests but also safety argued for an investment in the autonomy of each field. (The chair of my department strongly discouraged me in 1954 from taking a course on the philosophy of literature: what would he have said to one on the political economy of culture had such a course—unimaginably—existed?) At the same time, each field of inquiry must somehow align itself with all the rest, in the national interest. At an abstract level, truth must be the handmaiden of loyalty.

And of course one emphasis, in teaching and scholarship, did lie outside those broad limits of the thinkable: historical materialism. Marxism disappeared from the academy; the tradition dried up. The handful of its surviving adherents in the humanities—Gaylord Leroy, Robert Cohen, Norman Rudich, Paul Siegel, perhaps a dozen in all?—were isolated from one another, from interested students, from scholars in other fields (Paul Baran, at Stanford, was reputedly the only Marxist economist in any American university), from political allies and projects. Right across the humanities and social

sciences, this exclusion shut down certain kinds of inquiry, posted "no tres-
passing" signs around some topics (notably class struggle), and sanitized
others, such as exploitation and power. In English and neighboring fields,
the loss was, if not more damaging, at least more peculiar in its consequences: it left us with our moral critique of bourgeois society from the
standpoint of culture, while excising culture *from* bourgeois society, severing
it from its real historical and social relations, and exempting it from historical critique, as history declined into "background," biography, influence
studies, history of ideas, and the other maneuvers of sealed-off "literary"
history. The exile of historical materialism, along with the confidence inspired by expansion and prosperity, also turned attention away from the
conditions of our own cultural work and professional consolidation—away
from our embeddedness in relations of class and power, not to mention race,
gender, sexuality, and those other matters that had to be discovered or rediscovered from the late 1960s on.

The provincial flavor of this account is intentional. Needless to say, historical materialism remained a working tradition in Europe and elsewhere
through the 1950s, but literary studies in the United States paid little attention to Lukacs, Brecht, Goldmann, Adorno, the Marxian Sartre, even left cultural critique from Britain—though we appropriated Richards, Eliot, and
what was usable from Empson for New Criticism, and Leavis had a small,
embattled following. American military and economic dominance fostered
academic insularity and arrogance as well. The only continental European
work I remember as "must" reading for us was Auerbach's *Mimesis,* mined
for the brilliance of its formalism, with its history muted.

In the intellectual and institutional space demarcated by those cold war
intimidations, by U.S. world domination, by the rewards proffered for disciplinarity and socialization, and by the benign neglect of literary studies in
centers of power, an elaboration of structures and practices went forward
that has by now been the subject of extensive analysis. I wrote about it at
length myself, in the central chapters of *English in America* and will not
reprise the discussion here, beyond saying that its main theme still seems
apt, whatever amendments and corrections I would now make (see my 1996
introduction). That theme was the concealment and mystification of conflict, power, and privilege: in literary theory and criticism, in the curriculum,
in departments and professional organizations, in writing instruction, in
pedagogy. Practitioners of English sang the beneficence of Culture in the

abstract without taking account of the relations and institutions through which Culture circulates—without taking account of Culture's role in social reproduction and the hegemonic process, as I would later have put. Literary studies played a small part in the cold war, not by selling our unwanted expertise, not by perfecting the ideology of free world and evil empire, but by doing our best to take politics out of culture and by naturalizing the routines of social sorting.

Nonetheless, I want to reemphasize here, as I did not in *English in America*, the ways English defined itself in *opposition* to the social arrangements on the American side of the cold war—though not of course in support of those on the Soviet side. I have mentioned the mild critique of commercial culture and the business ethos that we brought with us to graduate study or took in as a corollary of our dedication to high culture, and have suggested that New Criticism, with its defense of poetry over and against the language of science, encouraged or at least accommodated such a critique. So did the theories of Russian formalism, when, at first mainly through the presence and work of Roman Jakobson, they came into our ken and were grafted onto New Criticism: literature as a special language or special use of language, one that lifted it from dull routine, estranged it, renewed its materiality, freshened consciousness. Those who embraced existentialism found another way to demote the categories of bourgeois morality, as did partisans of the modernist writers: ill-assorted and politically discrepant as they were, Eliot, Joyce, Woolf, Lawrence, Hemingway, Faulkner, Dos Passos, and so on all ranged themselves against industrial capitalism and counterposed something finer in the realm of avant-garde culture. Traditionalists in literary studies, who promoted the Great Books conception of the humanities and were often hostile to modernism, also deplored capitalist reality, though from the vantage point of the classical or Catholic or monarchist past.

Many but not all of these groups abstained, also, from nationalist fervor and from U.S. triumphalism in particular. America was raw and philistine; Europe cared about culture. Anglophilia colored the outlook of many— unsurprisingly, when one recalls that "English" did chiefly mean English, for people in our field in the 1950s. American literature had barely gained academic recognition. (Graduate students at Harvard could "specialize" in American literature only by substituting it for the medieval period, as one of the five fields on which to be quizzed in our Ph.D. examinations.) To the extent that American culture *had* become a legitimate field of study, in English and in the few American studies programs of the time, the judgment of scholars was mixed: alongside preservationist and triumphalist efforts, influential studies by left liberals such as Leo Marx, Henry Nash Smith, and the less easily classified Leslie Fiedler refused to whitewash American history, and allowed some nonelite voices to be heard, thus quietly heralding the "anti-American studies" of the 1960s and after. Of course few of those nonelite voices were female and virtually none were black, but oppositional undertones resonated; some younger people in English began listening to the Beats and, by the end of the 1950s, to Norman Mailer on the "White Negro."

Hardly the making of a counterculture in English, and the skepticism among us toward the cold war and the American project of development was entangled with complacencies of class, whiteness, and a still unquestioned male supremacy. Furthermore the spirit of vague alienation that permeated much of our training and work almost never spilled out into political activity, beyond voting Democratic. The exception, and an interesting one, was antinuclear work (I and a few in my cohort went on marches with the Committee for a Sane Nuclear Policy; a few were Quaker activists). It is worth remembering that for many of my age, graduate school was an alternative to the draft, and that those who chose the profession after Korean War service had gained little enthusiasm for cold war police actions. "Brinkmanship" scared us; the Cuban missile crisis was worse. An informal pacifism accorded with our allegiance to Culture. We were not a promising constituency for war on Vietnam.

This take on literary studies from the late 1940s to the early 1960s prepares the way for a particular story of what happened next. I have postulated a group of educational workers organized as a profession with a core ideology of redemptive Culture, beneficiary of vast expansion in the cold war university, yet not specifically favored or assigned cold war tasks as many other disciplines were, and pretty much left to work out its own practices, shape its own ethos. Though there was of course no possibility of its doing so independently of or in opposition to the hegemonic process, in a number of ways English and its neighbors imagined themselves as an alternative within the dominant. Yet this dissent, which in any case rose more from residual than from emergent values, found no political expression outside the timid and self-promoting learned societies and professional organizations. How would such a group respond to provocations and shifts that fueled its dissent and invited political response?

Even before 1960, it became clearer that the national leadership viewed education not only as building human capital for economic growth but also as a weapon in the cold war. The challenge of Soviet technical and scientific development to U.S. domination after Sputnik (1957) turned anxious eyes toward the American public school system, found wanting in service to the national interest by influentials such as James Bryant Conant, in a 1959 Carnegie-sponsored study, *The American High School Today*. Congress passed a frankly named National Defense Education Act (NDEA) in 1958. Such pragmatic attentiveness caused no more than mild concern among humanists who had quite different goals for education, in part because the NDEA and other efforts of the state contributed to the growth and prosperity of higher education as well. But the NDEA also required recipients of scholarships to sign loyalty oaths and noncommunist affidavits. Faculties gagged on this intrusion, which stirred memories of loyalty oaths imposed on University of California faculty members in 1949 and of the McCarthy moment in general. Many faculties (including Wesleyan's) voted noncompliance, and the issue reawakened the possibility of contesting our relationship to the cold war state.

The nascent civil rights movement also began to have a bracing effect. Little Rock, Montgomery, Greensboro, and other landmark confrontations brought the virulence of white supremacy and the courage of protesters inescapably to liberal consciousness. A handful of northern faculty members joined in the Freedom Rides; more joined in the Mississippi Freedom Summer and marched in Selma. Through this period, as confidence in the supposedly widening inclusiveness of U.S. democracy grew less and less tenable, so did complacency about fairness and meritocracy in the university itself, enclave of urbane culture. Were not our students and faculty members virtually all white? Were we not practicing segregation by methods less subtle but no less invidious than those displayed on national television? Agitation for the recruitment and admission of black students arose in different quarters on many white campuses. At Wesleyan, mainly younger faculty members quarreled with a director of admissions who repeatedly assured us that no qualified black students were out there. Our critique, augmented by a convenient scandal, led to his dismissal, the appointment of a new admissions man, and the arrival of a visible and soon militant cohort of black students in the fall of 1965, only a year or two before parallel events forever changed most elite campuses.

Even most of those who had favored desegregation of our colleges ex-pected black students to assimilate happily; but their admission turned out to be just the first stage of conflict and transformation. Civil rights, like the loyalty oath controversy, broke the membrane between national and univer-sity politics and involved even the most reclusive faculty members in both. Battles over racism in the academy are too familiar to call for narration here. What bears commentary, in the frame of this analysis, is that pressure soon built on people in history and various fields in the humanities and arts, but especially in English, to examine critically and wholesale the very subject of our knowledge and instruction: literary culture. Most black and many white students wanted curricular acknowledgment that more than one black American (Ellison) had actually made literature worth reading and study-ing. In response, and out of progressive commitments deepened by the civil rights movement, Americanist faculty members and graduate students be-gan an intense project of recovery and revaluation, the first stage of the canon wars. The *PMLA* bibliography for 1969 listed twenty articles by Americans on Richard Wright, more than the total for all the years from 1950 to 1968; production of scholarship on Wright continued thereafter at the 1969 rate. Even to speak of "the canon," as we soon came to do, was to grant its historical contingency and admit into our conversation questions of power and authority that had been muted or absent since the 1930s. New professional terrain, new rules of engagement: no such perturbations shook the foundations of other fields, not even American history.

To disrupt chronology for a moment, the women's movement, when it emerged first in oppositional political groups and then in the university, in-tensified the revisionist imperative in many fields. Feminism was perhaps less easily contained in women's studies programs than African American insurgency was in black studies, and again, the challenge in English was more immediate and direct than elsewhere. Our students were dispropor-tionately female; a fair number of women already held faculty positions, and many more were working on Ph.D.'s—a critical mass for consciousness rais-ing and academic strategizing; the canon already included a few women writers, though hundreds of others, much read at one time or another, had been excluded; many women were prominent writers *in* the 1960s. The in-gredients of a feminist literary and political culture were quickly catalyzed.

Professional consequences abounded. Courses on women writers prolif-erated; women's studies programs sprang up, along with a ferment of insurgent meetings, new discoveries and recoveries, curricular revisions, feminist journals, feminist book-publishing ventures. This movement deeply subverted the institution and ideology of literary studies. As feminists laid out the systematic male bias of canonical works, recovered women's writing for study and criticism, and then placed gender high on the theoretical agenda, they made evident the "unmarked" male position from which the supposed universals of literature had been studied. Who could believe now in the autonomy of the artwork, the disinterestedness of the critic, all those denials that had underwritten our professional charter and our claim of exemption from the oppressions and injuries of bourgeois society? There was no ignoring feminism.

Energy flowed into English from 1960s movements, calling into question both the grounds of professional legitimacy and the terms of our pact with the larger society—understood to be philistine but roughly just, within the framework of liberal political belief. Other minority movements, gay liberation, environmentalism, the "counterculture," and especially the student power movement had similar consequences, but resistance to white and male supremacy most profoundly troubled our dogmatic slumbers. Vietnam linked up these disturbances in two ways that are critical for my argument.

First, it brought large numbers of us, including white males, into sharp criticism of, then protest against, then open conflict with the government of the United States. From grousing to writing letters to signing and then circulating petitions to joining teach-ins to turning in draft cards to refusing to pay taxes to supporting draft resistance to helping actual resisters and deserters: enough academics followed such trajectories to constitute a lively culture of activism. It brought many into organizations and organizing. I worked in campus and town antiwar groups, helped found RESIST and the Radical Caucus of the MLA, joined the Students for a Democratic Society for a while, then the short-lived New University Conference, and endless ad hoc groups. To see oneself as an organizer, not to mention a criminal, was a far cry from defining oneself as a detached professional and bearer of cultural wisdom and solace. The antiwar movement also put thousands of academics in an adversarial relation to their own employers and to the leaders of their professional guilds.

Second, as opposition intensified, the accompanying analysis proceeded from picturing the war as a tragic error to understanding it as the natural extension of American anticommunist policy—imperialism, as we soon called it. This change placed the rapidly growing New Left in direct opposition to the cold war: not, to be sure, into alignment with the Soviet Union (only a tiny handful of New Left sectarians joined Old Left remnants there), but in sympathy with various other colonial and socialist revolutions and in strident opposition to the industrial-military complex. Furthermore, radical analysis from various quarters sought to unite critique of the war and militarism with critique of racism and patriarchy, of ecological depredations, of the bourgeois family, of the educational system in which we worked and studied. So, by the early 1970s, an encompassing oppositional analysis of capitalist social order itself circulated widely in and out of the universities.

Opposition to the Vietnam War spread across liberal arts faculties and student bodies (by contrast with those in engineering, agriculture, business, and so on), but was not limited there to English and the humanities. However, as the analysis broadened to take on bourgeois society as a whole, it did find especially fertile ground in English. That was true in part because the analysis tried to embrace insights of the antiracist and women's movements, which had a powerful and enduring impact in English. And it was also true, I suggest, because as argued earlier, English in the 1950s had already distanced itself—quietly and inactively—from the ethos of growth and consumption, as well as from the stupidities of official anticommunism. That disaffection metamorphosed rapidly into a more articulate and principled antagonism under pressure of 1960s movements and of deepening skepticism about the dependability of the liberal state whose benign embrace had seemed to promise laissez-faire for us and civil liberties for all—a skepticism fueled by attack dogs, water hoses, billy clubs, wire taps, CIA domestic spying, police riots, dirty tricks, assassinations (Fred Hampton and so on), infiltrations, and other indecencies, not to mention fragmentation bombs, napalm, carpet bombing, "pacification," My Lai, and other manifestations of liberalism abroad.

Thus, many of the challenges posed by 1960s movements to the postwar consensus were taken up and developed in English and neighboring fields. No one there could any longer take for granted—that is, without encountering dissident views among close colleagues—that American society was relatively just and marching toward equality under the banner of its corporate leadership; that policy elites were trustworthy guides in international affairs; that the war machine was an instrument of democracy abroad; that the state security apparatus was promoting democracy at home; that capitalism itself

was the handmaiden of democracy; or even that any regrettable shortcom-
ings in these areas could be justified by cold war urgencies—the implacable
enmity of the evil empire and the peril of domestic communism. What held
together pretty well as hegemony in the 1950s now took on the aspect of domination. Furthermore, as I have noted, English took 1960s challenges into its
own internal discourse, putting in question such givens as the autonomy of
literary works, the universality of the values attributed to them, and the permanent value of canonical works outside historical process. These debates
translated over a few years into curricular initiatives perhaps more disruptive than any that had occurred since the discipline took shape around the
beginning of the century.

Of course many opposed these changes, and no more than a tenth of people in literary studies, I imagine, subscribed to anything like the full critique
of the United States and international capitalism that accompanied them.
But neither was this fraction isolated, or on all campuses embattled against
conservatives. Bear in mind, as a measure of sentiment against the war, that
MLA members at the 1968 convention elected antiwar activist Louis Kampf
(from MIT) second vice president (i.e., president-to-be), and that a sizable
majority of the members affirmed by mail-in ballot the resolutions passed at
that turbulent meeting condemning the war as immoral and illegal and urging colleges and universities not to cooperate with the Selective Service system. Certainly a majority also endorsed the movement for racial justice (if
not in its "black power" form), and came around eventually to support of
women's rights and feminist academic projects. And certainly these sentiments were still more widespread among graduate students, who, in spite of
the job market crash of 1969 and some clearly political denials of tenure,
were working their way up in English departments. By the end of the 1970s,
radicals and sympathetic liberals constituted a solid bloc of people in literature whose thinking, teaching, and institutional practice were informed by
1960s movements and by the effort to preserve and unify the insights of
those movements.

I hope to have offered a plausible account of where English was located,
institutionally and ideologically, in the first decade and a half of the cold
war; of how 1960s events shifted those bearings and provoked a harsh re-
assessment of disciplinary assumptions, and thus led to many changes in
disciplinary practice; and of why the changes were more thoroughgoing and
less reversible in English than in most other fields. If the account *is* plausible,

it goes some way toward answering the question with which I began: How was the quiet enclave of 1950s English transformed into the site of 1990s culture wars? But not quite the whole way, because in the period traversed so far no concerted assault on English and cultural studies had yet been marshaled. To explore that development, I will turn to the aftermath of the 1960s convulsions.

We can understand the events of the 1960s as part of a social process that worked itself out over the entire cold war period. While the United States used military power and alliances to establish and secure domination abroad, capital sustained its rule at home more through hegemony than by force—at least after the height of the red scares.[15] In a working hegemony, power relations seem natural when not invisible. Education contributes to this aura of naturalness by fostering ideologies of equal opportunity and individualism, even as the whole system of schooling helps reproduce inequality. The academic professions enter this process in obvious ways, benefiting from and advancing ideologies of merit, claiming privileges accordingly, helping sort out those who will and will not succeed, administering systems of knowledge and expertise in service to (though often critical of) ruling groups, and singing anthems of culture. Within a discipline, rituals and assumptions reproduce hierarchies and proclaim the legitimacy—the objectivity—of the ranking and sifting. This particular hegemony functioned smoothly into the 1960s but lost its appearance of inevitable common sense when social movements rose in open resistance to the use of military force, to white and male supremacy, to the rule of corporate needs, and to many systems of control that had worked in near silence until then. The effort to defend and restore hegemony after that did not and could not proceed silently.

Let higher education stand as an example. It is not the most critical terrain of contestation. Still, both Left and Right have thought it moderately consequential over these three decades. Sixties movements took root especially in universities, noisily disturbing the smugness of meritocratic ideology and bringing in previously excluded groups of students, with different needs and earnest demands. Comprehensive schemes of oppositional thought—ecological, feminist, Marxist—took root especially there. Challenges to the authority of high culture, to bourgeois political economy, to the exclusions of traditional history, to Eurocentrism, to male and heterosexist assumptions in many disciplines, and to power relations embedded in the whole educational institution and its pedagogies, amounted to a running battle over cultural capital.

As the university system had expanded and taken on new tasks through the postwar period, it had become more vital than before to social reproduction, and a central locus, too, for the vastly expanded professional-managerial class, whose activities mediate and sustain the late capitalist social order in innumerable ways. The eruptions of the sixties showed that the loyalty of this class, particularly of its youth, is far from secure. So questions about who might act as organic intellectuals of the professional-managerial class and what forms its cultural capital might assume have taken on a good deal of political significance—the more so in a time when the place one may hope to attain in the social hierarchy depends increasingly on access to education. Such considerations amply explain why those seeking to defend and recreate domestic hegemony have chosen to engage in combat over the practices and content of higher education and concentrated their attack on English and the humanities, so distant from the practical work of capitalist accumulation and social control.

A number of skirmishes led up to the "PC" spasm that coincided with the end of the cold war. Although the efforts at conservative restoration itemized below had to do more with school than with college, that very fact demonstrates the integrity of the Right's project, even as its leadership and tactics have changed.[16]

1. *Vocational education:* Beginning about 1970, the Nixon administration and some allies began a campaign to promote "career" education, as they dishonestly if more palatably called it; Nixon's commissioner of education, Sidney P. Marland, put it at the center of his program. With backing from a Carnegie report and others, he advocated and supported tracking through secondary schools and community colleges to prepare students for the work they were likely to find, not the work toward which they might aspire. Vocationalism aimed also to forestall discontent by lowering expectations and by cutting back on liberal-arts work in schools and community colleges.

2. *Literacy Crisis:* In 1975, articles appeared in *Newsweek, Time,* the *New York Times,* the *Chicago Tribune,* the *Saturday Review, Reader's Digest,* and many other mainstream periodicals exploring—as the *Newsweek* cover story put it—"Why Johnny Can't Write." Academic authorities such as Jacques Barzun and A. Bartlett Giamatti, the head of the National Endowment for the Humanities (Ronald Berman), and a slew of pundits taught us that we

were in the midst of a literacy crisis, instanced by falling SAT scores and even or especially by the inability of college students to write standard English and put forth simple arguments in coherent prose. Since there was no unambiguous evidence suggesting that anything so dramatic as a decline in literacy had in fact taken place, the outcry was remarkable. I am unaware of a conservative design to scare the public in this way, but some familiar conservative bogeys figured prominently among the many causes assigned to the purported decline: open admissions programs, 1960s indulgences such as the free speech movement, popular culture, drugs, permissiveness, and so on.[17]

3. *Back to basics:* In any case, the literacy "crisis" was accompanied and followed by the usual spate of commissions and studies, and by concerted efforts to promote hard-line educational strategies that would curtail liberal and critical tendencies and oblige instructors to intensify drill in the supposed fundamentals of language.

4. *Excellence:* In 1983, several highly publicized reports came out from the National Commission on Excellence in Education, the Education Commission of the States, the Twentieth Century Fund, the National Science Board, and the College Board. Two of their titles, *A Nation at Risk* and *Action for Excellence,* defined the range of their concerns: our educational system was sinking into mediocrity and so endangering the future of our society, by now a familiar cold war theme. The remedy this time was not basic education but the boosting of higher-order skills, especially scientific and technical, for those who would be competitive, and for the national interest. George H. W. Bush, the "education president," gave a blunt justification for the Educational Excellence Act of 1989: "I believe that greater educational achievement promotes sustained economic growth, enhances the Nation's competitive position in world markets, increases productivity, and leads to higher incomes for everyone." The insistence on an economic rationale for education flatly ignored not only the liberatory ideals of the 1960s and 1970s but also humanistic ideals that dominated 1950s thought on the subject.

5. *Cultural conservatism:* By then, these efforts of the conservative restoration to make schooling basic and economically functional had joined uneasily with another project, one more centrally coordinated, more openly ideological, and more combative. The New Right identified its enemy from the start as people who had come out of 1960s movements, gained (in the Right's view) dominance in colleges and universities, and there orchestrated

an assault on core values of the free-enterprise system, the family, Christianity, and Western civilization. The Heritage Foundation, Free Congress Foundation, and other institutions founded and handsomely funded in the 1970s (by Coors, Olin, Bradley, and so on), attempted to advance a right-wing agenda in politics and the media, as well as in universities. The scandalized attention accorded to political correctness and multiculturalism from 1990 on has been a direct, intended, and largely successful outcome of this right-wing organizing.[18] Another was the elevation of such New Right leaders as William Bennett and Lynne Cheney to key positions in cultural policy (both directed the National Endowment for the Humanities).

So in its New Right phase, hegemony was conceived in very different terms from those of the postwar consensus that the 1960s had undermined, and the Right took aim not only at higher education but also with surprising accuracy at English and cultural studies. Much that has changed in those areas since 1965 has indeed carried forward the momentum of 1960s movements and affronted those who identify the well-being of our society with the alliance of Western high culture, Christian values, and free-enterprise economics.

Just to mention African American studies, women's studies, cultural studies, Chicano studies, Native American studies, Asian American studies, and lesbian and gay studies is to name some outposts of those movements and demarcate a new understanding of what culture might deserve academic study and appreciation. As noted earlier, these enlargements of interest affected English more quickly than other fields, inaugurating a debate over the canon and cultural value that has occupied us for twenty-five years, convicting us in the Right's eyes of relativism or, worse, of sullen enmity toward Culture itself.

The genesis and role of "theory" in all this is a vexed question, but clearly the poststructuralisms that came forward in the 1960s and after answered to strategic and theoretical needs of some critical groups in universities, including feminist and gay and lesbian activists as well as scholars. Although conservative critics have often seemed to dismiss theory as foolish preening, a kind of academic speaking in tongues, many (e.g., Lynne Cheney) have also taken it on as a serious antagonist. And no wonder: though some in our profession have deployed the thought of Foucault, Barthes, Derrida, Lacan, Cixous, and so on mainly to build reputations and harmlessly decenter meaning, poststructuralist theory has served others in the demystification of patriarchal and expert authority, and in the project of social constructionism, which has won academic ground well outside the precincts of literary study. All this is reasonably seen by the Right as a strong intellectual challenge to traditional hierarchies and cultural verities.

Equally vexed is the role of Marxism(s) in this redrafting of the academic agenda. Relatively few people in the humanities define themselves primarily as Marxists. These few have almost no allies in economics and political science, where a vigorous Marxism might connect to nonacademic political thought and to public policy. Still, it is more than an irritant to the Right that Marxism has regained influence and legitimacy even in a limited sphere, and that some terms of Marxist analysis—commodification, class, ideology, for instance—have lodged in the commonsense vocabulary of historical and cultural study.

In higher education as a whole, by contrast to English, the socialist and feminist Left amounts to a tiny minority (only 5 percent of faculty members place themselves on the "far left"), and a weak counterhegemony. Yet the Right accurately perceives that the academic wing of 1960s movements has over time redrawn the intellectual landscape. Look at English then and now. Feminists, Marxists, and Foucauldians hold major professorships. Journals put out endless issues and book publishers run series on a range of concerns from postcoloniality to the politics of knowledge to popular music to the construction of sexualities that were hardly on the horizon in 1970. The annual program of the MLA gives space and legitimacy to similar inquiries, providing an array of sessions that each year provokes risibility but also rage among New Right commentators and their media followers. (An obscure special session on "Teaching the Political Conflicts," in which I spoke at the 1994 meeting, attracted the dour presences of both Hilton Kramer and Roger Kimball.) I conjecture that many students choosing graduate work do so in part because in English they have found an ethos hospitable to the ideal of social justice and quite different from what they expect to find in law or business.

Nor has the teaching of writing eluded politicization. Because its work must respond to perceived economic needs, composition is under pressure to serve existing social relations. But even in this subfield of English, progressive ideas and methods contend seriously for professional space in journals, at the meetings of the Conference on College Composition and Communication, and in many a writing program—as witness the repression brought smartly down on the founders of a composition course, a decade ago, at the University of Texas (Austin) grounded in issues of social justice. When you look around at the English curriculum in the most generous sense—not only courses and requirements and majors but also the questions embedded in the course of study, the ideas and perspectives that students are likely to encounter in and out of class, the things we tell them are worth their intellectual work, the very academic agenda—the curriculum has been deeply altered, and indeed politicized since 1965. That is why the Right pays English the courtesy of its bellicose attention.

English and the university in general have also come under economic stress for reasons connected to the political assault, but of partly separate genesis. As I will argue at some length in this book (see in particular essays 2, 10, and 12), American capitalism encountered severe challenges around 1970, including a negative balance of trade, a weakening currency, the massive build-up of governmental and personal debt, a decline in corporate profits, a leveling-off of productivity, bankruptcies, takeovers, and so on. Responding to such difficulties and to European and Japanese rivalry, U.S. capital has pursued a variety of countermeasures, including rapid globalization and a reinvention of corporate practice to increase flexibility and reduce dependency on the well-paid, benefited, secure, and heavily unionized workforce of the postwar boom years. In order to downsize and to increase flexibility, corporations have come to rely more and more heavily on part-time and temporary workers, here and abroad.

Meanwhile, the traditional university, under analogous pressures, has resorted to labor practices of the same sort. In English even more then in most academic fields, this is old news. More than people in other academic fields, we know firsthand the use of flexible labor: adjuncts, part-timers, moonlighters, and an army of graduate students, paid at a national average of around $2,000 per course, usually with no benefits. In the mid-1960s over 90 percent of new humanities Ph.D.'s had full-time, tenure-track appointments; in recent years the figure has hovered around 40 percent. The full-time job market has never regained its capacity to absorb new aspirants, and at this writing it is disastrous. In short, the conservative restoration has combined with a global economic shift to put extreme pressure on English as reconstituted after the insurgent 1960s. Furthermore, the old Sputnik rationale for strengthening American education and for deficit spending lost its force as the cold war wound down.

The easiest way of responding to the "downsizing" imperative in English and in other fields that train Ph.D.'s mainly for academic employment has been to continue overproducing them and A.B.D.'s ("all but dissertation") by admitting more graduate students than the core labor market can possibly employ, and turning the unfortunate ones out into the peripheral market, thus haplessly following the script of flexible accumulation. The profession, however radicalized, is not well equipped to resist such developments. Organized as it is to regulate careers and maintain hierarchies of status among practitioners and institutions, the profession is all but unable to act in solidarity with its most weakly positioned members. Throughout the years of job famine, top departments have gone right on competing for "stars," not only at entry level but also at the top.

Economies made possible by the reserve army outside our professional gates have not escaped the notice of administrations. One department I visited put each of its new M.A. students to work teaching two sections of composition per semester and had a number of postdoctoral "fellows" teaching three courses per semester at meager salaries. Another, when I first visited, staffed its composition courses largely with experienced, full-time, decently paid, benefited, but non-tenure-track lecturers. By my second visit, two years later, these people had been fired and replaced with the usual cadre of part-timers, by order of the provost who said this campus had lagged behind the state system's "benchmark" for part-time employment. At my own relatively posh but financially straitened college, the English department used to hire a few part-timers to cover specific needs; now, in a given year almost as many of them may be on the roster as full-timers. The two-class system thus created—our own local version of peripheral and core labor—works to perpetuate the invidious opposition between literature and composition.

As the framework of global politics collapsed with the decline and disappearance of the Soviet Union, so did a durable structure of domestic ideology. Of what use now in galvanizing political emotion was the anticommunism that had been the air we breathed for forty years and more? With domestic dissidence pried loose from any illusion of links to the evil empire, the task of restoring hegemony in the United States requires a new basis, a new organizing principle. With internal challenges to domination and privilege no longer graspable as tentacles of communist subversion, the Right and many not on the Right turn to an assault on social movements that have in fact grown more and more separate since 1970, when the "Movement" began to lose what coherence it had and many of its constituent groups veered toward identity politics or, worse, a politics of lifestyle. The Right has picked up on that change in the forms of dissidence and has mounted one assault after another on entitlements won in the 1960s and 1970s: on affirmative action, women's rights, lesbian and gay rights, children's rights, workers' rights, welfare rights. We have seen a coordinated attack on multiculturalism and political correctness, specifically targeting colleges and universities, and with the crosshairs right on English (see the next essay). Yet, despite the forces arrayed against identity politics, with entitlements and affirmative action put under fire by the Right, and with the stakes raised by the pressure on schooling to track the young toward increasingly separate slots in core and peripheral labor, our existing social categories of difference remain explosive.

Black Americans continue to face discrimination and the hard choice whether to resist in separatist or integrationist terms; Afrocentrism and black Islam are insistent tendencies. Gay and lesbian people are finding more of a voice and forming more of a movement: queer politics, Queer Nation, and queer studies gain strength; Asian American studies appears alongside African American studies, Chicano studies, women's studies, postcolonial studies. The presence of these movements in and around English guarantee that it will continue in a gritty relation with strong political forces on the national scene.

Although I have concentrated on a chain of events that set English somewhat apart from other fields, the post–cold war university as a whole has been under ideological pressure from the Right and severe economic constraint brought about by changes in global capitalism and cutbacks in public funding. More and more tasks of higher education are shifting to other sectors, while the university itself turns more to private sources of funding and so bends its efforts to the bidding of corporations. These developments are beyond the scope of this essay, but it seems plain that English has a lot of company in this engagement, including those who will fight for public education at all levels.

Finally, I have suggested an obvious periodization of the cold war into three stages: postwar consensus from the beginning through the early 1960s; strong and open opposition through the rest of that decade and into the 1970s; and the conservative restoration thereafter. That restoration, however, has not restored hegemony, or anything close to it, in or outside the university. In the turbulence ahead, English will not become once again a pastoral enclave.

2

ENGLISH AFTER THE USSR

◆

Although the topic of this essay follows that of the previous one chronologically, I wrote this one first, in 1992. Its exploratory method reflects its closeness to the end of the cold war and expresses my willingness to speculate about the "new world order" in which we all abruptly found ourselves.

As I watched the geographical, economic, and ideological map of the world changing almost beyond recognition in the years just before and after 1990, I felt very much a spectator, yet of a drama that would surely involve us all as at least bit players, one that would change the terms of our lives in general and our professional lives in particular. How? I had only the vaguest ideas. I needed to think about it, read, talk with others. An invitation to speak to Chicago area English instructors afforded me the chance I wanted. I gave my Chicago host a title that would make me face my confusion at its deepest level, "English after the USSR," and allowed myself a few weekends to consider the strange-sounding conjuncture. Here are the speculations that ensued, as amended by welcome advice from friends and editors. Some of these thoughts pertain only to "English"; others apply to higher education across fields, or to education in general.

◆

What are some of the issues close to where we work—close to those committee meetings, stacks of papers, and other urgencies of life in English these days—that one might wish to grasp in relation to a large movement of history? I think of the questions and conflicts that surround our teaching of writing, from those about the nature and politics of literacy itself, including something called "cultural literacy," to the ever increasing demand for vocationally useful writing, professional writing, business writing, technical writing, and so on. I think of the infusion of new technologies *into* writing, bringing as always utopian hopes and monstrous fears. At the border between our two professional territories, the war of privileged literature against underprivileged composition simmers on, even while writing instruction makes stronger claims to professional standing. Meanwhile, the professional standing of both groups is under assault as budget cuts make the hiring of temporary and part-time workers seem imperative to administrations, creating a two-class divide between tenure track faculty and others, closely connected to the divide between composition and literature instructors; and as those budget cuts drive the work loads of many regular faculty members up to a level that calls into question the premise of a dual commitment to teaching and research, and the more basic ideal of every profession: that it control the conditions of its own work. Finally, I'd name as another set of issues very much on our agenda in the field of English, partly because they are on some rather more influential agendas, those having to do with canons, with cultural authority, with the multiplicity of cultures and identities and entitlements in this society: in short, the debates that have burst into the public arena under the headings of multiculturalism and political correctness. These are questions that still clamor for attention on the job and are thematized at conferences and in books such as this one.

I seek paths of connectedness between them and the world-historical events toward which my title gestures. More than the disbanding of the Soviet Union, of course: the abandonment almost everywhere of the project that called itself socialism or communism; the tectonic-plate shifts in relations among capitalist societies; the proliferation of new nation states even as many commentators are ready to declare the nation state itself a vestigial remnant; and the emergence, not of a new world order, I think, but of the conviction that some such order is slouching toward Bethlehem to be born.

I am looking, then, for ties between global dislocations and our local concerns in English. It may help to begin, however, by positioning our work in an intermediate sphere, that of *this* nation state's recent history, making clear as I do so my commitment to the idea of hegemony as an instrument for thinking about domination and resistance. Though the concept of hegemony was developed within Marxist thought, I think it useful to anyone who believes that some groups have relatively entrenched power and privilege in each society while others pursue their life chances in ways that accept, resist, or challenge that power. A signal advantage of the idea is its use in understanding societies like ours in which inequality is not *primarily* maintained by naked force but rests on a measure of consent, with force in the background.

In a working hegemony, power filters through innumerable laws, institutions, daily practices, attitudes, and needs, so that except to those directly under the heel of the policeman it feels less like rule than like what Gramsci called common sense. It saturates experience, consciousness, and customary relations with other people to the extent that inequality and domination seem normal or invisible. In this process, education helps reproduce the inequities of the social order but does so in ways widely accepted as fair and natural. The ideology of equal opportunity and merit rewarded has been quite serviceable toward that end, through large parts of our history, obscuring decisive advantages of family position and wealth, the differential access of young people to cultural capital and networks of privilege, the politics of tracking, and the operation of the hidden curriculum to discourage and derogate those not adapted by birth and rearing to the culture of school. When the system is working smoothly, not just its main beneficiaries but also its victims understand their life chances and trajectories as resulting from differences in individual ability, effort, choice, and luck.

No hegemony stays automatically in place or unproblematically retains its appearance as common sense. As Raymond Williams put it, "[A] lived hegemony . . . has continually to be renewed, recreated, defended, and modified. It is also continually resisted, limited, altered, challenged by pressures not at all its own. . . . At any time, forms of alternative or directly oppositional politics and culture exist as significant elements in the society."[1] Surely we are living in a time of strenuous effort to renew, recreate, defend, and modify the hegemony of dominant groups in the United States.

I think the reconstructive effort, including the "political correctness" campaign, is overdetermined in some obvious and some less obvious ways. There is the long decline of American capitalism since the postwar boom began to taper off at the end of the 1960s, while European and East Asian economies rapidly expanded. Also, in the 1960s, just when the economic system was reaching the limit of its ability to improve material life for each successive generation, political movements came along to demand more equal shares in the distribution of goods and in political power. Whatever the willingness of those in charge to respond to such demands, economic stagnation made it impossible to accommodate these new claimants, even to the extent that the white, male, industrial workforce had been grudgingly accommodated during the 1940s and 1950s. But the new movements did establish the state as a place to contend over entitlements and fix the social categories—African Americans, women, Latinos, and so on—by whose fortunes the legitimacy of the social order would in part be measured. Thus, for instance, decades later, the widespread perception of the Rodney King affair and the Los Angeles riots not as isolated outrages but as symptoms of profound social failure.

Sixties movements had also enabled that kind of perception through later decades, by insisting that the Vietnam War, white supremacy, male domination, environmental damage, and so on, were expressions of systemic malaise rather than separate problems to be solved by liberal management. Comprehensive analyses—Marxist, feminist, ecological—gained currency and remained available as challenges to mainstream common sense, even through the right-wing resurgence of the 1980s.

Needless to say, these strains of critical thought took root especially in universities. Among their targets were the educational system itself and the official knowledges it produced and purveyed. Taken together, challenges to the authority of high culture, to bourgeois political economy, to the exclusions and blind spots of traditional history, to Eurocentrism, to male and heterosexist assumptions in many disciplines, and to the power relations embedded in the educational institution and its pedagogies amounted to a running contest over cultural capital. Far from hegemonic even in universities, these projects have at best constituted a weak counterhegemony.

One more point: as the contemporary university system took shape in the postwar period it became a much more critical site of social reproduction than before, and a central locus too for the vastly expanded professional-managerial class whose activities mediate and shore up the system in innumerable ways. The 1960s showed that the loyalty of this class, especially of its youth, is far from secure. So the questions of who might function as organic intellectuals of the professional-managerial class and of what forms its cultural capital might assume have taken on a good deal of political importance—the more so in a time when the place one may hope to attain in the social hierarchy depends more and more on access to education.

If you accept this highly abbreviated and mainly political history you will be no more surprised than I that those seeking to defend and recreate the domestic hegemony of our system and its elites have chosen to engage in battle over the content and practices of education, higher education in particular. Why that battle has taken such specific forms as the assault on "political correctness" and multiculturalism is not so obvious; it is a question I will touch on before the end of this essay. But to get there, I want to begin stalking, from a distance, my announced prey, that which is named vaguely enough by the prepositional phrase "After the USSR" in the title. The pursuit will take me first, with dizzying simplification, back over the same period of our history, this time tracing a path more economic than political.

It has been clear for quite a while that long before the Soviet empire began to quake, its productive system had weakened and ossified, and that American capitalism too had run into a difficult patch. The trouble in the First World began to show—it had of course been brewing for longer—about 1970. This was a time marked in memory for many of us academics as the year the job market collapsed. Less parochial changes were also under way. National unemployment has never again dropped to anywhere near the level of 1969 (below 4 percent) and has stayed instead within a couple of points of a rate about twice that. Real wages, which had risen steadily since 1940, stalled for a few years after 1970, and then declined about 10 percent—a dull number, but realized in the lives of millions in terms of second jobs, more spouses entering the job market, kids working more after school, families struggling to stay even, young people facing expectations lower than those of their parents. You or I could cite many other indices of the decline—they're in the news and on the lips of pundits and politicians. The balance of trade went negative in 1975. The dollar faded against stronger currencies from the early 1970s. The federal debt began its notorious rise in the late 1970s (dropping briefly during the Clinton administration); so did personal debt, with corporate debt following a few years later. Profits as a portion of national income sagged after 1968. And so on.

Meanwhile, the nature of capitalism changed. This is a subtler transformation, not so easily captured in a few statistics, yet again everyone who reads at all about such matters knows it's happening. A variety of labels have gained currency to describe parts of it—globalization, finance capital, deindustrialization, the knowledge society, and so on. All ugly names, and I'll add one more that attempts to capture the change at a quite general level. It is richly analyzed in David Harvey's book *The Condition of Postmodernity,*[2] which helped me a lot in these ruminations. Harvey describes a "sea-change in cultural as well as in political-economic practices since around 1972," a change from what he calls "Fordism" to a regime of "flexible accumulation":

> It rests on flexibility with respect to labor processes, labor markets, products, and patterns of consumption. It is characterized by the emergence of entirely new sectors of production, new ways of providing financial services, new markets, and, above all, greatly intensified rates of commercial, technological, and organizational innovation. It has entrained rapid shifts in the patterning of uneven development, both between sectors and between geographical regions, giving rise, for example, to a vast surge in so-called "service sector" employment as well as to entirely new industrial ensembles in hitherto underdeveloped regions (such as the "Third Italy," Flanders, the various silicon valleys and glens, to say nothing of the vast profusion of activities in newly industrializing countries). (147)

We have all experienced the instability and excesses of this casino capitalism—the painful dislocation of the old industrial base, especially in the American Northeast and Midwest; the torrent of financial and industrial bankruptcies; the merger frenzy of the 1980s; the 1987 crash and subsequent boom; the internationalization of production, so that even when one wants to "buy American" it's hard to know how; the evolution of a world financial system so intricate that almost nobody can understand it. These upheavals began well before the 1980s and extend far beyond the borders of the United States: one could plausibly see deregulation, for instance, as a response to them, rather than as their cause.

Furthermore, at least from some stratospheric height where human lives look small, these shifts might even be a *successful* adjustment of the system, a tremendous reinvigoration of capitalism's old project of accumulation. They have certainly thrown the old, popular, labor-based opposition a curve ball, in the First World. And I would even suggest that flexible accumulation, as much as cold war fatigue and political tyranny, helped scuttle the Soviet Union and most of the other "actually existing socialisms," stuck as they were in a stale, rigidly enforced Fordism and unable to compete in a new game whose rules were drawn up elsewhere.

Be that as it may, it is not possible to think clearly about any part of our working lives without seeing them in the context of historical shifts in the world's productive system. And although from here on my ruminations will at last draw closer to their quarry, I want to insist that the demise of the Second World affects our professional lives not as an independent line of causation, but as an *additional* force, closely related to changes in world capitalism.

The first of six conjectures I will now venture about English after the Soviet Union is that the events of the last few decades in Central and Eastern Europe, Asia, and some other parts of the world that were within the Soviet sphere will feed into, and further, changes already under way in the national and international division of labor. Employers of all sorts have long been responding to increasingly worldwide competition, the weakening of unions, and the dispersed pools of cheap and surplus labor by moving production to wherever capital has the greatest advantage over labor, and by breaking up the rigidity of Fordist work regimes. Flex-time, part-time, and temporary labor; subcontracting and out-sourcing; job sharing, home work, and piece work; workfare and prison labor: these and other practices have eroded the old core labor market of full-time, long-term employees and surrounded it with a huge global penumbra of marginal, now-and-then labor. Part of this is no news to those of us teaching English in the United States. More than people in other academic fields, we know firsthand the use of flexible labor —adjuncts, part-timers, moonlighters, and an army of graduate students, poorly paid and usually without benefits. English has, it would almost seem, served as a small laboratory for innovative uses of flexible, highly skilled labor power. Within universities, we stand as a microcosm of the shrinking labor market core and the expanding periphery.

But this is not the full extent of the change. Education is itself, more and more, an internationally circulating commodity. As Nancy Folbre points out, when Texas Instruments hires fifty programmers in Bangalore, or when Saztec International (a Kansas data-processing company) has most of its work done in the Philippines, they are taking advantage not just of low-wage technical workers abroad but of cheaper teachers and cheaper education there.[3] Also, the dual labor market in this country has always been divided in part racially; now the global division of labor reproduces the color line, and of course the feminization of cheap, peripheral, flexible labor.

I suggest that the absorption of the Soviet Union, Central and Eastern Europe, more gradually China, and smaller pockets of so-called socialism (is Cuba next?) into world capitalism will greatly enlarge the labor periphery, opening up the possibility of new maquiladora schemes almost everywhere, and making it less and less urgent to improve American education, from the corporate point of view, unless political pressure weighs in heavily on the other side.

Two last implications of this conjecture: obviously, these developments put professions under stress. It's not just a matter of a two-class system; though one can see that widening fault even in the strongest professions such as law (paralegals, legal secretaries) and medicine (the proliferation of low-paid workers around doctors). In English, core professionals themselves find their work more and more driven by imperatives of higher productivity. In every department I've visited, the full-time people, the *tenured* people, are working harder and having more trouble setting their own professional standards than they had before.

And finally: in the regime of flexible accumulation knowledge is perhaps the most valuable commodity of all, and its rapid development and circulation are crucial. Universities are increasingly drawn into this regime in ways that reduce their autonomy. They become in effect subcontractors. (The University of California at Berkeley now [i.e., when this essay was written, in 1992] receives only 25 percent of its funding from the state.) We might wonder how this will affect English, which from the corporate outside looks more and more like an adjunct to the circulation of knowledge, and one among others that may well be cheaper, in the United States and abroad.

To reiterate: across a range of interlinked changes such as these, in the international division of labor, the disappearance of the Soviet Union and other communist regimes is not a fresh cause but may have an accelerator effect on processes already under way. I've spent a long time working toward this first conjecture about English and world events, because I felt it necessary to chart the fall of actually existing socialism in tandem with a movement of global and American capitalism. I can be briefer about my five other points.

The next one is the most evident. It's that the end of the cold war changes everything in this country. Most of the talk about this has been happy talk—the liberation of peoples, the release from fear of nuclear war, the peace dividend; and I do not want to spoil anyone's day by cynically refusing the grounds for hope. But I do want to flag some questions about the peace dividend and its potential for diverting money to education, thus improving our circumstances in English. I wonder. For decades the peacetime military, the cold war military, has not just been a *drain* on the economy: it has been a site of knowledge production, an alternative educational system, and a place where very many young people have jobs, who otherwise might join the reserve army of the unemployed. The expanding proportion of young people in universities and the lengthening period of their stay have served the same purpose and helped adjust the labor market to the boom-and-bust cycle. Were the army and other forces to spill a million or so people back into the private economy, along with those laid off from military production, would the colleges be able to absorb the surplus? And, since the enlargement of the college population along with the deskilling and exportation of work, has already made for a lot of overtraining and overcredentialing, I wonder how the awkward fit between college education and the job market might be worsened by an additional flow of young people into our institutions. Will colleges become, even more than now, a machine for sorting out those who will ride the high wave of flexcap into glitzy careers from those relegated to dead-end, insecure jobs in the trough of the wave?

Whatever the answers to these questions—and clearly they depend not just on grim economic law but on the politics and movements that will take shape in the near future—one thing is clear: the taxpayer revolts that dotted our landscape in the 1980s and gathered into a national strategy of the Republican Party have set in place a massive reluctance to pay for education and widened the "savage inequalities" described by Jonathan Kozol.[4] Now, the old Sputnik rationale for strengthening American education is gone with the cold war. Gone, too, is the cold war rationale for deficit spending, as we heard quite explicitly in the 1992 presidential election campaign. A Ross Perot commercial said, "The enemy is not the red flag of communism but the red ink of the national debt," and the other candidates gave at least lip service to that principle. If anything like the sacrifice that Perot and many businessmen call for in the interest of debt reduction should come about, it's hard to see how funding for the work we do can hold at even its present skimpy level.

Yet at the same time, a different rationale for policy comes forward with the fall of the Soviet Union, filling up space occupied by the old one, but doing so with needs and ideas that will not play out in the same way at all. Our competition now is not the Soviet behemoth but resurgent Europe, Japan, the Southeast Asian countries, China. And the competition is not military but quintessentially economic. The very national interest has been purified, distilled to its innocent, 1920s form: the business of America is business. And that's the premise of my third conjecture about English after the Soviet Union. To be sure, perils to the national interest remain here and there around the globe, and we can expect clean little wars now and then to fight back tyranny, "restore democracy," *and* defend oil. But mainly the national interest will be spelled out in terms of productivity, competitiveness, efficiency, technological development, and so on.

Where will English be borne by such imperatives? I can hardly guess; I'd be grateful for a conference on the question, where people could work through its labyrinthine paths. But for starters I will throw out a fact and a couple of leads. The fact: in the legislative and political arenas, the economic rationale for education reigns almost without challenge. Already in 1989, the education president, George H. W. Bush, stated just four goals of his education bill: "I believe that greater educational achievement promotes sustained economic growth, enhances the Nation's competitive position in world markets, increases productivity, and leads to higher incomes for everyone."

That's it. I don't think that the Democrats' understanding of education's task is much different; nor in fact was that of Albert Shanker, president of the American Federation of Teachers. We are not talking here (though a Lynne Cheney may do so in other venues) about citizenship in a democracy or about timeless values, but about economic measures of success. How does English contribute?

The first lead I throw out begins with an observation of Evan Watkins. He suggests that the abstract form of labor in our field, for students and instructors, is this: "A accomplishes a task of speaking or writing; B evaluates the performance of that task; and C reports the evaluation to A and/or C."[5] He has in mind work in literature, but the formula generalizes pretty well to cover work in composition. "A" may be living or dead, a student or a major author; "B" may be a student or an instructor; "C" may be an instructor or the readership of a journal. The point of looking at our labor in this abstract form is to see how much of what we perform—in English even more than in other fields—is a traffic in evaluations. Why? What use is that? I'll compress Watkins's subtle argument almost to the vanishing point by saying that the traffic in evaluations has much to do with the sorting out of young people into various career paths, with the attribution of merit, with a democracy's need to locate and justify social authority anew in each generation; or, if you like, with making inequality seem fair.

That need will persist and intensify, I believe; but what's interesting is that it can be met by widely shifting practices of *concrete* labor, including shifts back and forth between the uneasy cohabiters of English, composition and literature. From the perspective of abstract labor and its uses to the economic system, it doesn't matter whether we spend most of our collective time commenting on themes or writing articles on Kate Chopin; whether our students write seminar papers on Milton or computer-scored tests on usage. This means that the flow of concrete labor is free to respond to whatever specific needs and pressures are out there, insofar as English meets specific needs at all. And of course some of it does. Businesses and bureaucracies want some employees with writing skills. The post–cold war identification of national interest with business interest should give more force to that need. I imagine that composition will continue to grow in relation to literature as a portion of our work, a process aided by the moderately successful professionalization of composition during the past decades. But not just composition in a general way: I would expect our concrete labor to slide toward recognizably practical, vocational kinds of writing instruction, as it has been doing: witness the sharp increase of courses and programs in technical, business, and professional writing that I mentioned in my initial list of things to be explained. Some of the work we do is already, in effect, subcontracting for business, and it is altogether compatible with our work in class reproduction.

But that is not enough. We don't do enough for accumulation—for profits—that business is willing to consign to us, or to education in general, the task of matching knowledge and skills up to the job system; and this is the second of my two leads. Business is giving less to public education. It is doing more education internally—$50 million dollars a year at Ford, $30 million at General Motors, and so on and on. (See essay 10 for more on this topic.) And why not? If the only interest is competition in the new regime of flexcap, why not educate just the workers you need in just the ways you need? Why pay for literature and philosophy? If South Carolina can attract a new BMW plant partly by offering to supply the company with pretrained workers, isn't such an expenditure of state funds more obviously beneficial than increasing support for the state university system?

Privatization moves on quickly in another way, too. Whittle Communications made its Channel One required viewing, commercials and all, for about eight million public school students. Whittle then launched the Edison Project, backed by Time Warner and a British media firm, and headed by former Yale president Benno Schmidt, planning as many as a thousand for-profit schools within a decade of its founding. Should the voucher system become a reality, of course, it would open wide the education market to private investment and flexible accumulation. I'm not sure what the place of English might be in this new environment.

Now I will proceed to my final three conjectures. They have more to do with ideology than with hard economics; I can be both vague and brisk. Conjecture number 4: with the fall of the Soviet Union the framework of old global politics collapsed, and with it the durable structure of domestic ideology. Of what use now in galvanizing political emotion is the anticommunism that was the air we breathed for forty years and more? With domestic dissidence pried loose from any illusion of links to the evil empire, as it has long been detached in fact, the task of maintaining hegemony in the United States must find a new basis, a new organizing principle. This is a murky and fluid time on the ideological front, but it seems that a broad strategy is gathering force. With internal challenges to domination and privilege no longer graspable as tentacles of communist subversion, the Right and many not on the Right turn to an assault on social movements that have in fact grown more and more separate since 1970, when "the Movement" began to lose what coherence it had, and many of its constituent groups veered toward identity politics and even a politics of lifestyle. The Right has picked up on that change in the forms of dissidence and has mounted one assault after another on entitlements won in the sixties and seventies. On the ideological front this strategy materialized just after world socialism began to crumble, in the attack on multiculturalism and "political correctness" described in the previous essay. I need hardly tell you what bearing this strategy has on issues in our field—on two decades of rethinking canons and cultural authority; on the retrieval of lost texts and forgotten experiences; on the slow and painful effort to dismantle the white, male, heterosexual, upper-middle-class "we" that once put itself forward as universal. "Universities have become saturated with politics," says Benno Schmidt. Lynne Cheney picks up the assertion on the first page of her NEH report *Telling the Truth* (1992) and makes it her theme. She attempts to put politics to bed, not counterpose a politics of democratic capitalism to a communist challenge. The Soviet Union merits just one mention in her booklet, as an example of the impoverished life that results from "suppressing thought." Meanwhile, the fundamentalist right subsumes an older, class-based politics in the crusade for "family values," attacking much the same groups as Cheney, but from another flank.

My fifth conjecture is that in spite of the forces arrayed against identity politics, issues of racial and ethnic and sexual identity will continue to sit high on our agenda in English, and that the fall of the Soviet Union will make them more heated and volatile. We have seen in the Balkans, in Central Europe, in the republics of the former Soviet Union, an eruption of ethnic hostilities and national claims unmatched since at least the mid-nineteenth century; they find parallels in similar divisions from India to South Africa, from Spain to Britain to Canada. Nationalism seems now *the* privileged mode of resistance to domination, even as established nation states lose their autonomy. The great movements of people across national boundaries, following the imperatives of the flexible labor market, are augmented by movements of refugees. The United States is more a nation of immigrants now than at any time since the immigration law of 1924 shut down earlier migrations. New ethnicities gather; some old ones regroup as their homeland counterparts struggle for nationhood (Ukrainian, Croat, Serb, Lithuanian). Black Americans and other groups seen as *racially* different continue to face repression, discrimination, and the hard choice whether to resist in separatist or integrationist terms. Gay and lesbian people are finding more of a voice and forming more of a movement; new minority studies programs join the established ones in universities. All these movements overlap with and infiltrate English. Multiculturalism will be with us for some time, its forms changed in ways I can't predict, by ethnic wars in the old, so-called socialist sphere.

My sixth and last point hardly deserves to be called a conjecture. It's more a series of questions arising from the stunning collapse of the socialist project. To speak a little more personally than I've done so far, people like me in the socialist feminist left, formed politically in sixties and seventies movements, never had much use for the dreary regimes that ruled the earth from East Berlin to Vladivostok. For us, whatever historical allowances we made, these were deformed alternatives, betrayals or failures of an idea, false utopias. Many of us were saying, from 1989 to 1991: "Good riddance, and hooray for the peoples of that huge region: now maybe we can start afresh to imagine a democratic successor to undemocratic world capitalism, freed up at last from stifling ideas like the dictatorship of the proletariat and the vanguard party."

But what will the world be like without any living alternative to capitalism? What can serve as a focus of hope in Latin America if Cuba goes the way of Nicaragua? What can the idea of socialism amount to if nobody is trying to enact it? How can our students imagine any historical narrative that could take us out of the present world crisis, if they, like President George H. W. Bush (in one of the 1992 debates), encode the events of the past few years as the triumph of freedom and democracy? Now that freedom and democracy have won, why is there all that killing and oppression and greed in the newly free regions? Why are hundreds of millions dying of disease and starvation in the free world? What does this victory mean in our own troubled country? Are we to live happily ever after in consumer heaven, no longer bothered with the nuisance of politics and citizenship? What about the half of our people not invited to the victory bash? What ways do our students have to think their own futures, apart from the giddy logic of flexible accumulation, which nobody can understand? If our society and our world need some new social form, how can we imagine it in the cold light of a victory that has left us with no visible other to ourselves?

People my age taught for forty years within the ideological envelope of the cold war. I believe it confined our thinking—our sense of the culture we wanted to pass on and criticize, our pedagogies and our hopes for our students, our sense of the possibilities of English—within limits so natural, so tacit, so invisible, that it will take us years to figure out what they were and to get new bearings. It's a worthwhile task. The world will be very different when our younger students are middle-aged, but the course of its change will not follow the master narrative of old Marxism or the cold war narrative of democracy victorious in an epic battle against communism. If we and our students are to be agents rather than dupes in the process, we'll need to invent a new narrative. English, where we at least talk about empowerment and imagination, would seem a natural place for the utopian impulse to range; but if the conjectures explored in this essay turn out to be even partly right, there will also be much to check the utopian spirit.

3

SOME CHANGES ACROSS
THIRTY-FIVE YEARS

◆

*This is the lightly edited text of remarks I made at a March 9, 1996, sympo-
sium in honor of Louis Kampf, on his retirement from the Massachusetts Institute of Technology. I began by noting that English used to be a quiet academic backwater; by 1992 it had become a controverted discipline, with the
controversy spilling out beyond professional boundaries to claim the attention, usually outraged, of conservative officials and journalists. Then, in the
tradition of the celebrity roast, I proceeded as below. Aside from blaming or
praising Louis, personally, for a major passage in institutional history, the
points I made about changes in our professional outlook and practice across
the thirty-five years of his employment at MIT seem to me important, in the
way the obvious is important if you have forgotten that things used to be (and
will be) be other than they are now. So I include this account as a brief and
perhaps handy synopsis of matters I treated more generally in the two previous essays.*

*It's worth mentioning, as one instance of these modulations, that Louis
Kampf was himself persona non grata to many colleagues and bosses at MIT
for a number of years, as a consequence of his political and intellectual consistency and his antiwar activism, in violation of old professional conventions of
neutrality. He probably made some additional enemies by his principled and
vigorous work in support of Palestinian rights. That he retired surrounded by
friends and admirers from MIT and from English, and with institutional
huzzahs, reinforces in a small way my general point about the politicization of
our field and (as I see it) the enlightenment of the university.*

I don't hold with those who blame Louis Kampf, personally, for the changes in the practice and teaching of English that have occurred in the last thirty-five years, though God knows it wasn't Paul Lauter or I who caused the Modern Language Association presidency to speak in the brash accents of Washington Heights.[1] Whatever share of the blame or credit goes to Louis—and it is a significant share—there can be no doubt that the outlook and practices of literary studies have dramatically changed since he came into the profession. I want to say what I think the main changes have been, ask what difference they have made, and end with a suitable blend of despondency and good cheer.

First, let me articulate eight simple hypotheses that I believe will seem obvious to most here today, and to many in our area of intellectual work, not just to Lefties—hypotheses that would have seemed outlandish or even incomprehensible in, say, 1961, when Louis and I got our first full-time jobs.

1. *Culture is political.* Which is to say, the making, transmission, and uses of culture are history-making activities, related to the exercise of economic and political power, and to the legitimation and subversion of power generally. Back in 1961, to be sure, Raymond Williams and a few others had revived an old conversation about culture and power, but in the United States that conversation had been ridiculed, labeled vulgar, shunted to the social margins, and quite exiled from academic, humanist ideology, which identified culture instead with timeless universals.

2. *Literature is more than the Canon.* The literature worth preserving, celebrating, criticizing, teaching about—includes far more than the works majestically lined up in the syllabi and bibliographies of 1961, more than the writings of the now infamous dead white males and the five or six dead white females admitted to their company.

3. *Culture is more than Culture.* The culture worth our critical attention and our teaching energies includes more than literature, more than Culture, more than high culture. That proud, old term strikes many as having lost, not just its honorific resonance, but its very power to discriminate. Be that as it may—and I venture no hypotheses on postmodernity, here—we have greatly broadened the scope of our work, in what some see as a debasing of its currency, others as an opportunistic move to lure back students fleeing from the humanities, still others as a dilettantish encroachment onto the turf of sociologists and communications scholars, but *many* as a necessary opening into the popular and a rejection of disciplinary blindness. Whatever you

think, something changed that made it acceptable for Louis to teach about spectator sports in a literature department and for me to write about popular magazines and the advertising industry.

4. *Criticism is political.* It is inevitably so, if culture and literature are political, for critics to try to negotiate or control the meanings, and thus the social efficacy, of literature and culture: to control, in short, the ways they line up with or against the interests of social groups. Criticism is political, too, in that it is professionally driven and regulated, and so participates in the politics of the profession, its claims for itself on social terrain, and, by extension, the claims of the professional-managerial class. Of course not all criticism need do that, but our ability to do anything else, through criticism and teaching, has depended on understanding the institutional setting of our work, and dropping the Arnoldian premise of criticism as disinterested, as somehow above social process, that was such a flattering idea in the fifties, and such a high-sounding defense against attacks by the Bennetts and Cheneys[2] of those days, who nonetheless drove engaged criticism out of the university.

5. *Teaching is political.* By this I do not mean, as Lynne Cheney seems to think, that people like us assault the social order by injecting Marxism, feminism, and hatred of the United States directly into the tender veins of our students. For that matter, indoctrination and abuse of teacherly authority are concerns among us, as well, though I hope we've risen above the cretinous level on which Cheney and her allies propose to discuss these questions. But apart from the relatively banal matter of what statements we choose to utter in our classrooms, there's wide awareness now that as teachers we intervene, willy-nilly, in the making and unmaking of ideology. So, better willy than nilly. Further, it's a commonplace now that teaching, like criticism, can never be an entirely disinterested pursuit of truth. I do believe that few in our political quarter, unlike some of our poststructuralist colleagues who figure as coconspirators in the Cheney/Bennett indictment, have discarded Truth as an aim, but many have doubts about the "disinterested" part. Ideology aside, almost everyone understands teaching to be political in that by doing it we take part in social reproduction, not just when we give assignments, put grades on papers, break classes up into professorless groups, talk at or listen to students, arrange chairs in rows or circles, and so on. Not just in our local strategies and tactics (though hypothesis 5 has sponsored a thirty-year-long discussion of those, richer than anything that

passed for pedagogical talk before) do we as teachers join in preserving or amending the social order, but through our very placement in the institution, and through our work there.

6. *Students bring their lives into our classrooms.* Could this ever *not* have been known? In any but the most trivial sense, I think, yes; it was a secret. At least it figured hardly at all in talk about college teaching, which assumed that students all wanted or needed to learn pretty much the same things and did so in the same way, differences in intelligence aside. Who now abstracts students from their origins and circumstances and imagines them as similarly shaped vessels into which we pour knowledge? Students are people of various ages, sexualities, genders, races, classes—as we say in crude shorthand but try to think more subtly. The conflicts and inequalities and pathologies "out there" are also *in class.*

7. *Instructors are social beings, too, and citizens*—not just bearers of professional authority. You don't have to favor identity politics to believe it makes a difference who is teaching. Like students, we bring into the classroom our projects, our defeats, our tensions with the institution. Hypothesis 7 also allows that we are historical agents, maybe even activists.

8. *Teachers are workers; teaching is a job.* For this astonishing truth I cite Kampf and Lauter, *The Politics of Literature,* page 4.[3] Yes, in a way we knew it was a job; some even belonged to unions. But the ideological pressure was to think of our work as more of a cultural mission, soiled by conditions of employment—however lightly, in those days of expansion, of a seller's market, of professorial privilege. The work of sixties radicals taught hypothesis 8, and the collapse of the job market in 1969 underscored it, bringing us into the world of flexible accumulation and splitting the profession into a core and a marginal labor force, the latter no longer just putting in a few years as apprentices, with dignity and tenure to come.

Today it's possible to think more clearly about all these things, thanks partly to Louis Kampf and the movements he worked in, partly to the Right's resurgence against those movements, partly to bracing changes in the world's economic system.

How consequential have these shifts in understanding been? Mention of the Right will serve to remind anyone who has managed to forget that our movements (remember how fine it was just to call them "the Movement"?) have taken quite a beating over twenty some years, and that this is not a happy time for most of those with whom we cast our lot in the sixties. A reminder, too, that some of what we helped build *has* turned into the sort of identity politics the Right delights in attacking. Let's also acknowledge that for all our efforts to connect our teaching with the world outside—to insist that there really was no *inside*—many, many students who now learn to demystify power, injustice, male supremacy, capitalism, you name it, have little idea how to change any of these things or much hope that it's worth trying. The horses of instruction seem to have lost the tygers of wrath, somewhere between the lobby of the Hilton in 1969 and the year of Louis Kampf's retirement. "No socialism in one profession" might be hypothesis 9.

These remarks wouldn't reflect what Louis has taught me, unless strongly tinged by pessimism of the intellect. As for optimism of the will: let my eight hypotheses point to what change *can* be wrought in thirty years of struggle along with colleagues, friends, brothers and sisters, comrades.

TEACHING HISTORICALLY

◆

This essay, written in 1991, expands on my suggestion, in several of these essays, that the practice of English changed significantly after the early 1960s. One way is the inclusion in courses (as in scholarship) of texts from commercial culture, such as the advertisements I discuss below. Another is the teaching of literary texts as participants in historical process, including contestation over power along lines of gender, race, and (in this instance) class. I see these two themes as critical in the modulation of an older literary study into cultural studies, and in a widening of pedagogical openings and challenges. Obviously, I see the changes as improvements, but not without complications, and I hope to have at least acknowledged the latter in my commentary toward the end of the essay. One complication is that often we teach with colleagues, not as untrammeled individuals; the small political questions that arise in collaborative teaching about history also come forward in this essay. I need hardly add that the argument for historical teaching put forward in the first few paragraphs, below, applies with double force after September 11, 2001.

When I think about the great, blank space in our national consciousness that in part justifies historical teaching, I often think of an exemplary memory. One night in 1979, shortly after the Iranian takeover of the U.S. embassy, I was watching television coverage of a spontaneous demonstration on a Washington, D.C., street. A man repeatedly shouted, "We're *tired* of other countries telling us what to do," and then led people around him in a scraggly rendition of "God Bless America." In his frustration, the man spoke for millions of citizens. I doubt he knew what almost all had forgotten, that in 1953 our secret government had shanghaied a nascent democracy in Iran and put the shah in its place.

That would have been pertinent knowledge. It would not have freed the hostages, and it would have come too late to change the dismal course taken by the Iranian revolution. But it would have suggested two crude lessons. First, when people are trying to push the United States around, their actions may be the long-muted reflex of a push in the other direction. Second, if you steal a society's right of self-determination, you may not like what it does when it takes back that right. Applying those crude lessons to Central America in 1979 might have led people who could remember what the Monroe Doctrine had concretely meant for those countries, to demand a posture toward Nicaragua, Guatemala, and El Salvador different from the one adopted by our leaders—who are incapable of learning such lessons except in those few occasions when citizens raise the issue of what is quaintly called the "political cost" of killing peasants, as did the movement against the Vietnam War.

These are and will be matters of life and death, in which the sense of history plays a role. Of course, more than one sense of history is at play on this stage. The historical vision given currency by our leaders and their complaisant friends in the media sees an endless struggle between two great forces, one for good and one for evil, with freedom or slavery as the stakes. Here, in the bastion of freedom, a smiling, progressive evolution was set going by the American War of Independence and the U.S. Constitution, by the Puritans and the pioneers, and that history keeps delivering the fruits of democracy and hard work so long as we do not betray it or let the Evil Empire terminate it. Within that historical vision, the overthrow of a Mossadegh, or Arbenz, or Bosch, or Allende, or Bishop takes its place as a minor act of altruism, or at worst, an unfortunate necessity, and is easily forgotten—except that these forgotten bits of history sometimes snap up to bark our shins later on.

So a historical sense is not enough. Official history is apologetics; maybe its salience is one reason so many students write off history in general as bunk. Maybe they get the idea that history supports a crackpot reality they can do nothing to change. Obviously, I think that a sane historical sense has to define itself as *critical* of both official history and the power relations that sustain it and are sustained by it.

My subject is teaching historically about cultural texts, not teaching about American adventures abroad, but I frame it in this way to indicate the urgency I feel about the project. That urgency does not entail a particular vision of history, or a particular way of teaching about it, and the ways I will sketch here raise theoretical problems that I will acknowledge at the end of the essay. Also, the dangerous historical void in our public life is not the only reason for teaching historically about texts. We should do so because, in addition, we and our students cannot understand texts very satisfactorily without making them part of some historical narrative. With those premises out, I will try to suggest through two examples how a critical historical sense might come into play in our classrooms.

The first example concerns teaching about mass culture, in particular, about advertising. Consider the series of ads that probably gets into as many classrooms where advertising is taught as Shakespeare sonnets get into classrooms where poetry is taught: those for Virginia Slims cigarettes. You know the genre: an "old," brownish photo, usually in the upper background of the ad, evokes the bad time before women were free. Perhaps it shows a turn-of-the-century woman sitting demure and alone at one end of a dinner table, while three or four men at the other end exclude her from their talk, brandy, and cigar smoke; perhaps it just shows a group of Klondike miners with a subservient woman or two off to one side.

In the foreground of the ad, striding forth in brilliant color and bold, idiosyncratic fashion, is the Virginia Slims lady, confidently, even defiantly flourishing her cigarette, yet gorgeous and still somehow quintessentially feminine. The familiar slogan, "You've come a long way, baby," annotates the contrasting images with the correct historical reading of their juxtaposition.

Everyone who has thought for five minutes about these ads understands how they mean to turn critical history into good marketplace behavior—how they swallow up 90 percent of what is creatively critical in the women's movement of the last twenty years, convert it into freedom of self-presentation in public, and hand it back to women as inseparable from commodified glamour. And of course they subsume the women's movement within official history: just part of the long forward march of progress, a natural outcome of our social and economic system, rather than a battle against persistent inequalities of that system. So the Virginia Slims ads, like all others, but more openly than most, do not just ignore history, they enter into a contest over its meanings and direction. Awareness of that contest is essential to the critical sense one needs to keep one's bearings in mass culture and in the politics of our lives.

What might historical teaching contribute here, beyond rescuing the development and ideas of contemporary feminism from the ad agency's cynical assault and extending the reach of an eighteen-year-old's memory? I suggest contextualizing the Virginia Slims ads more deeply in the commodification of desire and in mass culture's characteristic attempt at sanitizing and incorporating whatever threatening tendencies arise outside its sphere. One might, for instance, look with students at commercial and ideological uses of the flapper image in 1920s advertising. Or one could trace this strategy farther back, to an ad like that for a dentifrice called Rubifoam, that appeared in several popular monthly magazines around 1896. This was the moment of boldly independent "New Woman," the much controverted feminist of the 1890s. Like Virginia Slims today, Rubifoam appropriated both the appeal and the scandal that surrounded this figure. The ad showed a woman in knickers, a vest, a shirt with bow tie, and a riding jacket and hat, standing informally with hands in pockets. The text linked image to product thus: "THE NEW WOMAN whatever costume she may wear, will be particular about her teeth. Fashion decrees changes in wearing apparel, but it will always be fashionable to have the teeth white and the breath sweet." Then followed specific claims about Rubifoam. The image itself represented the New Woman mockingly—her stylized outfit, her mannish pose.[1] The text neutralized the politics of dress reform by calling her clothes a "costume," by recuperating them within the familiar dynamic of "fashion," and by making it clear that even the defiant feminist will seek conventional beauty, presumably with the aim of attracting a man.

While enlisting a social movement in the promotion of a humble domestic commodity, the Rubifoam ad did a number of other things that are common in advertising today, of which I will mention just three.

1. It connected meanings in a way that was semantically (though not politically) arbitrary: a tooth cleanser signifies women's liberation. Such links were constituting a *language* of advertising, an essentially magic system of meanings.
2. The ad hinted at the possibility of raising oneself socially, of attaining distinction, of standing out from the crowd, not by actually gaining in wealth or status but by using a product that cost twenty-five cents. It promoted the "democracy of goods" that was feeding on and supplanting the old Horatio Alger dream of success.
3. It addressed the reader as valuing *modernity*, indexed here as advanced dress, "the New Woman," "fashion," "fashionable," and "up-to-date."

It hailed her as one hoping to ride the wave of historical progress, *and* it invited her to take that historical part by a private act of consumption.

In short, the ad mystified human relations and the social process in ways extremely familiar to us today, displacing needs that are intrinsically social into that arena of individual choice, the marketplace.

Finding such antecedents does not in itself do much to nurture a historical sense, though it is a beginning. A danger is that by stressing likenesses between this ad of 1896 and many ads of the 1980s, one may seem to imply that the more things change, the more they remain the same—that advertising is advertising. Not so. You could search the ad pages of national magazines just fifteen years earlier and find nothing like the Rubifoam ad in appearance or technique of signification. In fact, in 1881 publications, you can find few ads of any sort for nationally sold, brand-name commodities. Those you can find are small, without sophisticated graphics, and printed in tiny type, more or less like classifieds today. Their texts all read like this one for a baking powder: "Absolutely pure, grape cream tarter and bicarb of soda; contains nothing else. . . . All other kinds have filling, as starch, flour, . . ." This might well have been false, but my point is that earlier ads gave information and made offers instead of magically linking products to social ideals and personal dreams of glory.

Why? What happened between 1880 and 1900? Very many related things, including the birth of both the national mass circulation magazine (*The Cosmopolitan*, not then a women's magazine, was one of the leaders) and the modern advertising industry (led by ad agencies, specialists in consciousness): linchpins of the national, mass, commercial culture that surrounds us today. Behind those new cultural institutions was the sudden development of the large, integrated corporation, drawing together the entire productive process, from raw materials to sales, in strategic response to the instability and repeated crises of entrepreneurial capitalism. Through the new arrangements, businessmen sought to organize markets rather than just get out the goods and hope for the best. Advertising as we know it was a byproduct of that need; in turn, national mass culture was (I exaggerate only a bit) a byproduct of national advertising and the circulation of brand-name commodities such as Rubifoam, Ivory Soap, the Gillette safety razor, Cream of Wheat, and dozens of others—including cigarettes, transformed from a rare luxury into a common necessity by the wonderful new Bonsack machines and the promotional genius that James Buchanan Duke employed to market their output. The magical language of advertising was and is both specific to our social formation and responsive to the needs of powerful actors within it.

In teaching critically about mass culture, I find it essential to explore this network of economic and social relations. Otherwise, the critique stays on the surface and tends to promote a shallow cynicism and a false, conspiratorial understanding of cultural production, the notion that media corporations are intentionally brainwashing audiences into zombielike acceptance of the status quo. That is better than the *non*critical understanding, that we have a cultural democracy in which audiences get just what they want; but it misses the depth, the rootedness, of cultural relations and renders the critical attitude ineffectual, leaving us with the feeling that "we" sophisticated college people can see through these crude deceptions, whereas the masses remain forever victims. And that points to a second way in which the historical sense can be empowering, if sobering. By dissipating the solipsism of the present moment in which many students live, owing partly to mass culture itself, it lets them and us see that things could be different because things *have been* different—and very recently. Social formations are temporary. Something worse or better will supplant this one. We who are living will, by action and inaction, give it shape. Historical teaching can awaken a sense of agency outside the sphere of the personal.

My second example, which moves away from my individual teaching practices, concerns not the historical contextualizing of recent texts but the approach to texts from other societies and other times. I refer to a course in the historical study of literature that my department at Wesleyan has been teaching for about five years. It is the second semester of a year-long sequence for sophomores considering an English major. There are usually about one hundred students in that category, and the course usually has around five sections. About half the members of our twenty-person department now have the course in their repertories.[2]

First, I need to say a word about the course's genesis. Like anything that an eclectic department agrees on, it is the product of a compromise, and one that interestingly embodies some of the divisions in literary study today. Eight or ten years ago it become clear that most of my colleagues wanted to reconsider the no-requirements free-for-all that had been our response to the late sixties. In the curricular discussions that followed, however, we were naturally up against a range of disagreements about the premises of literary education, indeed, of literary study. What might we all agree to say through a required sophomore course about the kinds of reading we thought essential? Nothing, obviously. But we could and finally did agree to suppress our differences beneath two platitudes: every student should know how to read a text with careful and subtle attention to its language, and every student should be able to read a text with some appreciation of its historicity.

From this plain credo we developed two semesters of study with a chasm between them. In English 201 the students read mainly lyric poems in the way that became traditional after World War II. One poem per fifty minutes; no intentional fallacy, no context, little intertextuality; key in on voice, register, metaphor, syntax, dramatic situation, prosody, and so on. In English 202, suddenly, the texts are fat novels surrounded by journals, memoirs, documents, historical arguments, criticism, and so on, all somehow to be grasped as participating in the historical process. It is as if the English Department were kidnapped and taken en masse to a reeducation camp over winter break. The schizophrenia makes for quite a pedagogical jolt that I will not attempt to rationalize; I am speaking of what one disparate and overworked group of people actually does, not about a utopian scheme.

To suggest some implications of the pedagogical shift, and to give an idea of what we try to do in the course, I will focus for a while on issues we engage in a unit on Jane Austen's *Emma*. A characteristic passage of exposition in the novel begins this way: "The Coles had been settled some years in Highbury, and were a very good sort of people—friendly, liberal, and unpretending; but, on the other hand, they were of low origin, in trade, and only moderately genteel."[3] Well! This sort of judgment, fundamental to Austen's narrative, troubles most of my students. It expresses an outlook that puts the novel at a considerable distance from them, temporal, cultural, and indeed moral, as if one were to say, "She is a wonderful person but, on the other hand, a dental technician." (Never mind that few of my students are likely to marry dental technicians and mechanics, or even drink beer with them; the *sentiment* is old-fashioned, snobbish, and offensive.) How do we bridge, historically, the gap between this twentieth-century American response and the early nineteenth-century English context? One way would be to grant that, yes, by our standards Austen was a snob, and go on to praise the counterbalancing virtues of her work. But this is to endorse a dismissal of it as simply

outmoded, a dismissal that not only could be extended to most older literature but also denies our own connectedness to history.

A more common strategy among critics is to save the work from the scrap
heap of outmoded values by claiming it as universal, or modern, or at least
in advance of its time. Nonhistorical techniques of reading in service to this
strategy are readily available. For instance, a New Critical close reader, after
noting the tidy opposition of triplets ("friendly . . . of low origin"), might
look for internal evidence to determine whether the opposition is ironic.
And such evidence is abundant. After explaining that the Coles have experienced a rapid increase in prosperity, the narrator continues: "Their love of
society, and their new dining-room, prepared every body for their keeping
dinner-company; and a few parties, chiefly among the single men, had already taken place. The regular and best families Emma could hardly suppose
they would presume to invite—neither Donwell, nor Hartfield, nor Ran-
dalls." Until that last sentence, no distance seems to separate the narrator
from Emma; but here, surely, is the tip-off. Emma will swallow her pride and
do likewise. Thus, the Coles gain admission to the inner circle on at least
probationary terms, and Emma learns yet another lesson about rank, social
mobility, and true gentility of conduct.

The close reader may now confidently label as ironic the narrator's balancing of "friendly, liberal, and unpretending" against "of low origin, in
trade, and only moderately genteel." Here, one may conclude, the narrator
voices the inhumane class feeling of Emma (and of "every body") only to
discredit it and to establish a higher moral community between the narrator
and the democratic reader, to which Emma will be fully admitted only at the
end of the novel. In such ways, I believe, teachers and students often enlist
close reading in tacit defenses of writers, aligning their values with ours and
claiming them as advocates of universal values, or at least of the "modern"
ones that inhabit the American classroom. Lionel Trilling is one of many
who have claimed Austen for modernity. In English 202 we ask students to
read his well-known essay "*Emma* and the Legend of Jane Austen," in which
he credits Austen, "conservative and even conventional as she was," with
having "perceived the nature of the deep psychological change which accompanied the establishment of democratic society." And he argues that the
novel shows Emma's initial snobbery to be "a mistake of nothing less than
national import," a "contravention of the best—and safest—tendency of English social life," in that it would have excluded not only rising tradespeople

like the Coles but also members of "the yeoman class" like Robert Martin.[4] This is indeed to make Emma's moral education an education in democratic sensibility and conduct, as well as to naturalize the novel for young readers in this society.

But in calling Robert Martin a member of the yeoman class Trilling makes an interesting error that perhaps is nonetheless understandable: he took his lead from Emma, who, in her famous put-down of Martin to Harriet Smith, says, "The yeomanry are precisely the order of people with whom I feel that I can have nothing to do."[5] Although she knows well enough that Martin is a tenant farmer, already prosperous and likely to become rich, she chooses to place him in an older social structure that by the beginning of the nineteenth century was in an advanced state of disintegration. Some families, like the Martins from the old yeomanry, had made it in capitalist agriculture, forming a new class adjacent to, and in partnership with, the great landlords. Most yeomen and peasants, done in by the enclosures of the eighteenth century and by the new rules of the game, had slid off the edge of respectability and disappeared into the great mass of agricultural laborers, by far the most numerous class in the time and place of Emma's story. Students in English 202 read about the three rural classes and the new exploitative basis of agriculture in a chapter from *Captain Swing*, by E. J. Hobsbawm and George Rude.[6] In Hobsbawm's *Industry and Empire*[7] they also read more broadly about the industrial capitalist transformation of English society—the proletarianization of labor, the polarization of city and country, the assimilation of successful merchants like the Coles into the class of "gentlemen," and so on: the entire, dynamic, world-transforming process from which Austen abstracted her "little bit (two inches wide) of ivory."

Such a reading does more than merely ground the questions of the Martins' and Coles' proper social rank in a historically specific process of class formation and assimilation, one that Austen understood very well and in which she chose to give Emma a moral education. It also prompts the following question, an odd one for literary study: where are the rural masses in Austen's world? And that leads us to scrutinize their very few appearances in *Emma:* the "poor sick family" of cottagers to whom Emma and Harriet pay a charitable visit, resulting in the brief ennoblement of their sensibilities; the gypsies whose rude assault on Harriet faintly indexes a challenge to the social order administered by magistrates like Knightly; and, similarly, the anonymous poultry thieves whose depredations hasten the happy end of the story by reconciling Mr. Woodhouse to the treachery of his daughter's marriage. I will not recapitulate here the sorts of discussion that ensue. What I want to emphasize are two premises of our course that emerge from such inquiries.

First, we unabashedly encourage mimetic questions often thought to be illegitimate, like the one about the rural poor. Whom did Austen virtually delete from the social milieu of farmers like Robert Martin, and how does Austen's novel represent that condition? To ask this is to commit what Trilling called the "notable error" of believing that "the world of Jane Austen really did exist," though "any serious history will make it sufficiently clear that the England of her novels was not the real England, except as it gave her the license to imagine the England which we call hers."[8]

But what *kind* of "license" was that? What authority issued it? What did it mean for Austen to give only the rarest glimpses of rural laborers, and those only through stereotyped images of the deserving poor and the dangerous poor? "Where only one class is seen, no classes are seen"; so says Raymond Williams in a section of *The Country and the City*,[9] which is also part of our packet of readings. We want our students to consider what kind of "seeing" this was.

That brings me to the second premise. Our effort is not to provide a true picture of early nineteenth-century, rural, southern England, by reference to which students may judge Austen's novel to be a faithful or distorted representation of reality. Rather, we assume distortion and conceptualize it as mediation and ideology. Trilling opposes the mimetic premise by insisting that the England of *Emma* was an "idyll." Fair enough, but questioning does not end there. An idyll grounded in whose values, whose interests, whose project of idealization, whose project of social order? Questions like these are central to the course. We encourage their careful articulation through discussion of an essay by David Aers, in which he argues, powerfully if contentiously, that Austen's mediation of her world is governed more by her ideology than by some abstract "imaginative insight" and that we should see her, in company with Edmund Burke and the like, as a "polemical tory ideologist, a most accomplished partisan in a period of open and intense ideological controversy in which novelists played a significant role."[10]

It is our task, of course, to keep such a position from being reductive; we try always to return such claims to the novel—for example, by considering Williams's point that "the paradox of Jane Austen is . . . the achievement of a

unity of tone, of a settled and remarkably confident way of seeing and judging, in the chronicle of confusion and change."[11] This idea takes us back to
passages like the one about the Coles and to the precise mobilization of values entailed by balancing "personal" qualities such as friendliness against
social givens such as birth and the sources of one's money, education, and
manners. With luck, this movement brings ideology into focus as permeat-
ing every line of the novel and inseparable from its esthetic texture, so that
history takes shape *in* the text, not just as an external standard by which to
measure it.

I hope that this example has provided at least a rough idea of how we
conceptualize the task of reading literary works as they participate in the
historical process. I have been ruthlessly selective, of course. Our unit on
Emma devotes little time to the rural poor, more to the intricate matter of
gentility and class accommodation, and more still to marriage, sexuality, and
gender. In addition, we raise questions of biography and reception, dealing
with gentle Janeism through several sources: the Austen Leigh memoir of his
aunt, selections from Austen's letters, and Harding's article on "regulated hatred" in Austen's works—in particular, his well-known statement that "her
books are, as she meant them to be, read and enjoyed by precisely the sort of
people whom she disliked."[12] The "historical process" is more than the class
struggle, in English 202 as in life.

Now let me quickly sketch in the rest of the course. It has four units, each
lasting three or three and a half weeks and centered on a major fiction. Each
year we replace one unit to keep us fresh and to allow us to keep rethinking
the aims and methods of the course. Last year *Moll Flanders* was the first
main text, buttressed by Ian Watt's *The Rise of the Novel* and by a brief comparison with *Pilgrim's Progress,* a text that both provides a sharp contrast to
the "economic individualism" Watt finds in early eighteenth-century novels
but in some ways presages their concerns. There were also readings on marriage and the condition of women in eighteenth-century England, on crime
and prisons, and so on. After the unit on *Emma,* we vaulted the Atlantic and
130 years of history to read Faulkner's *Go Down Moses* against material on
slavery and plantation life; readings, including Thoreau's "Walking," that
delineate an American relation to nature quite different from that expressed
by Emma's rhapsodic thought of "English verdure, English culture, English
comfort";[13] and readings from the debate initiated by the agrarians on southern culture. Race was even more central to the final unit, along with gender,

as we concluded with Morrison's *Song of Solomon,* pondering various strategies for black liberation, various relationships of writers to black oral culture, and so on. (The writers included Hurston, Gwendolyn Brooks, and Ellison.) This year, Faulkner gives way to a section on Hemingway's *A Farewell to Arms,* contextualized, especially by reference to 1920s writers, in main currents of U.S. culture.

Naturally, this course works less smoothly in the classroom than in my retelling. I want to name some problems that arise for us, and doubtless would arise in any course that attempts a serious engagement with history and literature for first- or second-year college students. First and most obviously, the task is impossible. The students know too little, we know too little, the semester is too short, the leaps from text to text are irreducibly speculative, and so on. To this objection—which is not just theoretical, but which makes itself felt in our and the students' frustrations at hundreds of loose ends, at lack of closure, at uncertainty—I can only say, yes, it is hard to understand the world, including literature and history, but we have to start somewhere or accept the false reassurance of a narrow, formalist definition of ourselves. I myself am glad my department insists on a course that many students initially find uncongenial, precisely because in doing so we directly confront the blank refusal of history endemic in this society.

Second, there is a constant risk of privileging the nonliterary texts in the course as unchallengeable reports on how things really were, in a neat reversal of the way English departments usually privilege the literary—as if Hobsbawm did not have his own ideological project; as if Bennet Barrow's *Plantation Diary* were not itself a mediation of slavery, comparable in that way to Faulkner's "Was." We try hard not to sanction two different ways of reading and a simplistic view of direct access to historical truth through "nonfiction," but I know we sometimes fail.

Third, as we enlarge the usual mandate of criticism from interpreting texts to explaining them, we sometimes inadvertently give students the idea that the game is to *see through* literature: for example, either by discovering what dirty business Jane Austen was "really" up to or by casting her as the helpless instrument of historical forces. Our aim is indeed to dissipate some of the aura that surrounds Holy Literature, as we challenge the idea of its autonomy, but we do not want to leave students thinking that literature is only a self-interested scam. Certainly we do not want the challenge of historical thinking simply to dislodge the pleasure of the text.

Finally, there is the closely related danger of actually promoting a kind of ahistorical feeling and thinking to which some students are already inclined, even as we combat the ahistoricism that conceives literature as timeless, universal masterworks. I have in mind the tendency to confront the ideology of an older text as if its writer were an entrant in our own arena if discourse. Jane Austen may not have been the precursor of democracy that Trilling casts her as, but neither is his a totally misguided way to judge her. A difficult relativism is necessary in such matters, but hard to achieve. Most canonical writers were both progressive and reactionary in relation to the possibilities of alignment and feeling available in their own times. English 202 insists that they can be held accountable, just like the mass of human beings who are not writers, but it is another thing, and a bad one, to ride through literary history on an ideological white horse from the left-liberal barn of Wesleyan's political culture. After all, students can censure Austen's class consciousness well enough without taking English 202.

Beyond these pedagogical problems, and related to them, lie vexing theoretical issues that, because they permeate the cultural atmosphere of this discussion and of any attempt to teach historically, claim at least a brief acknowledgment on my part. As noted, English 202 tends to privilege a version of what really happened in history and use it to explain and interpret the literary texts at hand; my strategy for teaching about advertisements certainly does so. It is easy to see in such pedagogies the specter of a master narrative, subject to attack as both an illusory metaphysical presence and an instrument of coercion. To the second charge I reply that everyone—even a poststructuralist—is willy-nilly involved in a contest over the understanding of history. There is no way for teachers of literature not to be. One can *limit* the intrinsic risk of coercion by promoting generative historical thinking and an awareness that any master narrative is controverted and provisional, but that is hardly more than an ethical given in the liberal academy. I myself insist in addition that to counter the official master narrative with more liberatory ones is an act that empowers. The coercive power of even dogmatic feminist and historical materialist teaching is, in our present situation, no more than disruptive or subversive.

The other charge is more difficult. A story like that of capitalist crisis and transformation, which I often use to situate and explain texts, is itself a distillation of other texts, read in a certain way. It can have no epistemological priority over, say, *Emma;* indeed, its coherence dissolves along with its explanatory power when submitted to poststructuralist scrutiny. Thinkers in that mode tend to reconstitute history as a parity and interaction of infinitely many structures, with no center except language—and at that, a language diminished in its capacity for reference, expression, and action. Small consolation that on this view language itself is historical, for this is history without causes and without agents. To the extent that it admits change at all, it attributes change to something like the collision of molecules. The "randomization of history," to use Perry Anderson's term,[14] leaves the pedagogies I have recommended hanging over the much-touted abyss.

Of course that consequence is no argument against the theory, which is notoriously hard to combat on its own ground. I tend to think the theory fails at its origins, inferring from the arbitrariness of the signifier far more than Saussure's observation warrants. I do not think that signifiers are arbitrary in the sense required, which must bypass their social rootedness (and, if Chomsky is right, biological rootedness) or write it off as a delusion. That move led—again, in Anderson's words–to "the exorbitation of language" and "a gradual megalomania of the signifier,"[15] but I am not sufficiently versed in these debates to argue the point, nor are most of us who must choose one way or another to teach about history and culture. For those who want to do and teach explanatory history, I think the apt counsel is Jonathan Culler's suggestion that for the nonce we try to *ignore* deconstruction as irrelevant to our concerns[16]—not kick the stone in useless refutation, like Dr. Johnson, but adopt the double consciousness of Hume when he repaired from his skeptical labors to dinner and backgammon. Ignoring deconstruction will not put its skepticism to rest, but neither will ignoring history stop it from happening, or perhaps from doing us in. We must intervene as if history had causes and we might be agents. History, even without foundations, goes on.

The claim is often made that poststructuralist ideas and methods can ground a truly radical and subversive pedagogy. As S. P. Mohanty writes "[If] the mastery of the human subject over its meanings and its consciousness is rendered uncertain and spurious ... [then] pedagogy, particularly in the realm of culture, needs ... to face the fundamental challenge to escape both the transmission of coded knowledge and the coded transmission of knowledge."[17] The "archeological examinations performed by deconstructors," says Vincent B. Leitch, "are frequently corrosive insofar as the formations of history are subject to irreverent critiques of founding categories and operations."[18] Does not the "challenge" challenge too much, given our actual circumstances? Does not the "corrosive" reading corrode too much? An early and influential advocate of deconstruction suggested to me, modestly enough, that the method could serve teachers and students as a "crap detector." It surely is that. But when everything smells like crap, we need a more sensitive instrument that will identify the *dangerous* crap. Even if deconstruction should turn out to be "right," a true end to metaphysics rather than one of the innumerable blind alleys of system-building philosophy, that would not entail the rightness of its deployment in our classes—though it *would* enjoin us to remind ourselves and our students that the level of analysis at which we argue for one or another version of history is provisional and vulnerable. But so is every academic discourse.

Mohanty suggests that de Man's position in "The Resistance to Theory" is seductively attractive because it "makes possible a radicalism without the messy implications of *engagement*."[19] After all the caveats are registered, I favor politically engaged reading and teaching. For what is the alternative? Sartre describes it well, I think, in his caricature of "the critic," who contemplates with equal distance the racism of Gobineau and the humanitarianism of Rousseau (between whom he would have had to choose, had they been alive) because both Gobineau and Rousseau are "profoundly and deliciously wrong, and in the same way: they are dead."[20]

"Which side are you on?" is a question we should keep in close proximity to our classroom teaching of literature, however much it needs to be complicated by the passage of time. We, the ad man of 1896, and Jane Austen all are part of the same historical process. As we historicize their texts, we should see ourselves and our students as both bearers and creators of history.

GRADUATE STUDENTS,
PROFESSIONALS, INTELLECTUALS

◆

This essay is based on a talk I first gave at the University of North Carolina in 1988, on invitation by its organization of graduate and professional students. Like several other pieces in the book, this one is about how professions are constituted, about how they might be changing, and about what it means to join one of them. But here I put the role of professional into play with and against that of intellectual, in a hopeful effort to see the roles as still (or again) compatible. I imagined activist professionals working more or less anonymously in groups or movements and did not expect the role of "public intellectual" to be reoccupied or reinvented. As I scan the public arena now, I wonder if the prominence of such wildly diverse academics as Henry Louis Gates, Camille Paglia, the late Stephen J. Gould, and (after decades as a voice from the margins) Noam Chomsky is calling that part of my argument into question. I will not try to recoup or amend the argument here, beyond wondering also if the general commodification of flexible capitalism is at work here, especially its organization of and response to niche markets. (See essay 12.) And what would happen if in painful times the niche market for, say, Chomsky's ideas grew larger than that for Pat Buchanan's? But I grow fantastical.

I have a standard opener for talks like this. It is to cite the old definition of an expert as someone who is more than thirty-five miles from home. Given the topic I've taken on tonight, I might modify that: an intellectual is someone more than thirty-five miles from home. Back there, I was reading students' essays, teaching about Fitzgerald and West, and worrying with my colleagues over the shape that the second half of our required sophomore course for majors should have. Then, a surge of jet power, an interlude at the Atlanta airport, another jet, and here I stand before you, to talk about class, history, and the responsibilities of intellectuals. This is very grand—but also appropriate, since what I want to urge upon you is the ineradicable presence in our lives of just such incongruities and tensions. We often feel them as a kind of role dissonance, yielding malaise or worse. There are historical reasons for those feelings, and I plan to touch on our history today; but not with the intent of arguing that we are its helpless pawns. I think there are openings out from the contradictory position of professional-and-intellectual, and eventually I'll get around to such upbeat thoughts. First, though, I will speak of the contradictions.

In doing so, I address—most directly—the graduate and professional students. I hope I won't, by taking long views, show insensitivity to the very real, immediate problems you face. I remember clearly enough, over the lapse of three decades, the intimidating weight of professional expectations, the crush of daily labor, the monumental anxieties produced by qualifying exams, the impossibility as it seemed, of producing a discourse of three hundred pages or so that some human being would care to read. I know too—though not from my own experience, since jobs abounded in those ancient days—the desolation of spirit into which the job crisis of the past twenty years has plunged many arts and sciences students. I have little to say about these good causes for worry, and to any who may have come hoping for practical advice, I apologize, and suggest you step out for a beer. Nor will I talk much about the bright side of your experience, the challenge and exhilaration of higher learning. That's part of what you came for, and I hope you're getting some of it.

Let me make some assumptions. For instance, that most of you came from liberal arts backgrounds and that you experience professional or graduate education partly as an enlargement of scope and competence, but partly also as a narrowing of the interests and vision you brought here. I assume that you wanted to be, in a broad sense, intellectuals (you didn't choose on-the-job training in sales or computer programming) but find, if you didn't already know it, that you can qualify for that life only by becoming specialists—specific *kinds* of intellectuals, holding your most serious conversation with ever smaller groups of peers. I assume that you wanted the kind of autonomy offered by professional life but are experiencing along the way enough subservience and deflection of individual purpose to make you wonder. I assume you wanted what I'll call social authority, and will achieve it, but only in a small compartment assigned you by the division of labor. I assume, finally, that you came with concern about social problems and hoped to address them responsibly with the aid of what you are learning and of the social authority conferred by professional membership—issues like health care delivery, nuclear power, crises of the family, racial inequality, the physical and cultural environments. You can name your own issues, and I'm sure you have plenty of them, as we do in English: literacy, the relations of elite and popular culture, the status of minority dialects and languages, the continued subordination of women, and so on. If I'm right, I imagine that you are finding, too, or will find, that your expertise and concern run more into small local channels than you might have wished. Hopes for deeper literacy shrink into schemes for writing across the curriculum; hopes for racial equality come down to inclusion of a black writer in English 202 —to call on examples from my own field once again.

Now, there is nothing particularly new or surprising in this. I do no more, perhaps, than name the familiar discontents of specialization. The immediate occasion for reviewing them in your presence is my bemused reading, a while back, of Russell Jacoby's book, *The Last Intellectuals,* which puts the matter in a startling enough way and makes the case that something new has indeed happened. His title refers to the generation that includes Galbraith, McCarthy, Howe, Kazin, Carson, Riesman, Bell, and so on, and he holds that they are indeed the last of their kind. He challenges us to "name a group of important younger American critics, philosophers, or historians," sociologists, psychologists, and so on.[1] As recently as the 1950s, he says, that would have been easy to do—and the names would have been those just mentioned, along with perhaps two dozen others. They have virtually no successors.

Of course it would be easy for those of you "in" history to name important young historians and for me to name important young critics. Jacoby's point is that few outside our credentialed ranks could do so; and even those who could—perhaps because of hostile notice taken in the *New York Times Magazine* or the *Wall Street Journal*—would have little interest in reading their work, and little understanding of the debates that animate their writing. Jacoby is concerned with "*public* intellectuals, writers and thinkers who addressed a general and educated audience" (5). They were "freely speculating minds" who pursued "wide-ranging, curious, adventurous, and humane study" (72–73), but the main point is that they did so in accessible language and in arenas that could carry their ideas far beyond professional bound-aries. Why is there no successor generation?

To put it sharply: the habitat, manners, and idiom of intellectuals have been transformed within the past fifty years. Younger intellectuals no longer need or want a larger public; they are almost exclusively professors. Cam-puses are their homes; colleagues their audience; monographs and special-ized journals their media. Unlike past intellectuals they situate themselves within fields and disciplines—for good reason. Their jobs, advancement, and salaries depend on the evaluation of specialists, and this dependence affects the issues broached and the language employed. Independent intellectuals, who wrote for the educated readers, are dying out . . . .

Jacoby sees the migration into universities as critical, and not mainly out of a nostalgia for shabby cafés on the Left Bank or in Greenwich Village. Not the security and comfort of university life, but its way of organizing knowledge is the main trouble: "[P]rofessionalization leads to privatization or depoliti-cization, a withdrawal of intellectual energy from a larger domain to a nar-rower discipline. Leftists who entered the university hardly invented this process, but they accepted, even accelerated it. Marxism itself has not been im-mune; in recent years it has become a professional 'field' plowed by specialists" (147).

That last point is close to the heart of Jacoby's concern; like me, he is es-pecially worried about the shriveling into professionalism of critical and op-positional intellectuals, those who would search for the roots of social and cultural change, cry halt to processes of corporate domination, and put forth alternate visions. About the activities of such critics in their university perches, Jacoby is gloomy indeed, especially with respect to those who took part in sixties movements and then carried their politics into professional careers. His survey of radicals in academic philosophy, international studies, political science, history, economics, literary theory, geography, and so on makes his point well enough, though in my view hyperbolically and with a skewed emphasis to be explored toward the end of this talk. To look about us is on the one hand to confirm the worst horrors of the *Wall Street Journal,* the *National Review, Commentary,* and the Heritage Foundation—the uni-versity gives sustenance to thousands or tens of thousands of radicals—and on the other hand, and from the other side of the aisle, it is to fear that Jacoby is right in his ironic message: "Not to worry, they are only talking to one another."

Having laid out these propositions for your consideration, I now want to put them in a slightly longer historical perspective than Jacoby does. History can help us see where we are—particularly we intellectuals, who, as Alvin Gouldner observed, tend to see everyone else's condition as historically grounded, but ours as self-grounded and autonomous. Of course it is not. For those who work as professionals, our history is in fact highly contingent and brief. Professionalism as we know it gradually took shape—through the efforts of occupational groups to control their work, regulate entry to it, and claim privileges and benefits—only in the second half of the last century. Before that there were the three recognized professions of law, divinity, and medicine, but they bore little resemblance to the forms of organization that characterize professions now. (The word "professional" was first used as a noun, in the modern sense, about 1850; and the word "professionalism" appeared even later.) Professions affixed themselves to, or grew out of, universities toward the end of the nineteenth century, when modern universities themselves first came into existence. Professionalism seems to have been an integral growth within advanced capitalism, which first offered the opportunity for such specializations of knowledge, status, and power.

As this development implies, no line of work is intrinsically a profession. People settled disputes before there were certified lawyers, healed before there were licensed physicians, built bridges before there were professional engineers, did science before there were academic degrees in it, and so on. Contrariwise, no logic prevents shoe repair or rock 'n' roll performance from being a profession. The important thing to see is that professions are socially made categories, and processes. A group that is doing a particular kind of work organizes itself in a professional association; appropriates, shares, and develops a body of knowledge as its own; discredits other practitioners performing similar work; establishes definite routes of admission, including but not limited to academic study; controls access; and gets recognition as the only group allowed to perform that kind of work, ideally with state power backing its monopoly. The process doesn't end there. Every constituted profession must continue to defend its rights and its borders. For the weaker ones, like secondary school teaching, this is no hollow threat, as proposals regularly come forward to bring nonpros into the schools, or eliminate job security from outside, or stratify teaching so that only a few would ever become full-fledged professionals ("master teachers"), or as instructional materials prepared by business groups and other outside agencies flow into the classroom. Most high school teachers experience their profession as sustained through daily conflict in ways hardly imaginable to economists or physicians. But the possibility of challenge and even defeat always in principle exists.

Now this is not to say that every line of work is equally amenable to professionalization. Magali Sarfatti Larson, whose book *The Rise of Professionalism* will be the main source of my remarks for the next few minutes, lists a number of conditions favorable to professional monopoly:

1. That almost everybody needs the service being sold.
2. That its dispensation can be kept relatively private, even invisible.
3. That the clientele be unorganized individuals.
4. That the profession's cognitive basis be well-defined and esoteric.
5. That the market for the service can be kept independent of other markets.

Clearly conditions like these favor medicine over high school teaching and high school teaching over fast food work. But nothing is determined or eternal here. Professions, in the modern sense, can exist only in the context of commodity and labor markets—that is, in the context fully created only by capitalism, so far. But Larson interestingly points out that professions did not automatically or easily find a place for their wares, even in that context. It is worth quoting her at some length on this:

> For a professional market to exist in a modern sense, a distinctive "commodity" had to be produced. Now professional work, like any other form of labor, is only a fictitious commodity; it "cannot be detached from the rest of life, be stored or mobilized," and is not produced for sale. Unlike craft or industrial labor, however, most professions produce intangible goods: their product, in other words, is only formally alienable and is inextricably bound to the person and the personality of the producer. It follows, therefore, that the producers themselves have to be produced if their products or commodities are to be given a distinctive form. In other words, the professionals must be adequately trained and socialized so as to provide recognizably distinct services for exchange on the professional market. . . .
>
> Because of the unique nature of the products to be marketed, and because their use value to the large public was as uncertain as it was

new, control had to be established first "at the point of production": the providers of services had to be controlled in order to standardize and thus identify the "commodity" they provided. For this, a cognitive basis was crucial. . . . However, a cognitive basis of any kind had to be at least approximately defined before the rising modern professions could negotiate *cognitive exclusiveness*—that is, before they could convincingly establish a teaching monopoly on their specific tools and techniques, while claiming absolute superiority for them. The proved institutional mechanisms for this negotiation were the license, the qualifying examination, the diploma, and formal training in a common curriculum.[2]

Precisely because there is no natural market for services provided in the professional format, in order to gain market control, professionalizing groups have to standardize their entry rituals and create a body of knowledge whose mastery will serve as prerequisite for novices. This is not to say that the knowledge and training associated with various professions have no social and intellectual value—though members of one group have occasionally been known to hold such views about the cognitive basis of another group—but just that it's wrong to think of bodies of sound knowledge as logically or historically prior to movements toward professional power.

This suggests, to no one's surprise, that in any profession's address to the public there will be a certain amount of ideology. To that I now turn, with the intent of explaining some of the contradictions I assumed you to be experiencing. The first two derive from claims that must be advanced— and accepted—about a profession's body of knowledge. First, that knowledge must appear objective and disinterested, transcending the preferences of those who produce and transmit it. That requirement stands directly athwart the fact that we all are interested parties with social and moral projects that are partly responsible for our wanting to be professionals in the first place. Everything in the professional ethos urges that we lay aside those interests, at least in our professional roles, and especially during our training. Second, the body of knowledge and its regulation and advancement must be closed to outsiders—in effect, private—or there is no reason to demand long specialized training and no justification for banning amateurs from practice. But that requirement conflicts precisely with the wish many of us have to converse with wider groups of citizens—to be, in fact, public intellectuals.

Let me mention—still drawing on Larson's analysis—just a few other contradictions and tensions that arise from the historical contingency of professionalism:

1. Successful professions have gathered in the social authority that Jacoby attributes to older generations of free intellectuals but, as specialization increases, have done so by delimiting the field of that authority to the extent that few outsiders know what the specialists do, or care to seek their counsel. (This is especially true in academic fields.)

2. To warrant their privileges—freedom from the most intense competition and relatively autonomous conditions of work, to mention the two most important—professions have proclaimed an ideal of service to the whole social body and initial independence from the rich and powerful. Yet since we offer our services either on the market or through institutions like colleges that express social inequality, we tend generally to serve those who pay. Willy-nilly, most of us spend at least part of our energies reproducing the injustices of the social order.

3. Professions justify their rewards, similarly, by announcing their openness to anyone who qualifies and forsaking all barriers of heredity or class. In so doing they shore up the ideology of equal opportunity, actually providing a justification for inequality, which, when ideology is working smoothly, will seem the natural result of different abilities and different degrees of effort.

4. Finally, professionals claim autonomy, both in their work and from the market, while using socially produced knowledge to gain, collectively, an advantageous position in the market. (Obviously some do this far more successfully than others.) To add one more twist, autonomy translates, partly, into careers, wherein one gains public advantage by winning the approval of specialist colleagues. Thus public recognition in the form of earnings and prestige gravitates toward those who speak with the least public voice.

I've been generalizing over a broad range of professions, ignoring the differences among them and between those that sell services to individuals and those that work for salaries, and abstracting rather madly. Still, I hope that even this distorted account helps explain both why so many professionals and professionals-in-training feel conflicts between their original goals and the means of achieving them and also why the disappearance of public intellectuals is about as historically inevitable as such changes can be. The only puzzle is why this one took so long to complete itself—for it was well under way in the first two decades of this century, as contemporary observers such as Veblen and Randolph Bourne often complained. I think the answer is just that, in spite of rapid growth from 1880 on, universities and professions remained a small part of our society until after the Second World War. Then they quickly enlarged to encompass almost all possibilities for intellectual inquiry, overwhelming alternatives like Jacoby's much-lamented Bohemia. Further, as professional bodies of knowledge grew exponentially and increased in sophistication, professionalized intellectuals gained real advantages, along with spurious ones, over generalists, so that it takes a truly heroic effort now, by someone like Chomsky (is there anyone like him?), to compete legitimately with professionals in other fields for their own terrain. Clearly, this is not all bad.

And with that grudgingly cheerful remark, this talk has passed its nadir. I will now begin to loosen the net of contradictions I have drawn so tightly around our best hopes and your life chances. Before waxing too optimistic, though, let me pause to deal with a phenomenon that might seem to call Jacoby's thesis into question. At about the time when his book was granted the modest success he would have predicted, two other books by intellectuals stood week after week at the top of the *New York Times* nonfiction best-seller list; as everyone knows, they were Allan Bloom's *The Closing of the American Mind* and E. D. Hirsch's *Cultural Literacy*. I shall pass over the first of these, because I don't plan ever to read it (I have enough ulcers without that; but I'll be glad to debate it anyhow in the question period). In any case, Jacoby has a place for it in his scheme: the conservative jeremiad against the university, so familiar in recent years, can reach wide audiences because conservatives continue to write plain language for general audiences, and they can do that because . . . well, because they have big conservative bucks behind them, supporting a conservative public sphere.

Hirsch is another matter, a liberal, and a highly professionalized academic. His case for the inseparability of literacy from cultural knowledge is strong. The point is important and could easily sponsor a more fruitful debate than the one that has ensued. But Hirsch encouraged the kind of reception his ideas have in fact had by espousing the very traditional American hope that a technical reconception of learning and modification of educational policy might, without any significant change in our society, ameliorate its inequality and injustice. His program, he insists on the first page of the preface, would not only serve all classes, but "constitute the only sure avenue of opportunity for disadvantaged children, the only reliable way of combating . . . social determinism" and breaking "the cycle of poverty."[3] Since Hirsch seems to attribute class to "class distinction" (91), implying that it would go away if we could eliminate ignorance and invidiousness, this hope is no surprise. The fact that the distribution of wealth has remained roughly constant through a century in which education has changed beyond recognition, the fact that it has gotten steadily more unequal during the last twenty years, regardless of 1960s experiments in open education or 1980s movements back to basics, the fact that the top 10 percent now own close to 90 percent of productive wealth and the top 1 percent nearly half of productive wealth—these facts might suggest that there are unjust forces at work in our social process, not just bad theories about the teaching of eight-year-olds.

But our leaders, intellectual and political, prefer not to think of matters in this way and welcome programs that offer to channel social conflict into technical resolutions. This gatekeeping process is evident from Hirsch's account of his project's genesis and development: an article in the *Journal of Basic Writing,* a fellowship at the Center for Advanced Study in the Behavioral Sciences, support from the National Endowment for the Humanities, encouragement from Gerald Graff at a 1981 conference of the Modern Language Association, urgings from Joseph Epstein to develop the MLA paper into what became very influential articles in *The American Scholar,* a suggestion from Diane Ravitch that Hirsch write a book and call it *Cultural Literacy.* Then, as he puts it, "the tenor of my life began to change. I received a letter from Robert Payton, president of the Exxon Educational Foundation," whose "kindly and idealistic challenge pulled me away from scholarly concern and into educational activism." I could go on through his acknowledgments, which tell a story of patronage and affiliation that says much about the ideological and hegemonic processes in a society like ours and about the attainment of influence.

One shouldn't make a single instance bear too much interpretive weight. But I suggest that we can understand the Hirsch event only in part by reference to Jacoby's categories. An academic professional can become, at least briefly, a public intellectual if he (probably not she) taps into liberal myths, adopts the problem-solution format, eschews the deeply critical, and advances a striking and hopeful thesis in accessible language. Yet the interpretation seems forced; another frame for the Hirsch event may be more helpful. Couldn't we see him as an action intellectual, like so many who went to Washington in the sixties, and who, whatever publics they reached with their writings, were finally addressing policy-makers in the seats of political power? Or, might we better still understand Hirsch in his present situation as an organic intellectual (Gramsci's term), advancing the social vision and project of a powerful class? What class, in that case?

Here I must touch on a part of the historical picture I have so far left out. In speaking of emergent professions a hundred years ago, I treated them strictly as occupational groups, coping with the challenges and opportunities history had dealt them. Needless to say, there were affinities of interest, outlook, and experience among these rapidly enlarging groups; and their growth was accompanied by that of managers, administrators, and officials. Barbara and John Ehrenreich, Robert Wiebe, and others have persuasively urged that we think of all of these groups as constituting a new class, between labor and increasingly remote corporate capital, and quite distinct from the old petty bourgeoisie. They were mental workers; they did not own a significant share of the means of production; their broadest social role was reproduction of capitalist culture and class relations. The Ehrenreichs call them the "professional-managerial class." This class, to which most of us surely belong, stands in a complex relation to labor, which I won't try to describe here, and also to capital: we can see it as carrying out tasks of social control, ideological production, and supervision more or less on behalf of the dominant class; but also as critical of unrestrained capitalism and market processes, right from the outset. It has aligned itself with rational management of production and of the social process and with culture, broadly speaking. It offers a vision of intelligent, liberal society.

The main point I wish to make is that the professional-managerial class has grown enormously from at most two million in 1900 to something like sixty million today, with much of that growth in the postwar period, accompanying the explosion of the universities mentioned earlier. In the process, it has gained influence, confidence, and political cohesion (think of Gary Hart and the yuppies), to some degree apart from and in conflict with big capital. I think we can understand liberal intellectuals—the Bundys, Rostows,

Schlesingers, and so on of the 1960s, perhaps intellectuals like Hirsch today— as the active, public voice of the professional-managerial class. Clearly such a role in formation of ideology and social control is not what Jacoby has in mind, but I suggest that it's a parallel role, today, to that of the older public intellectuals and that it is the main channel of influence for people in our class.

That will hardly comfort Jacoby, nor does it comfort me. But it's not the whole story either. Within the class and especially within universities, critical and radical intellectuals obviously also exist in larger and larger numbers. I would hold that their—our—significant presence is in fact guaranteed by the contradictory position of the professional-managerial class and more narrowly of professionals and university intellectuals. To mention just one key reason: the claim of autonomy, the aspiration toward a free life of the mind, so embedded in professional ideology, is always in some tension with the large institutions that structure our work and with their relation to centers of real power in our society. "Cooptation" was the word for that, in the sixties, and what happened then suggests that critical intellectuals can in certain circumstances become a significant social force, when in alliance with other groups.

Of course Jacoby is right, that rebels of the sixties who have continued as intellectuals have largely done so in the quieter venue of faculty ranks. And he is right that the move there has called forth from them a more specialized voice, that Todd Gitlin, professor of sociology at Berkeley, is not the same as Todd Gitlin, president of Students for a Democratic Society in 1964. Yet the example is not the best one Jacoby might have chosen, for with Gitlin's books on SDS and the media, on prime-time TV, and on the sixties, he has in fact reached a wide audience with no sacrifice of intellectual scope, professional rigor, or critical edge. That his audience consists mainly of university people and media professionals hardly makes it insignificant.

Beyond that, I think Jacoby is looking in the wrong place, for the wrong kind of relationship between intellectuals and the rest of the society. His ideal is that of the brilliant individual, wide-ranging and autonomous, precisely the sort of person who lurks in the background of professional ideology: the lone hero of intellect. I too regret that there are no more Edmund Wilsons, but in the new context their role cannot often, if ever, be taken up by unattached intellectuals, or by heroes of the economics department.

This does *not* mean that critical academics lack a public voice or social authority. Consider a remarkable blind spot in Jacoby's book. He names Betty Friedan as one of the last intellectuals, for *The Feminine Mystique;* apart from that, no feminists, academic or otherwise, appear among the hundreds of names in his index, except for Jane Fonda, who is mentioned in the text as Tom Hayden's wife. Nor does the word "feminism." Yet imagine the absurdity of thinking that feminism vanished from the public arena in 1964 or that its contestation of power and privilege depends on, say, Gloria Steinem stepping into the shoes of Betty Friedan. If any group of academic and nonacademic intellectuals has changed minds and changed the world over the past twenty years, it is feminists; but they have not addressed society through the lone, heroic voice. They have done so in ways familiar to us all: through self-organized small groups, through conferences and journals, through a body of revisionist scholarship that has changed how we understand reality, through challenges in the streets and in the electoral process, through the building of thousands of feminist organizations and institutions, through pressure on gender relations in the recesses of the professional-managerial class domestic sphere . . . and the list could go on.

That Jacoby missed, or chose to ignore, this social upheaval and the role of professionals in it surely owes in part to good old-fashioned male thick-headedness. But I think it owes also to the way in which he conceives the public sphere and the activity of intellectuals. He does not allow for a relation more complex than that of single voice and general public. He does not consider how ideas flow through organizations and movements. He does not see how critical thought sometimes spills out of universities, rather than always being neutralized within them. He does not ponder how the growth and consolidation of the professional-managerial class creates new frictions and new articulations of critical thought, along with the siren songs of research grants and tenure.

Thus he is silent, not only on feminism, but also on black intellectuals, the black studies movement, and struggles against racism. He ignores the role of both specialists and academic nonspecialists in resistance to the rape of Central America. (Though a merciless gang of action intellectuals have for eight years promoted the ideology of intervention, and, with the public voice and the power of the president behind them, have kept the policy in effect, a substantial majority of the people oppose it, and that, along with the vigorous efforts of activists—including professionals—has at times deterred a pusillanimous Congress from exacting the full measure of presidential brutality.) Jacoby passes over the critical legal studies movement, Physicians for Social Responsibility and their place in the fight for disarmament, the professors and students who have at times led the antiapartheid movement in this country—and you or I could extend the list.

Critical intellectuals are in fact far more active and consequential now than in the early sixties, the last great moment, in Jacoby's view, of the public intellectual. They work in different sites and in different ways and will have to elaborate and sophisticate those ways enormously before gaining the power to challenge seriously the centers of ideological and social power. That will not happen apart from a gathering of oppositional forces comparable to what took place in the sixties. But critical intellectuals will play a role in that gathering—are playing a role in it—albeit not on the star system. They are doing so collaboratively, both within the university and in the relation to movements outside it.

I risk sounding more triumphalist than I feel here. Obviously, this is not an exhilarating moment for radical intellectuals or for oppositional movements. But I want to sound the optimistic note in speaking to you who are entering the professions and who cherish hopes that by doing so you will not, at the end of your entry rites and ordeals, find yourselves in some small, dark, padded corner of the labyrinth. There is no need to put aside hopes of making a political and cultural difference. You can work where you are and will be to challenge the entrenched inequality and the arrogance of power that nearly saturate our main arenas of public discourse and social action. You will have social authority: the question is, how to use it in collaboration with others; how to be consciously political agents, both in the narrowest professional sites (the syllabus and pedagogy of English 101 do make a difference) and in negotiating alliances beyond your certified competence and beyond the academy. Prior to that tough political question, of course, there is question of resolve. In closing, let me quote a passage that did a lot for my own resolve, when I first read it more than twenty years ago. It is from Noam Chomsky's essay, "The Responsibility of Intellectuals."

> Intellectuals are in a position to expose the lies of governments, to analyze actions according to their causes and motives and often hidden intentions. In the Western world at least, they have the power that comes from political liberty, from access to information and freedom

of expression. For a privileged minority, Western democracy provides the leisure, the facilities, and the training to seek the truth lying hidden behind the veil of distortion and misrepresentation, ideology, and class interest through which the events of current history are presented to us.

It is the responsibility of intellectuals to speak the truth and to expose lies.[4]

That's not a bad place to start.

6

POLITICS AND COMMITMENT
IN WRITING INSTRUCTION, AS IT
BECAME A PROFESSION

◆

This essay is based on a talk I gave at the first Watson Conference on Rhetoric and Composition at the University of Louisville, in 1996. It tells of an unusual twist in the story of composition and rhetoric, as practitioners in this field won professional status from the mid-1960s on. I include it in this collection not just for whatever interest that topic may have to my present readers, but because the essay includes specific details about the professionalization of one group of workers, a subject considered more generally in the previous essay. I hope the two pieces, taken together, will also help clarify what professions lose as they weaken, a process I examine several times in this book.

Another oddity about rhetoric and composition is that practitioners put together the apparatus of a profession at a time when other professions were losing coherence. That may help make sense of the fact, noted in passing below, that writing instructors failed to secure some of the usual benefits of professionalism, most notably decent working conditions, pay, and job security for most people in the field. The front-line troops in composition are chiefly adjuncts and graduate students, especially at the large universities where a few regular faculty members with Ph.D.'s in rhetoric manage the labor of the part-time instructors who teach first-year students. To put this fact in the framework I build in the essay that follows this one, writing instructors have taken part in creating a two-tiered profession, just at the time when older professions were dividing internally in the same way. It seems unlikely that practitioners of rhetoric will make further gains in the mode of Fordist professions. But perhaps, in part because of the egalitarian edge this profession has kept, its leaders will offer more understanding and help to graduate students who are organizing to improve their work conditions than have leaders in many other fields.

This essay is about the troubled relations between professionalization and politics in general, and about some agenda setting that went on from the 1950s through the 1970s, as composition professionalized itself, in particular. I will point to what seems an anomaly in the brief professional history of writing instruction, and end with questions about that anomaly.

A group of workers turns itself into a profession by grounding its practice in a body of knowledge, developing and guarding that knowledge within a universally recognized institution such as a university, limiting access to its lore and skills by requiring aspirants to pass through graduate or professional programs, and controlling the certification of those aspirants for practice either by widespread agreement among employers (for example, to hire only those philosophers or biologists who have earned Ph.D.'s) or with the backing and enforcement of the state (as in medicine, law, public school teaching, and so on). When a group fully achieves these goals, it turns its resources into artificially scarce commodities, creates a monopoly over their sale, and controls the conditions of its own work with little or no regulation by outside agencies.[1] Of course no group of workers could make such a safe and comfortable haven for itself in a market society without persuading consumers and authorities that the service it renders is a needed one, that only certified practitioners can meet the need, that they understand it better than their clients do, and that they will supply it in an objective and disinterested way—that is, in the interests of the client and by extension of the whole society, but to no special advantage of the practitioner, other than his or her fee. Professionalization is a social process, not an achieved and static condition, as witness heavy losses suffered even by physicians—the supreme professionals at mid-century—since 1976 when I wrote about these things in *English in America*.[2]

The historical condition of possibility for modern professions was the triumph of industrial capitalism, with its more and more specialized division of labor, its huge expansion of goods and services and infrastructures, and its incorporation of ever more needs within markets. For instance, it built great cities; created intricate systems of energy, water, and waste; and spanned a continent with canals, railroads, and bridges. This project offered *engineers* an unprecedented chance to specialize and elaborate their practices, demonstrate the absolute need for their expertise, build a wall of "cognitive exclusiveness"[3] around it, and turn that into monopoly—though never so successfully as did physicians, mainly because engineers' clients were powerful corporations rather than individuals. Again, capitalism needed to clarify and limit risk, redefine rights, and solidify control of property and labor power in the era of the corporation: this project offered *lawyers* their main chance to professionalize. *Doctors* were able to make their move for more complicated reasons, including the cacophony of practices and theories after mid-century, the virtual absence of regulation, the outrageous lies of proprietary healers and patent medicine makers, and the consequent public distrust of almost all practitioners other than the beloved family doctor. Then there were the manifest successes of medical research—anesthesiology, bacteriology, epidemiology—and the practical control of diseases such as typhus and cholera. Professionalizing "regular" doctors really did, for the first time in history, have more to offer the sick than a kindly or imposing manner. But the capitalist transformation of U.S. society was critical for medicine, too, as the massing of people in cities and factories brought new health crises, and new risks to the affluent from the illnesses of the poor. Doctors offered both public hygiene and private cures in response to the hazards of industrial capitalism.

The academic fields that professionalized around the same time intervened similarly in the new economic order, promising to help make it run efficiently, rationally, and without devastating social conflict. The point is especially clear for the emergent social sciences. The American Economic Association (AEA) offered (at its founding in 1886) to speed "human progress" by rationalizing the economy, and help bring peace in the "conflict between capital and labor."[4] Professionalizing political scientists offered expert and disinterested help a bit later in mediating political conflict and smoothing the political process, at a time when machine politics and corrupt government were scandals to the middle class and fears of anarchy or revolution were widespread. These occupations professionalized through a period of conflict at least as distressing and systemically profound as the conflicts of the 1960s and 1970s, during which composition made its move. In such times the first modern professions claimed neutrality; they would take no sides in, for instance, the "conflict between capital and labor" that figured in early AEA discussions but instead show a way toward peace in such conflicts through social planning, meliorative legislation, and expert management.

The AEA flirted with class-aligned views; one of its founders was Richard Ely, who identified "human progress" with Christian socialism. But he took much heat for such ideas both within the association and from public figures in Wisconsin, where he taught at the state university through the 1890s. By 1900 most economists seem to have agreed with Arthur T. Hadley of Yale, who in his presidential address held that the economist would have most influence if he maintained a "dispassionate and critical attitude ... that it is his mission to be the representative and the champion of the permanent interests of the whole community, in face of conflicting claims from representatives of temporary or partial ones."[5] Never mind that Hadley was himself a partisan of laissez-faire; the point was to perform neutrality, convincing colleagues as well as the laity that the profession stood above class and faction, partisan only for modernity and the common good—and, of course, that laissez-faire was itself neutral, natural, inevitable. Successful in this maneuver, the new professions and the new class of which they were the core made themselves indispensable, winning authority and comfort in the social order of this century.

In the years after they cleared pathways toward professional standing, familiarized all with its conventions, and established the legitimacy of its claims over a broad range of fields, many other groups of workers sought to gain the obvious advantages it afforded, often in connection with new technologies, products, and economic activities. Some groups have succeeded unequivocally (psychiatry, computer science), others partially or unsteadily (journalism, advertising). Composition seems a late arrival in that intermediate state. It has a moderately cohesive though also variable and contested base of knowledge, or at least a disciplinary conversation with recognizable topoi. That conversation goes forward at conferences and in learned journals and professional publications of all sorts. Practitioners have a well-established professional organization (nearly fifty years old, now) and many specialized or regional groups. The field has M.A. and Ph.D. programs whose graduates have privileged or exclusive access to some well-paying jobs, and substantial control over content, method, and working conditions in those jobs. I won't comment on the obvious shortfalls in professionalization, most notoriously the failure of composition to secure a lucrative monopoly in the provision of its primary service, writing instruction. The field *has* professionalized, if unevenly, and a comparison to other professionalizing groups is legitimate.

One could, for instance, focus on the historical conditions of possibility for its emergence. As at the time of the first wave of professionalization one hundred years ago, there was when composition set its course a very rapid expansion of the economy (the postwar boom) and of demand for the kind of service composition offered: skill in the organization, development, and transmissions of knowledge, for an "information society." There was virtually open warfare in the 1960s over the nature and control of that society, as there had been in the 1870s, 1880s, and 1890s. At the two times there were also comparable realignments of capitalism—from competitive to corporate around 1900; and from a Fordist regime to the flexible, global capitalism we now know, through the time when composition professionalized.

To be sure, many particular and even peculiar conditions made an opening for composition, including its prior embodiment in a college course that was required for almost all students; its subsumption within English during the first wave of professionalization; its eighty-year subordination to literary studies; the failure of English to theorize composition; and its exclusion of *pedagogy* from a place among its professional secrets—as if medicine had left clinical practice to the whims of individual physicians! For all these local contingencies, the professionalization of composition seems to have gone forward in the sort of historical conjuncture most hospitable to such transformations.

And along the usual paths. Those who sought to make the Conference on College Composition and Communication (CCCC) a semiautonomous professional organization from 1950 on announced goals that resonate with those of other aspirant groups. They wanted better pay and lower teaching loads (to end the "drudgery" of writing instruction). They wanted respect for their work from English department colleagues. Departments should recognize the centrality of composition; every member should share in teaching it; and when the department hires, it should look for people with credentials in composition. That proposal of course entailed that there *be* such credentials: that Ph.D. programs in English offer composition studies and prepare graduate students to teach writing, rather than assuming that the practice was an art, an innate ability, or a craft learnable only from experience. CCCC leaders wanted to behave like a profession, with a systematic exchange of ideas, a "coordinated research program,"[6] and normalization of procedures and standards across the nation. Like doctors earlier, they did not have to persuade the public that it needed their service, but they did have to distinguish that service from the public's image of it—the much disdained "Miss Fidditch" approach, with terroristic enforcement of spelling rules, grammar, correct usage, and the mysteries of the five-paragraph theme. Like any professionals, they knew better than their "clients" what the latter needed.

What these people lacked was a way of theorizing their work, a coherent body of knowledge that would organize practice and validate composition in the eyes of university peers and administrators. On the written record in *College Composition and Communication,* the professionalizers were slow to take up that challenge. Only in the late 1950s did some begin to propose a revival of rhetoric. By the mid-sixties a number of voices nominated rhetoric as, in effect, the theory of composition. In an article of 1965 (interestingly, in the first issue of *CCC* edited by William Irmscher), Virginia Burke wrote of the "chaos" in composition, attributed it to the absence since 1900 of an "informing discipline," asserted the "power of a discipline [i.e., a body of theory] to identify and maintain a field," and invited her colleagues to "restore rhetoric as the informing discipline in the practice of composition at all levels."[7] Over the next few years, many noted a revival of interest in rhetoric, hoped it was not a fad, and proposed one or another rhetorical tradition as theoretical foundation for their field, maybe even for all liberal education. These advocates included such influentials as James Murphy, Richard Braddock, Robert Gorrell, Richard Hughes, Edward Corbett, and Joseph Schwartz. Others began domesticating rhetoric, connecting it to the practice of composition; the work of Francis Christensen seemed especially promising for a while.

Alternative candidates for the role of theory came forward through the fifties and sixties: semantics, structural and then transformational linguistics, Bruner's psychology, tagmemics, and of course, communication theory, whose affinities with composition had been hopefully anticipated in the naming of the organization. Unless I've missed something, composition never did agree upon a single "informing discipline" or theory but has made do with a shifting assortment of issues and texts that frame the professional discourse and give it continuity. This has sufficed to mark composition off from other fields and build its scholarly respectability—and why not, given that a number of more established professions, including the parent field of English, are even less focused?

What struck me in scanning *CCC* from 1960 to the mid-seventies was that the moment of professional articulation and purposeful disciplinarity did not damp down political engagement, as in economics and other professionalizing fields of the last century, but quite the reverse. That is, in the *pre-professional* phase of composition, up through the early sixties, *CCC* admitted virtually no explicitly political discussion—for instance on the cold war, anticommunism, and matters of free speech—and in fact published a few pleas for professional detachment.[8] But by the end of the 1960s the journal was addressing a range of issues taken from the noisy arena of national politics: disadvantaged students, two-year colleges and egalitarian education, racial oppression (indeed, the assassination of Martin Luther King),[9] the question of dialect and power, campus uprisings, the rhetoric of confrontation, student power—almost everything except Vietnam itself and, until much later, feminism. Furthermore, these political energies invaded discussion of teaching practices, putting up for debate the decorums of classroom hierarchy, standards, grades, and even the question whether composition can be systematically taught at all. In short, the conventions of authority and dignity a nascent profession would ordinarily call upon to set practitioner apart from client were all interrogated, and in the core venues of the discipline. Likewise, questions of political derivation were allowed to subvert academic conventions of writing *in* the journal: the passionate appeal, the free-form essay, the collage, gained admittance to *CCC,* as if to forgo the exclusions and reassurances implicit in a shared, specialized, and emotionally restrained style of address. Composition was airing unseemly questions about neutrality, detachment, and partisanship, and even about whether to act like a profession. I recall vividly, of course, the flow of politics into the pages of *College English* at the time, facilitated at first by my editorial tolerance and then by my more principled determination. William Irmscher, who edited *CCC* through the same years, espoused politics very different from mine and was more committed to sober professionalization; yet *CCC* put on display the same tensions and disruptions.

Now, for a brief while it might have seemed to a reader of *CCC* that politics was allowed an occasional hearing, in segregation from the ongoing disciplinary project. The December 1968 issue dealt with education and inequality, the question of black language and identity, teaching Native Americans, the troubles at San Francisco State, and more. The next issue (February 1969) returned to a scholarly conversation about rhetoric and allied topics, with no effort to bridge between these and the politics of December, and no acknowledgment of a disjunction. Soon, however, the theoretical conversation began to notice the political. A pivotal moment, perhaps, was the publication of Edward P. J. Corbett's celebrated article "The Rhetoric of the Open Hand and the Rhetoric of the Closed Fist,"[10] which accorded radicalism the dignity of rhetorical analysis even while preferring the disinterestedness of the open hand and mind. Increasingly, over the next few years, the professional and political conversations mingled. Can one say that the professional internalized the political? That composition took social conflict as part of its domain, rather than exiling it or offering to resolve it through the ministrations of experts, as with economics and political science earlier?

I'm not sure, but my strong impression is that although the disciplinary project went forward briskly, it did not leave behind the political themes of 1960s movements. Questions of inequality (including now of gender as well as of race and class) remained on the professional agenda. Language retained its political dimension, as in the famous 1974 statement on "Students' Right to Their Own language." CCCC, along with the National Council of Teachers of English, engaged vigorously in battles over testing, basics, literacy, and so on, right through to the culture wars of the 1980s and early 1990s. And as Patricia Bizzell has suggested,[11] much of the most notable work in composition through that later period has dealt with "multiplicity and conflict," the social and the historical. Moreover, the profession seems to me to have taken *sides* in social conflict—taken sides, broadly speaking, with the less privileged and against centers of power.

Be that as it may, I hope to have sketched out a reasonable case for seeing conflict and politics as durable presences through the time of composition's professionalizing movement, and for seeing that presence as unusual, across the range of such movements in U.S. history. The obvious questions, then, would be: Why did it happen this way? And with what consequences for current work and future prospects in composition?

7

WHAT'S HAPPENING TO THE UNIVERSITY AND THE PROFESSIONS? CAN HISTORY TELL?

◆

I first presented some of these ideas to audiences of graduate students and faculty members, and this essay probably retains some of my and their sense of grievance at the desperate state of the academic job market, the inability or unwillingness of the profession to find remedies, and the commercialization of the traditional university. I am indeed sad and angry about the personal hardship brought on by these conditions (both for former students and for one member of my family), but I do not want to be read as nostalgic for the good old days before 1970 or contemptuous of new formats for postsecondary education that are available through proprietary colleges and universities, on the Internet, and so on. There are gains and losses for different groups of students in the new arrangements. The traditional university conveyed inequality as effectively as does "market-driven" higher education today.

Privatization moves on apace. Since I finished this essay early in 2002, an educational consulting firm has reported that revenues of for-profit colleges increased by 20 percent in 2001 and are expected to grow at nearly the same rate through 2004.[1] In this essay I bring together a lot of facts and guesses of this sort and try to make sense of them as part of an historical pattern. The task is daunting, and I have surely made significant errors. I hope others will press on with the effort.

History cannot tell anything. But we can tell history so as to locate a present situation within a large narrative; then we can project how that situation will change if the main story goes as expected. This can be a loony activity, a paranoid exercise, a workout in millenarian fantasy. It can also disperse illusions and clarify choices. Readers will judge how the present effort turns out.

Here's my narrative line and the way I propose to interpret it. About a hundred years ago, a new middle class formed, between capital and labor and distinct from the old middle class of small merchants and craftspeople. Following a common usage, I call this new group the professional-managerial class (hereafter, PMC for short).[2] It formed in the context of an emergent and newly dominant social formation, variously called "advanced capitalism," "corporate capitalism," "monopoly capitalism," "Fordism,"[3] and so on. That formation, on many accounts, is today modulating into another one— again, with a choice of ill-assorted but partly compatible names: "globalization," "turbo-capitalism," "agile capitalism," the "knowledge society," "the new information age," and, best for my purposes (because balanced against "Fordism"), the "regime of flexible accumulation." Social classes are specific to social formations: they never survive into a new epoch without significant change and may gain or lose much in coherence and power. So if we are indeed in the vestibule of a new capitalist regime, it would not be surprising for a class that found identity and agency with the old capitalism to be transformed. It might become dominant, for instance. It might weaken, fracture, or dissolve.

Plainly, each term in this loose and extended syllogism is as unstable as the flamingos and hedgehogs used in Alice's croquet game. At this point in the exposition I will not attempt refinement. At the end, you can consider if the argument earns its way by clarifying our present circumstances and shining a beam along our future path. In using the term "our" I am imagining PMC people as the most likely readers of this essay; I myself grew up in a suburban PMC family and spent a working life in the university. Furthermore, this essay comes out of reflections upon thirty years of economic and political troubles for English departments, literary studies, the humanities, American universities, and the people who work there.[4] Yet, although I focus on our class and take its interests seriously, my aim here is not to champion or defend the PMC or press on you the urgency of its survival but just to attempt a better understanding of it. Of us.

The troubles: centrally and painfully, thousands of aspirants to university posts find themselves shut out of the job market; they have invested five or seven or more years of study and teaching to enter careers that are not there for them—and this in the flourishing economy of the 1990s, with full employment for almost every other group of workers. Many of these young people do teach for a sort of living, often for years, before giving up: they become irregulars with no chance of achieving tenure. Close to half of college teachers are part-timers now, and a third of the full-timers are on short contracts—figures that leave out the army of graduate students teaching for small wages on the way to careers that may not happen. Many in this casual labor force work at for-profit institutions like the University of Phoenix, with its hundred "campuses" and no permanent faculty. Some work on-line for traditional universities as well as for virtual universities, in innumerable projects of distance learning. The market affords bleak prospects for young academics, and many voices accompany its impersonal workings, proposing that universities run more like efficient businesses, urging cuts in their funding to make them do so, advocating an end to tenure or a system of posttenure review with termination of senior professors who won't or can't shape up, and so on. Obviously these trends are hard on many college teachers, among them former students of mine, good friends, and family members, whose anxious and exhausting efforts to qualify themselves for academic careers (far beyond what was required in my youth) have often been rewarded with defeat and exile. Their stories sadden and anger me, but my subject is not the distress of individuals. It is the coherence of a class and of the professions that have given that class much of its authority and power.

A profession is a group who have established their exclusive right to do work of a particular kind—for example, drill teeth, design tall buildings, argue in court—under conditions they largely control. To achieve these market havens, they have convinced many people, including potential clients and (often) legislative bodies, that they have knowledge whose mastery is critical for practitioners; that they will augment, test, and verify it; that they will initiate new practitioners into it and certify their competence; that they will as a group regulate the work of all members to guarantee its quality and honesty; and that they will disinterestedly serve their clients and society as a whole. Within the market haven so justified, a profession can regulate study and research, determine who qualifies to do both theoretical and practical work in the field, screen aspirants and control their numbers, set favorable terms of work for members, and ensure good pay. A healthy profession also commands respect from the public and is able to influence policy in its area of expertise.

The difficulties mentioned above show that the market haven of professors is no longer in good repair. They apparently cannot limit the number of new recruits so as to guarantee jobs for them. Along their path through graduate school, many of those recruits in all but the scientific fields have come to think of themselves less as privileged apprentices than as exploited workers and are vigorously unionizing. Professors cannot protect good conditions of labor for those with the Ph.D. credential, or protect them from the necessity of competing with less credentialed workers. Although professors never had the fee-for-service arrangements and posh incomes common in law and medicine, salaries for most were decent or better. Now, highfliers make news while pay for the great majority declines. People with the right degrees used to have secure, full-time employment; now many work on short-term or part-time contracts, essentially doing piecework like any casual labor force. Many have been forced out altogether, or have voluntarily left the profession to seek more rewarding employment. Professors used to set curriculum in their fields according to rational plans for general and special education; now, except in relatively elite colleges, curriculum is increasingly shaped by demand for discrete units of knowledge and training and by competition in markets to sell this "product." Some Ph.D.'s in academic jobs can pursue the kinds of research traditionally validated by peers in their fields, but many need to look sharp for practical applications and for "partnerships" that will provide alternate sources of funding. The ideal of leisurely research in the disinterested pursuit of truth has given way to the imperative that graduate students and untenured faculty members start bibliographies early and lengthen them fast.

In sum, I think the academic hard times that dominate insider conversation in the humanities and stir concern in all fields had best be understood not just as difficulties for some in the profession but as serious threats to the profession itself, as a whole system of practices, institutions, and privileges fairly well insulated from the rigors of the market competition. If so, a search for reasons will not be satisfied by citing economic downturns. The professions have handily survived business cycles far more brutal than any recent one, and in any case the current troubles—though they began in the crisis of the early 1970s—have intensified through almost fifteen years of unprecedented growth in the general economy. Labeling those troubles an academic job "crisis" badly underestimates a tendency that has accelerated for thirty years. So deeper explanations seem in order, and maybe broader ones, too. That's why my title refers to a social class, beyond the academic profession or even all the professions. Now I want to be more specific about that class and its narrative, before returning to the university and the professorate.

A Professional-Managerial Class

First, a brief genealogy of that concept. Marx and Engels wrote near the beginning of the *Communist Manifesto* that capitalism had simplified class antagonisms until just two great classes directly faced each other: capitalists, and workers with no resources but their labor power. On this hypothesis, the aristocracy, the gentry, the small bourgeoisie, the peasantry, and other classes or fractions were becoming marginal, or dissolving—for the most part, into the proletariat. That was 1848. Already by 1900 a look around the social landscape, especially in the United States, revealed a more complex situation. There were growing numbers of people who were not big capitalists or small entrepreneurs, but who had more than simple labor power to sell and enough income and authority to differentiate them clearly from the industrial proletariat. By mid-century, their prominence was still more marked and their place in the class structure much disputed.

Mainstream sociology had scrapped the Marxist problematic and arranged people in capitalist societies into as many as nine strata, from lower-lower to upper-upper (with professionals and managers somewhere above the middle), on criteria of education, income, and occupation. Analysts on and toward the left—C. Wright Mills, Nicos Poulantzas, Alvin Gouldner, Eric Olin Wright, Andre Gorz, Barbara and John Ehrenreich, and others—continued to work with or against classical Marxism. Some of these argued that people such as us belong either to a new, expanded working class or to an expanded petty bourgeoisie. Others held—and hold—that the scope of Marx's vision had temporal limits and that it is best to think of us as a new middle class, variously named but distinct from the petty bourgeoisie; or that we occupy a mixed class location, sharing some features with the capitalist class and some with the proletariat. I have found it fruitful for a while to take my lead from the Ehrenreichs, who in the mid-1970s defined the

PMC as "salaried mental workers who do not own the means of production and whose major function in the social division of labor is the reproduction of capitalist culture and capitalist class relations."[5]

I will not step into the quicksand of endless controversy around this idea but will modify it in three ways for my present purposes. First, not everyone in the PMC is salaried. Many doctors, lawyers, management consultants, architects, and so on are self employed, yet otherwise match up to the definition, and differ sharply in what they sell from the shopkeepers and artisans of the petty bourgeoisie. Second, the Ehrenreichs' definition stresses the PMC's usefulness to the capitalist class, in keeping up the culture and social relations that maintain its rule. The PMC has indeed patched and reinforced and justified the social order, to the long-run benefit of capital. But PMC groups have often, too, stood in temporary antagonism to the bourgeoisie: as in the Progressive era, through antitrust legislation, regulatory movements, social work, and agitation to improve the lot of workers; and in the 1960s and 1970s, through oppositional movements of various sorts.[6]

Third, I agree that the PMC's main work in the division of labor has been reproductive: that is, has helped preserve the contours and power relations of capitalist society from one generation to the next. Think of "scientific" management and organization of the workplace; of how engineers and applied scientists have put knowledge to use in factory production; of how lawyers have facilitated contracts and expanded property rights, including those to intellectual property such as patents and copyrights; of the criminal justice system, public schooling, public health efforts, city planning, and the whole twentieth-century apparatus of social amelioration and control. Think too of the PMC's role in advertising, public relations, the development of official knowledges, foundation work, the churches—labor of complex political valence, perhaps adequately if rudely captured by the term "ideology." Yet mention of these latter PMC efforts reminds us that reproduction is often also production, for the market. Certainly the culture industries, where PMC work has been critical, are fundamentally involved in material production. Or consider design of the workplace, which materially embodies and enforces relations of production; or, more inclusively, design of the whole built world from city layouts to the edifices of business and government and domesticity that complete them.

My study of mass circulation magazines, the advertising industry, and the corporate sales effort convinced me that PMC people were both active shapers and eager consumers of a burgeoning commercial culture, as well as of the new, brand-named goods—and their meanings—from which it was inseparable.[7] Beyond that, I came to see the PMC as not just securing a place within corporate capitalism, but taking active part in creation of that social order. The reproductive tasks just mentioned were in the 1890s far from routine. Lawyers helped imagine and actualize the great corporations that arose, most of them hurriedly, in a wave of mergers, just before 1900. Managers staffed and rationalized the vertically integrated structures of these companies. Sales executives collaborated with ad men (who themselves were inventing the modern ad agency) to plant the need for Ivory soap and Cream of Wheat and Gillette razors in middle-class souls, thus to guarantee steady sales of what the factories made, and so temper the instability and intermittent chaos that had plagued the post–Civil War economic system. Bureaucrats, city planners, health professionals, social workers, and improvers of many sorts went to work on the untamed city to rationalize its growth and intervene strenuously in the lives of the immigrant working class. Administrators, educational planners, and teachers standardized the high school curriculum and articulated it with college study. Academic professionals invented the new university, consolidated the production of knowledge, and in doing so established the key site of PMC advancement and self-reproduction. No wonder that people in this class tended to see themselves as the modernizers and perfecters of society, not as factota of the capitalist class.

As striking: these people, drawn variously from among the old urban middle class, the respectable folk of small towns, and the more prosperous farmers, were visibly and half-consciously organizing themselves *into* a class: I can see no more perspicuous way to sum up their activities. Around their work they wove a net of scholarly, professional, trade, and civic organizations—essentially the structure that persists today. At leisure, they remade social geography, including a distinctive space in it for themselves. That was the suburb, with its rural echoes (the yard and the curved streets), its segregation from industry, its gentrification of commerce, and its patterns of travel to city centers for work and entertainment. Home architecture departed from the Victorian, which had embodied old middle-class decorum and stiffness: now came more functional design, the open plan of the ground floor, the demise of the parlor and emergence of the living room, modern heating and plumbing, the valorization of efficiency and sanitation.

Outside the home, PMC people now delineated their social space less by elaborate rules of etiquette that the old middle class had used to signify Christian morality and character, and more by the institutions and pathways of daily routine. Those paths took young people of this class through the rite of high school, now all but universal for those not going off to college preparatory schools. Women gathered in improving clubs and took shopping trips to the sometimes elegant and always reputable new department stores. Men went to civic and social clubs as well as to their corporate or professional offices. All traveled together along the newly plotted tourist routes (Yellowstone, the Rockies) and to resorts in the Adirondacks, Cape Cod and the Islands, the Jersey shore—as socially distinct from the Newports and St. Augustines of old wealth as from the Coney Islands of the working poor. They mingled somewhat uneasily *with* the upper class in concert hall, opera house, and art museum, as well as at the university or college. These institutions, however, had a different meaning in the life trajectories of PMC people: there, they acquired the training and knowledges and credentials and habits of thought that constituted their *own* cultural capital. (Children of the rich at Vassar or Princeton or Williams already had such capital, along with the kind that sits quietly in trust funds.) In college, too, PMC youth met with peers and experts from around the country, building a fund of shared experience and aspiration that held them together as a *national* class.

Many scholars dissent or abstain from the conceptual language I have used in telling this narrative: "class," "cultural capital," "reproduction," and so on. But few disagree with the observation that a social group distinct from its predecessors gained cohesion, strength, and self-awareness at this time. Nothing like what I am calling the professional-managerial class had existed in 1875. The arrangements it contrived just before and after 1900, however, stood in place at least until the day before yesterday, historically speaking. The PMC grew and prospered well past 1950, along with the university, where professors created the knowledge and ideology and did the social sorting that made us helpful (though often irritating) to capitalists, and in so doing, secured our own continuance and well being. PMC people made up perhaps a tenth of the population in 1910, more like a fifth in 1960, and still more in the 1980s.

What, besides energy and ambition, empowered this group? They were able to consolidate as a class around 1900 only because the transformation of capitalism opened a way for them to do so. The giant corporation required an ever more articulated internal structure, with layers of semispecialized managers between owners and line workers. It put new knowledges to use both in the making of goods and in "scientific" control over the labor process. Instructed expertise was at a premium, not just finger knowledge acquired on the job. The redirecting of some corporate energies into a sales effort made room for new specialists in marketing, in the needs of consumers, and in consciousness and symbols generally. The culture industries flourished partly in response to this corporate initiative, and some became engines of corporate wealth in themselves, incessantly bringing within the compass of the market activities previously carried on outside it. Most generally, the large surplus that industrial capitalism was generating allowed the appropriation of knowledge for profit; provided funding for universities, libraries, and such; and enabled those with special access to knowledge and expertise to claim benefits such as autonomy, good pay, and job security. As John Frow put it, for a class such as the PMC to form required "the structural possibility of converting knowledge into cultural capital."[8] I will, however, distinguish between the marks of social distinction that Pierre Bourdieu labeled "cultural capital" and the aggregations of knowledge that fund professions, referring to the latter as "intellectual assets," to distinguish them from capital in the Marxian sense.

PMC initiatives joined with those of big capitalists (uneasily) and of the state, in new kinds of response to social disorganization and resistance. The violent repression that had marked 1877, 1885–86, and 1892–94 by no means ended. But other strategies of control came to dominate. PMC activists helped organize an embryonic welfare state—making food and water safer, offering various social services, regulating workers' lives on the job, in school, at home. Agencies and governmental bureaucracies proliferated, in time staffed by newly minted experts. More broadly, the PMC—its academic wing in particular—took on the ambitious project of understanding how society worked as a whole, and guiding its progress. To put it crudely, corporate capitalism both needed and could afford a professional-managerial class.

A Tectonic Shift?

Now, deep social and economic transformations not only make possible the creation of new classes; they pull the foundations out from under old ones. To cite familiar examples: the English peasantry vanished by around 1800, dispersed among tenant farmers (that is, agricultural businessmen), farm laborers, and factory workers. Industrial capitalism also pushed aside many artisans and crippled the guilds that were their characteristic form of organization. In the United States, the Civil War not only eliminated the class of slaves but completed the ruination of a slaveholding class already depleted by having survived in a society dominated by industrial capital. Twentieth-century corporate capitalism, expanding into area after area of production, virtually eliminated independent farmers as economic or historical agents. And so on: if one accepts the Marxian story, as augmented by new class theories, no significant class from two hundred years ago survives in the United States today, except the resilient small bourgeoisie, itself changed beyond easy recognition by shifting relations with other classes.

Suppose next, with many present-day observers and analysts, of all political stripes, that corporate capitalism might itself be modulating into a new and distinct formation. The staid, Fordist corporation gives way to the "agile" company, with its hectic innovation, proliferation of goods and services, invention of new markets, freedom of movement domestically and around the globe, fluid partnerships and deals with other companies, elaboration of corporate forms and financial instruments, and constant metamorphosis through subcontracting, outsourcing, downsizing, spin-offs, buyouts, and mergers. I will not defend or expand here upon the idea that we have entered a distinct phase of capitalist history, a "regime of flexible accumulation,"[9] though much of this essay will consider its applicability to the university and the professions. For now, just suppose that a transformation of the economic and social order began around 1970 and is progressing smartly now: if so, might the conditions of possibility for a stable and vigorous professional-managerial class be eroded or dissolved, along with Fordism? This is a fuzzy thought, which I hope will gain in definition as I put it to analytic use.

To begin with labor: all agree that the old, industrial working class has come under severe pressure in recent decades. People such as David Harvey, who propose that capitalism has reconfigured itself since 1970, emphasize the shrinking of its core labor force—the chiefly unionized, secure, well-paid, and benefited workers who staffed the Fordist corporation. The agile company moves production to wherever labor is cheap and docile and does so more quickly than did its predecessors, with the help of trade agreements fruitlessly resisted by American workers. Casual labor and job changing become the norm. We hear much about these arrangements, about a widening gap between rich and poor, and about the American family trying to compensate for a long decline in real wages by working extra hours and extra jobs.

What has received less commentary in major media, though it is obvious from a standpoint in the university, is the extension of similar pressures to the mental work that has grounded the PMC—academic downsizing, the resort to casual labor, the disappearance of traditional jobs for Ph.D.'s (our core labor force), and so on. These trends are often understood as a "crisis," whose likely causes might be discovered within the university and remedied by tinkering (cut back admissions to Ph.D. programs, encourage early retirement, etc.). But the market for academic labor collapsed over thirty years ago and in many fields, including language and literature, has remained dismal ever since. This is a story, not of crisis, but of long decline and maybe of permanent restructuring. It is a story with multiple agents. No doubt some of them qualify as opportunists or villains. But what has provoked even the most benign administrators and far-sighted professional leaders to streamline the university and its core labor force? I suggest that they are following a script drafted elsewhere, a more inclusive story in which academic woes form a small subplot. On this hypothesis, it is no coincidence that they set in at just about the time when other crises—a rapid increase in debt of all kinds, the peaking of real wages in the United States, declining corporate profits, a negative turn in the trade balance, daunting competition from Japan and Europe, and a cresting of the dollar's value—signaled a crisis for American capital and led it to adopt new strategies.

Now follows a detailed discussion and analysis of those strategies as played out in higher education. Since the university is a key site in the social reproduction of the professional-managerial class, as well as chief incubator of professional and managerial knowledges, I hope that the detail and my attempt to organize it will help clarify the main argument of this essay, and give substance to the hypothesis of a changing social and economic formation in our time.

Higher Education's Funding

Since the whole process under study is (to simplify) one of privatization, let us begin with the decline in public funding for colleges and universities after their great postwar expansion. Federal support of universities peaked in the late sixties. Cuts in government support, generally, began around 1970 and accelerated after 1980, since which year state and federal funding of U.S. public universities has dropped about 25 percent. Now, for the first time, more than half of these moneys come from other sources.[10] More than a few major state universities, such as Berkeley and the University of California–Los Angeles, receive less than 25 percent of their revenue from state budgets, with the rest coming from federal grants, private sources, tuition, and the sale of various resources (of which I will have more to say shortly). Even more service-oriented institutions have had to cast about for support; New York City provides less than a quarter of the cost of education at its community colleges (and none for the four-year colleges), with about 35 percent coming from the state and the rest to be raised through tuition, at these formerly free schools. Rudolph Giuliani made an effort, when mayor, to withhold all city support unless the community colleges stopped doing what he and his advisers considered remedial work, and the assault on the City University of New York continues. Resistance to sudden or dramatic cuts has sometimes burst out into strikes and demonstrations. But by and large, erosion of support from tax revenues has been steady and widespread for nearly three decades. For a few years during the prosperity of the 1990s, it seemed that this tendency might be reversed, but as I write, it has picked up momentum again, with tuition rising sharply at public institutions. Meanwhile, although some elite, private universities and colleges have escaped budgetary crisis, most have not; and at almost all, income from endowment has covered a smaller and smaller share of costs. We can best grasp this entire process as a decline in the portion of the whole social surplus going into higher education via state appropriation and private philanthropy.

Since postsecondary education has greatly expanded, not shrunk, through this period, it makes sense to ask what has replaced these transfers from the social surplus. I begin with traditional, nonprofit, public and private institutions, though theirs is only part of the story. The most obvious answer is that customers (students and their families) have directly paid a steadily rising portion of total costs. Tuition has risen especially fast at public colleges (7.7 percent in 2001–2),[11] where it used to be negligible, and now pays close to 20 percent of the tab. The boom of the 1990s slowed down the rate of increase, but it has picked up briskly since 2000, with record-setting hikes at many private universities, from Texas Christian and Baylor to Cornell, Dartmouth, George Washington, and Emory. At the last four, tuition is about $27,000, with room and board bringing basic costs to $35,000.[12] Needless to say, the impact of this historic change upon financially strapped students—who take on heavier and heavier loads of work-for-pay, accumulate debt, and take five or more years to finish B.A.'s—has been severe. With the change, now, comes a variety of schemes at private colleges and universities and even some state systems (e.g., Georgia) to compete for the most desirable students by offering merit scholarships or (at Princeton) grants instead of loans. This hustle threatens to repeal universities' uneven but telling effort, through the postwar period, to give students support according to their needs, thus making higher education accessible to most young people and lending support to the professions' implicit creed of careers open to talents—of success based upon merit rather than inherited position or wealth.

Administrators have addressed their budgetary problems[13] in several ways; first, by cutting expenditures. That's an old story, needless to say: when recessions lead states to reduce funding of public institutions and shrink the endowments of private ones, there will be freezes on hiring, across-the-board percentage cuts in departmental budgets, occasional elimination of programs with (in extreme cases) their tenured faculty members, and so on. But the emergent university seeks to replace or supplant helter-skelter measures like these with a fresh style of management, more in line with the way things are done in business. Here are some examples.

1. The University of Florida has for several years rated its seventeen colleges on productivity in "activities that generate revenue—teaching, research, and fund-raising." They must set their own "benchmarks" with an eye on competing programs at other institutions. The colleges that perform best each year receive payments from the University of Florida Bank, as it's called. This system for articulating goals and providing incentives and rewards has received praise nationally and is being imitated elsewhere.[14]

2. Northwest Missouri State University combines a "seven-step quality-oriented planning process," modeled after systems used at IBM, GE, and elsewhere, with activity-based costing, an accounting method that links activities and costs to results, and that has become widespread in business since Texas Instruments developed it in the 1970s. For thus showing how to connect quality and costs, the university has won awards, a Sloan Foundation grant to "share" its system with other

institutions, and an advisory appointment for its president (Dean
Hubbard) to the U.S. Department of Education.[15]

3. At Rensselaer Polytechnic Institute's Center for Academic Transformation, Carol Twig oversees a $9 million project funded by the Pew Trust
to save money and improve quality in large courses. "A revamped
introductory chemistry course at the University of Wisconsin saved
the school close to $300,000 a year. The per-student cost of teaching
linear algebra at Virginia Tech dropped from $78 to $24."[16]

4. Probably every college and university in the country now outsources
work previously done in-house. Sloughing off food services, bookstores (Follett and Barnes & Noble alone run about a thousand),
building maintenance, and the like has been a common tactic for
some time. More recently, universities have taken to outsourcing student health services, heating and power generation, the construction
and management of student housing, and even financial operations
such as purchasing and payroll. Unsurprisingly, a host of companies
(the March 2001 issue of *University Business* describes a hundred such)
have risen up to sell universities electronic services, from e-mail and
specific administrative tasks to the whole of technology operations
(Salt Lake Community College).[17] Needless to say, many of these im-
pinge on teaching and learning—courses, instructional design, "learning management," for instance—and many companies sell on-line
courses themselves. Chatham College outsourced the management of
its library. A company called Smarthinking formed in 1999 to sell colleges tutoring services for their students.[18] Clearly, all these arrangements can cheapen and divide labor, and the ones toward the end of
my list undermine professional labor.

Such tales could be multiplied a hundredfold. My point is not the detail
of any one case but the imperative that now dominates university administration: learn from business how to manage higher education, how to make
it lean and accountable.

In this project, administrators can draw upon analysis and encouragement from the business press, which has generally interpreted the budgetary
troubles of higher education as a failure to run colleges rationally and helped
popularize the idea that the university is bloated, inefficient, and retrograde.[19] Now comes *University Business*, a spin-off from *Lingua Franca*, to

offer specific counsel and inspiration, as well as high-powered conferences such as the one described in chapter 9 of this volume. Hundreds of consulting firms sell modernizing advice to individual colleges. Some consultants stay on as administrators, like Penn's John A. Fry, whose innovative cost-cutting saved the university $60 million a year (5 percent of its budget).[20] Inspiration of a harsher sort comes from regents and trustees, who demand high-stakes testing of university students, to see which programs and institutions are "working" and which not; and from legislatures insisting that appropriations of new money include "spending formulas," tying state support to perform-ance measures and forcing public colleges to compete for state aid.[21] This broad movement to reconstitute higher education on a corporate model has incensed many faculty members. I make no comment here on their objec-tions, noting only that in a world of corporate universities the academic profession would be much enfeebled—would have no more autonomy and coherence than do nonacademic engineers, distributed as they are across innumerable companies, whose managers direct their work and deal with them as individual employees.

While universities devised new strategies of cost cutting, they also pur-sued new sources of income. The traditional university had just one main product, which it sold to students for tuition or (at free colleges) gave them. That product was the chance to register and study (usually in a bundle of courses at one time) under the supervision of qualified professionals who would judge students' work, credit it course by course, and, acting as facul-ties, convert it into degrees or certificates. Some of the knowledge generated by those faculties was in the process transmitted to students but not thereby taken away from professors, who retained rights to it, used it to make repu-tations and advance careers, and collectively organized it into bodies of knowledge that sustained the various professions (i.e., that made up their in-tellectual assets). Colleges and universities also built rankings and reputa-tions around knowledge made by researchers but did not, by and large, own or sell that knowledge.

Everybody knows that this bundle of relations has changed dramatically in twenty years.[22] Colleges and universities still sell their old product, for more money than before and in more varied packages (a subject to which I will re-turn). But they sell much else, and the competition to develop, uh . . . , new product is fierce. Most evidently, they sell knowledge created by faculty re-search. Market opportunities in this area widened hugely in 1980, with passage of the Bayh-Dole Act (much revised and expanded since then), allowing universities to patent and commercialize discoveries made through research for which the federal government had paid. Before then, universities were averaging fewer than 250 patents a year. By the late 1990s that figure had increased more than tenfold. Universities licensed these inventions at first only to small U.S. companies but later to companies of any size based anywhere, which paid for the licenses through royalties, equity, options, fees, and so on. Universities (and entrepreneurial faculty members) often took the initiative here, helping to start up more than two thousand companies, and more recently establishing "incubators" where university people give new companies technology, capital, services, advice, and often a place to set up shop—as in North Carolina State University's thousand-acre Centennial Campus, a town-like settlement where sixty companies do business. At least a dozen other states are appropriating large sums to stake such ventures. More than 150 universities have incubators, and smaller institutions—especially community colleges—are initiating them.[23] Unsurprisingly, the initiative runs in both directions: opportunities opened up by Bayh-Dole have led corporations to invest heavily in academic research. Their funding of it has increased tenfold (to more than $2 billion annually) during the last twenty years.

Contractual arrangements between nonprofit universities and for-profit companies vary widely. The university may sell individual patents, or—as in a controversial deal between Berkeley and the Swiss-based multinational Novartis—first rights to all the research done in a single department (plant biology) over a period of time; in this case five years, at $5 million a year. A few universities, including Yale, are "monetizing" future royalties on patents, taking lump sums now instead.[24] Others launch venture capital subsidiaries to sift and develop that research themselves. Some deals involve several universities or several companies. Nonprofit institutions found and own for-profits; for-profits organize groups of nonprofits; and so on and on. From this galactic soup will surely come many fizzles along with brilliant successes. It's too early to foresee the results for university funding but not to make three observations. First, a great deal of socially funded knowledge is being privatized, both by corporations and by universities themselves—nothing new here, except this new method of making it happen. Second, researchers have every incentive to think like entrepreneurs and to guide their inquiries with corporate needs in mind. And third, new conditions have stimulated universities to think like agile corporations.

That last point allows us to bring a number of their other current practices into the same analytic frame. Take the soft drink wars. Coke and Pepsi spent $2 billion or more in the late 1990s for exclusive rights to sell their lines on campuses. Individual universities have received as much, up front, as $28 million (University of Minnesota) for a ten-year contract, in addition to annual commissions of 50 percent and more.[25] In a word, these institutions are selling their students' effective demand, as well as taking a large cut of their expenditure. Strategies of this sort are proliferating. Administrations often sell their students' attention, much as TV networks do, except that the students cannot switch channels or turn off the set. Portal companies like Campus Pipeline provide a college with sophisticated software to use for registration, billing, loan servicing, course enrollment, campus announcements, e-mail, and so on. Students logging in for these often-obligatory activities will encounter ads and marketing offers from a variety of companies.[26] Similarly, identification cards used for library checkouts, campus events, computer lab sign-ins, and so on can lead students to phone service and voice mail (with ads) from a particular phone company, as well as to a particular bank.[27] And speaking of banks, some universities have now created their own, for profit, in connection with student and staff financial operations. Sale of stadium-naming rights may go with the sale of services (e.g., cable TV) that students must then pay for as part of their regular fees.[28] The nation's 14 million or so college students are a valuable demographic to marketers, and hence a potential gold mine for institutions willing to act as brokers.

But of course the primary commodity that students buy through these years is education itself. I have already remarked the ever higher price charged for it, as tuition. Traditional universities are also elaborating the channels through which they provide it, and elaborating the product itself, for sale to customers who have different needs. Taking these points in order: distance education is no longer experimental. Little need be said here to emphasize the magnitude of this innovation in what is now quite appropriately called "delivery." Well over half of nonprofit colleges and universities offer at least some on-line courses. The figure is much higher for public institutions (79 percent in 2000 for four-year colleges, 72 percent for two-year), but private ones are moving quickly into this area, including Cornell, Columbia, Yale, and other elite universities. Some handle the operation in-house; some establish for-profit subsidiaries; some work through unaffiliated learning companies: here as everywhere in the managed university, arrangements are varied and fluid. There were 54,000 on-line courses in 2000, and 1.6 million students. Merrill Lynch estimated that the market for virtual learning will amount to $7 billion by 2003.[29] Furthermore, although many denigrate or fear this development, it is becoming a normal branch of higher education. Despite obvious differences between campus and on-line instruction, the regional accrediting agencies are figuring out how to rate the latter. A provider of distance learning for profit, Jones International University, was the first to be accredited. Others have now cleared this hurdle, including the state-sponsored Western Governors University (which gives credit not just for courses but for knowledge gained in whatever way, so long as students can pass tests on it).[30] From a student's point of view, this validation officially makes on-line credits and degrees the same commodity as those offered face to face.

How this mushrooming project fits into the balance sheets of universities is not yet clear. E-learning companies close down when broke; for example, Hungry Minds, a marketer of 17,000 courses from everywhere, which used up $100 million of its founder's cash. Universities such as Temple and the University of California survive the failure of their on-line divisions (Temple On-line, California Virtual University). But their troubles signal that early predictions of big revenues from distance education were wishful. Nobody knows, at the time of this writing, just how much it costs to produce an e-program in comparison to face-to-face education, or to what customers will pay. Some, including the National Education Association,[31] think on-line instruction will usually cost more than the other kind. My own conjecture is that it will be reasonably profitable, and that present uncertainty results from myopia about likely markets. In spite of abundant, visionary, and often crudely deterministic prophecies that education will be wholly transformed by new technologies, universities have tended to look no farther than selling their present courses and degrees via the Internet. And indeed, some of the more inflammatory prophecies have encouraged such thought: the bricks-and-mortar university is on the way out, everybody except Harvard students will learn in cyberspace, and the like. But business schools are finding that few want to earn their traditional M.B.A. at home. Enrollment for degree programs at Governors State University reached only 200 after two years, in contrast to the 5,000 expected. When the now-successful Kentucky Virtual University started up, offering only degree and certification programs, it enrolled 237 students; the next semester it raised that figure to 1,700, chiefly by allowing already registered students on existing Kentucky campuses to take its on-line courses. Nationally, the dropout rate for students in on-line degree programs is extremely high, but many students who dropped out from regular colleges take on-line courses to finish up, often many years later.[32] In short, except for older alumni (often of elite colleges) looking for culture and for news from the liberal arts, shoppers for distance learning generally want something other than the same courses undergraduates are taking on campus, or want them for different reasons.

A critical fact is that adult students account for about half of all enrollments in college courses. Urban universities have long recognized and encouraged this trend, as a moneymaker. Harvard, for a rather extreme instance, has three times as many part-time, continuing education students (60,000) as are in all its regular programs. The University takes in 10 percent of its annual budget ($150 million) this way. Like Johns Hopkins, another leader in this area, Harvard instituted adult education in 1909 and works chiefly on the old "night school" model, not on-line.[33] Apart (again) from those pursuing history or Chinese or music for enrichment, these are people who want to gain something practical in exchange for their tuition: a life skill such as financial management or tax preparation; completion of an interrupted course of study; a skill or small packet of knowledge that will win advancement at work or qualify its owner to look for a better job; or a certificate giving him or her the formal right to do a certain kind of work. Employers pay to send some of these people back to "college," but most adults are using their own money and studying on their own time to satisfy a present or future employer.

Certificates deserve a short paragraph to themselves. According to one estimate, there are now seven people seeking certificates for every student in a degree program. New York University (a leader in adult education) has 107 certificate programs. In the University of California at San Diego's extension division, 7,000 students are working for certificates in engineering, ten times the number seeking degrees in that field. The 7,000 already have degrees; they want more advanced and specialized qualifications. Other popular certificate areas include computer technology, accounting, paralegal studies, environmental technology, biotechnology, and aquaculture (and these are in addition to innumerable proprietary certifications such as "Oracle Database Administrator").[34] Universities and community colleges in this vast area of higher education sell parcels of certified knowledge in highly precise if slightly complex markets: the institutions must know that there is effective demand for particular certificates, because potential students know there is effective demand on the part of companies (and of course governments, etc.) for specific kinds of complex labor power.

That way of looking at universities today explains a lot. Those—a great majority—that have to think like businesses must then look around carefully to see what kinds of skill, knowledge, and worker actual businesses in the region need. It is now common for community colleges, city universities, and state university systems to survey employers and to adapt curriculum or start new programs according to the findings. "The views and the needs of businesses are at the heart of nearly all of the long-range higher-education plans that states have adopted or are considering."[35]

Moreover, the regular on-campus curriculum of traditional colleges and universities is gradually shifting, without the benefit of visionary planning, but simply in response to what students see as their practical needs. Music, art history, American literature, developmental psychology, organic chemistry, and the like disappear from lists of courses most frequently taken by B.A. candidates, to be replaced by business law, management, computer programming, marketing, finance, and the like. Over a quarter of these students major in business, and well over another quarter choose majors, such as computer science, that may ticket them through to high-paying jobs in industry. They are accumulating units of knowledge and skill that they can trade for income, rather than more abstract, class-signifying culture. In the annual surveys of first-year students, the number who check being "well-off financially" as an essential goal in their educations has risen above 75 percent, compared to 41 percent thirty years ago. Back then, 82 percent saw development of a sound "philosophy of life" as a main aim in their studies; now just half as many do.[36] They may enjoy studying Shakespeare and drinking in local pubs, but for them, education is less a conventional rite of maturation than the route to a good job.

This completes my tour of developments since 1970 or so in the traditional system of higher education—a tiny sampling, yet doubtless more than some readers wanted to know. My reasons for putting forth such a display are to show how fluid, multiform, and—to the untutored eye—disorderly these changes have been; yet also to argue for a way of understanding them that makes sense of the clutter. Universities become not just more like corporations (as is frequently observed) but like the agile corporations that have emerged from the ruins of Fordist capitalism. Those corporations, if they make old-fashioned commodities, scramble for knowledge to make and market them more elegantly. They build more and more complex knowledge into their products, and increasingly they sell knowledge itself. So do universities, to students and to corporations, in a great variety of ways. By itemizing a few, I have meant to explicate what is intelligibly and usefully meant by speaking of the whole process as a commodification of knowledge. It has also been a massive privatization of knowledge and education that used to be public goods. Finally, to anticipate a later stage of the argument, it has commercialized large portions of the knowledges that count as intellectual assets for the academic professions.

A close look at any one traditional university will show this transformation at work: Columbia, for instance—though a pioneer and hence not typical—may afford a glimpse of the academic future. The university leads all others in income from patents: $143 million, or close to 10 percent of its whole budget, in fiscal 2000. Behind that figure is a cornucopia of licenses, deals, and partnerships. Eye drops to treat glaucoma, a way of making protein for drugs using animal cells, a dot-com that dispenses information about nutrition, Biosphere 2 (now partly supported by the Department of Energy), the Lamont-Doherty Earth Observatory, a Washington think tank on science policy, and so on. Columbia Innovation Enterprises, the umbrella licensing operation, also seeks revenue from teaching: for instance through a for-profit subsidiary, Digital Knowledge Ventures, which works to create advanced placement and continuing education curricula. The university also started up Fathom in 2000, a collaboration with such nonprofits as the New York Public Library, the Victoria & Albert Museum, the American Film Institute, and the Woods Hole Oceanographic Institution. After many changes of direction and a good deal more support out of Columbia funds than initially expected, Fathom looks to be selling books, on-line cultural offerings, corporate training courses, and advertising space on its sites. With more publicity (because the original backing came from Michael Milken's Knowledge Universe), but perhaps less significance, Columbia and other prestigious universities have signed on as providers of business course content and prestige with UNext—another venture with lots of capital and an uncertain future, but one that has paid $20 million to Columbia for its contributions.

These deals, though more numerous at Columbia than elsewhere, are not otherwise unusual. Two of its practices are. Under leadership of its spirited and freewheeling vice provost, Michael Crow, and through the vehicle of its Strategic Initiatives Fund, Columbia has reinvested more than 10 percent of its patent revenues in new experiments and research projects that are expected to become self-sustaining or profitable in time. "We are expanding what it means to be a knowledge enterprise. We use knowledge as a form of venture capital," Crow says. A second of his projects, still germinating, is to join with other universities worldwide in selling patents to corporations, and become a truly "international university." [37]

There you have it, in one conceptual—and increasingly actual—unity: the university as agile, post-Fordist, global corporation, with knowledge as its chief asset.

The For-Profits

Columbia and the other institutions featured in the last section are nonprofit organizations. The money they gain from selling knowledge in new and varied ways makes up for loss of more traditional funds and (as entrepreneurial administrators all declare) goes to support the university's main "mission" more handsomely. Readers will form their own opinions on whether the priorities of these universities have deeply changed or only the means of realizing them. I suggest that working to enrich stockholders is and will be a social project in sharp contrast to what traditional colleges do, although quantitative changes in the latter may be adding up to a qualitative one—producing hybrids that merit names such as the "managerial" or "corporate" university. What is beyond question is that competition *from* profit-making institutions of several kinds has provided at least as much of an incentive as state budget cuts or changes in patent law for old-fashioned universities to reconfigure themselves. To that competition—and so to the rest of the universe of postsecondary education—I now briefly turn.

For the sake of a simplification that will later collapse, I divide this sector into three parts. First, proprietary colleges and universities. The largest and by now most famous is the University of Phoenix. It has close to 100,000 students and over one hundred sites in thirty-some states. Many people suppose it to be an on-line operation, and it does have a financially separate on-line division, but most Phoenix students drive to its "campuses" (office buildings or floors of rented space in them), for evening courses, of which a theoretical full-time load costs around $7,000 a year. Most of its 5,000-plus faculty members are part-timers teaching for about $1,000 a course; none of the few full-timers have tenure. Courses and degree programs are standardized across the hundred campuses, a fact that makes it almost as easy to establish a new one as to start up a burger franchise. It has moved aggressively into new states, often over considerable resistance from administrators of nonprofit colleges. And when barred from entry, as in New Jersey, it comes back again with a new plan to meet objections, such as that it has no library. It competes with traditional colleges also by recruiting community college graduates to finish B.A.'s with Phoenix in space rented on their original community college campuses. Aside from cheapness and convenience, its main appeal has been the practical value of its courses and degrees in many technical and career-related fields. It is taking students and revenue away from the nonprofits and so driving them toward strategies like those surveyed in the last section.[38]

Phoenix's parent company, Apollo Group, is one of a dozen or so publicly held and traded, degree-granting, for-profit companies. DeVry Institutes has 38,000 students on seventeen campuses; ITT has 26,000 on sixty-seven campuses in twenty-eight states; Strayer Education has thirteen campuses in the Washington, D.C., area; Whitman Education Group has twenty-four in thirteen states. All these specialize in engineering, information technology, business, finance, and such areas. A smaller company, Argosy Education Group, awards hundreds of doctorates in psychology, education, and business each year. Most of these institutions can boast to prospective students of very high job placement rates—about 90 percent at DeVry and ITT. As you would expect, they achieve that result by responding quickly to what local businesses want. An executive at Strayer commented that its curricular agility gives it a big advantage over public universities, which "can't change their curriculum every six months," or spend $500,000 a year to "retrain" faculty members.[39] Nothing could make clearer the contrast between such companies and the universities they are challenging. If a faculty must jump to change its curriculum and retool itself each year in response to the wishes of outside groups, it is doing without indispensable prerogatives of professionals as we have known them. To the extent that traditional universities emulate the for-profits, they, too, contribute to displacement of the academic profession.

This is a turbulent field of enterprise. Consolidation goes on apace. Kaplan, the old test-prep company, started up an on-line law school (Concord) in 1998, recently bought forty-one for-profit undergraduate colleges, and is looking to buy an established M.B.A. program. This list barely hints at the complexity of Kaplan, whose parent is the Washington Post Company.[40] Dot-coms in higher education took a serious drubbing along with their high-tech cousins in the 2000 crash, and a wave of mergers and acquisitions followed, from Education Management Corporation's purchase of Argosy for $78 million to tiny Provo College's acquisition of a faltering college of court reporting. In 2000, there were 125 changes in ownership among for-profits.[41] Yet in the slightly longer run, stocks of companies in higher education did far better than the market in general: the *Chronicle of Higher Education*'s index of for-profit stocks rose 156 percent in just two years, leading up to the end of 2001 (February 8, 2002)—one more datum on the fierce pace of commercialization in this area.

The second of the three for-profit activities made numerous appearances earlier in this chapter: selling not just campus management, food services, and so on, to the nonprofits, but technology, courses, portal services and other goods integral to education; and repackaging or brokering the "products" of the traditional university for sale to individual and corporate buyers. I will not revisit this subject except to remark that higher education has come a long way from the time not so long ago when colleges and universities bought only food, heating oil, furniture, and the like from outside companies—not to mention from the time when my alma mater was founded with the motto "Learning and Labor" and an ideal of cooperative self-sufficiency in everything. Now, it is impossible to draw clear lines between universities and education companies.

So too in the third area, that of corporate universities, where companies provide their own managers and technicians with precisely the knowledge they need, to do what the business strategy calls for, when it calls for it. General Electric founded the first corporate university in 1955; now there are more than two thousand of them. Motorola University, the best known, has sites in thirteen countries. This seems to be the fastest growing sector of postsecondary education, and a costly one. Fifty-two corporate universities covered in a recent survey had budgets that averaged $24 million. Many of them offer courses to wider publics than their own employees, so are serving two groups of students that might otherwise buy from traditional universities. But this way of putting it misrepresents the main threat to the latter, because more than 90 percent of corporations outsource "delivery" and 60 percent outsource "some aspect of course design" to traditional universities—which, in other words, have met the competition by supplying curriculum that corporations will buy. Jeanne C. Meister, head of Corporate University Xchange and author of the main book on these institutions, advises nonprofits to "redefine their business models," "think of themselves as business entities offering specific marketable services," and aggressively seek corporate partners with whom to "design, develop, and deliver courses."[42] Again, the line between these two categories blurs. We find universities looking to meet corporate needs more and more directly, and higher education sliding farther and farther into what Marx rightly saw as an ever more encompassing, ultimately universal, capitalist market.

Reflections

This tight and layered integration of nonprofit universities with businesses, of corporations' needs for specific kinds of labor with what individual consumers of education need in order to get jobs, of public funding of research with profit-making uses of knowledge derived from research, and so on, makes it impossible to answer what seems like a simple question: how far has privatization gone, in higher education? Or, even simpler, what portion of all the goods and services that add up to postsecondary education are sold by companies? If the denominator is around $750 billion (and I have seen widely varying estimates) then a numerator of $125 billion—the estimated revenue of companies that sell courses and degrees and certificates directly to customers—would give a fraction that reduces to one-sixth. Yet clearly a lot more than that portion of teaching and research is done in the profit mode, as this and the previous section have shown. The sellers of courses and administrative systems, the corporations that run internal universities, the innumerable corporate "partners" of nonprofit institutions in licensing, their for-profit distance learning subsidiaries, their sale of students' needs and eyeballs, and much else falls outside that one-sixth. Is half of higher education a business, now? The question cannot be answered, and an effort to answer it would be misplaced empiricism.

What my survey purports to have shown is the permeability of this sector to initiatives by post-Fordist business, the determination of business to colonize it, its rapid progress in doing so, the responsiveness of universities to the incursion, and their new agility in streamlining operations and finding new sources of cash. They have not gone so far along this path as some critics fear, but their ethos is changing with their practices, as corporations trespass on their near-monopoly. On this account, as American capitalism has reconstituted itself since 1970, the structure and practices of higher education have changed in homologous ways. So have traditional colleges and universities. In addition, the activities of higher education they manage constitute a smaller portion of the whole now, than in 1970. A number of the epithets and formulas used to characterize the new capitalism—flexible accumulation, agility, privatization, the knowledge society—also have some descriptive power when applied to the university.

So, I note in passing, does "globalization." Through these years there has been a rapid increase in the flow of students to universities across national borders. Twice as many students from the United States (114,000) were studying abroad at the end of the 1990s as at the beginning. The number of international students at U.S. universities also grew rapidly, but the total impact of educational visitors is greater in countries such as Britain, where over 10 percent of students are from elsewhere, and Australia—nearly 13 percent, with education at all levels now a ranking seventh among that country's "exports."[43] The for-profits are suddenly making an imperial move that may overshadow this migration. The British Open University has come to the U.S. Sylvan Learning Systems, and the Apollo Group are starting chains of universities abroad. For-profit universities, many bankrolled from abroad, proliferate in China, the former Soviet Union, South Asia, and Latin America, hastening everywhere the decline of the traditional university linked to national culture and interests, as described by Bill Readings in *The University in Ruins*.[44] In 2001 the World Trade Organization took up various proposals that it regulate higher education, thus confirming higher education's status as a commodity. Its internationalization proceeds in a less obvious way, too: if well-trained engineers in India earn 15 percent of what their North American counterparts make, companies can take advantage of the difference both by hiring immigrants and by locating facilities in India, where the low-paid professionals are. U.S. companies have large contingents of programmers and other information technology workers in Bangalore, the Philippines, and so on. These corporations are in effect buying advanced technical education abroad, on the cheap, and in the process undermining control of these branches of higher education by U.S. universities and professional groups.

Professions have more cohesion across borders than do unions, but as this example shows, not enough to contest the export of their work to where it may be done for less pay. Seen that way, globalization contributes to the same lessening of professional control over a defined area of work as does competition from for-profit universities that hire only adjuncts at hourly or piecework rates; or from on-line subsidiaries of traditional universities that use ill-paid tutors working at home; or from the profession's own apprentices (teaching assistants), floating A.B.D.'s, and rejected Ph.D.'s, working as a cheap, casual labor force in the same departments as their luckier colleagues on the tenure track.

The developments traced in the last two sections challenge in other obvious ways the autonomy and privileges that the profession won a hundred years ago and consolidated in the postwar period. The commercializing of research not only takes its products out of the public domain, but applies to them a different logic from that used by professionals to guard and develop their central bodies of knowledge. Along with corporate funding of university research, it also mocks the idealistic but professionally indispensable idea that the guild generates its questions internally and pursues them wherever the qualified mind can go. If corporations can pay university researchers to work on profit-making knowledge, a major argument for professional autonomy evaporates. Professors are also threatened with loss of their ownership in courses and class materials, a right that was too obvious even to need articulation before the days of videotape and then the Internet. Now it is being contested vigorously.[45] More consequentially for education, the curriculum is passing out of the faculty's control, and into a market where effective demand is directly or indirectly created by business. At the college where I taught, the faculty's *only* sovereign right, by charter, was to set and administer "the course of instruction." Formally, most academic professionals still retain that right, but it is becoming more of a fiction. As for university governance in general, it has come increasingly under management by administrators attuned to bottom lines and market forces. And as I argued earlier, whether they like it or not, administrators are forced to act more and more as curricular brokers between businesses and faculty members. This is not a lament, but an effort to understand how the world is working, these days. Piece by piece, and with no central design or main antagonist, the market haven of the academic profession is being disassembled and higher education removed from its charge.

Clearly the leading agents in this complex process are corporations. They pursue the strategies I have discussed in order to find new markets, reduce costs, and raise profits, not in order to undermine traditional universities or harm the people who work and study in them. On the contrary most business leaders believe that their project will improve both nonprofit and for-profit education: competition benefits all, in the long run. But undermining the traditional university and the academic profession has been a main effect of privatization—and not really an incidental one. For if knowledge is in fact the most important resource and one of the most important products in the new economic order, why leave its care, development, and transmission to academics and others with their own distinct or even hostile agendas? Why, in the cauldron of global competition, allow knowledge to serve as capital for semiautonomous and sometimes unfriendly professions? And why would the capitalist class want to foster even a submissive rival, the PMC, when history does provide instances of that class, or parts of it, turning on its masters? Whatever degree of conscious intent one attributes to capital in such matters, its post-1970 project has been hard on the Fordist university—chief locus of PMC reproduction, headquarters of its self-organization, and institutional base for professional privilege and authority. To be sure, ideologues paid by the right wing of the capitalist class have for over a decade been openly attacking the university. The culture wars—attacks on multiculturalism and "political correctness"—amount also to an assault on professional vows of neutrality and claims to a proprietary right in the control of knowledge. But that challenge has done no more than supply a public rationale for changes already under way (especially cuts in public funding) and driven mainly by forces other than the Heritage Foundation and its privatizing allies.

Other Professions

These shifts in the organization and circulation of knowledge have been most directly consequential for professors, whose well-being is closely linked to that of the colleges and universities that employ us. But other professions have also lost ground through this period: most strikingly, medicine. Over the last century, it became in this country the model of robust professionalization. Doctors won almost complete control over an area of practice they themselves defined, over the body of knowledge that grounded the practice, and over admission to their ranks. They had great respect, influence in many matters of public policy, and high incomes determined largely by themselves, within the context of monopoly, and through fee-for-service charges. Their incomes, though comfortable enough, have been declining.

In other respects, their profession has gravely deteriorated. It is losing control over its body of scientific knowledge, whose formation was critical to the early success of the guild (e.g., germ theory). As government funding failed to keep pace with research costs, and Medicare payments declined, medical schools turned to corporate support, with the predictable result that sponsors have a big say in what will be studied, with what goal (commodification is at work), and what can be published. There's also trouble where theory connects to practice, knowledge to art. Computer programs for diagnosis, based on hoards of data, may not put the family doctor in company with the family auto mechanic but will reduce the former's interpretative scope and put him or her in competition with less highly educated practitioners. More famously, the "sacred" relation between doctor and patient has been wrenched open by government agencies and malpractice lawyers. Administrators now supervise much of physicians' work, intervening in what used to be considered purely medical decisions. They try to fix the length of the medical work week—that is, increase it—and limit the time spent with a single patient. Most doctors work on salary, so with much less control over their compensation than before. More than 30 percent of hospitals are profit-making businesses, as are most of the ubiquitous health maintenance organizations, with which 90 percent of doctors have one or more contracts. These erosions taken together, rather than any one of them, have stimulated a movement among doctors to unionize, and, in response, led the decrepit American Medical Association (to which only 35 percent of physicians belong), to restyle itself as a union—an unthinkable conversion, until recently.[46]

Like many such affronts to the PMC, the loss of medical autonomy had multiple causes. Well before the HMO revolution, regulatory agencies began taking a keener interest in the work of physicians. Then with increased government support for medical education and research in the fifties and sixties came more supervision. Critically, pressure to increase medical school enrollments cut into the profession's ability to regulate its size (there were twice as many doctors per thousand Americans in 1990 as in 1970), and so into its members' affluence and power. Medicaid and Medicare brought regulation of practice, and, as costs soared, regulation of fees. But probably the greatest counter force to professional autonomy came from U.S. corporations that rebelled against the high cost of health insurance for their employees—a drag on profits just when global competition was heating up. All these tendencies fed the transformation of medicine into a business, and the commodification of medical knowledge.

Challenges to the legal profession have been quieter, yet bracing. Scandals like the savings and loan crisis brought more regulation. Tort reform threatens the self-determination of trial lawyers, and suits against them have doubled. The legitimation of advertising puts professional "brothers" in open competition with one another for trade and makes the law more like a business. Competing practitioners have invaded areas of prior monopoly such as real estate and auto insurance work. The laity can write their own wills and various contracts by using software (e.g., WillMaker) that costs one-third of an attorney's hourly rate. Perhaps most consequentially, the ranks of lawyers (like those of doctors) have swelled through this period, from 125 per 100,000 people in 1960 to thrice that ratio now. As new entrants carve out new specialties and form their own organizations, the old bar associations have lost some of their august power, and the profession some of its solidarity. There are many more associates now, in comparison with partners, and a host of paraprofessionals to divide and cheapen legal labor. More than half of all lawyers are now on salary, and average income has dropped. Even the upper tier of corporate lawyers, though paid extravagantly, find themselves in a buyers' market, and the corporations that pay the tab take more directive power over the work such lawyers do.

The legal, medical, and academic professions were in many ways models. Now, they have suffered real losses of control, as well as of public confidence. People tend to blame lawyers for everything from the lengthening and tabloidization of criminal trials to the increase in malpractice suits against doctors. At the same time, the percentage of Americans who think the average doctor is mainly interested in helping people has dropped by half since 1970. And then there are the familiar accusations of political correctness against academics, along with the spreading conviction that they drag themselves to work only a few hours a week, though studies show that in fact those hours increased from an average of forty in the 1970s to fifty-three in 1992. The time of modernizing, professional leadership broadly accepted as in the interest of the whole society is passing. Indeed, it is hard even for professionals to represent *themselves* in such confident and lofty terms.

For many reasons, then, it is hard to disagree with Andrew Hacker that "all three professions face similar futures," including "the prospect of unemployed physicians," the failure of lawyers to attain partnerships, and an end to "the salad days of the academy."[47] Nor is the disarray of these groups localized in the United States. Elliott Krause's thorough survey shows widely differing histories and forces at work in France, Italy, Germany, and Britain, but with similar adverse outcomes. Krause titles his book *The Death of the Guilds*.[48] He argues that when early capitalism destroyed most of the old guilds, it spared these three, basically because they made nothing that could be mass-produced for profit. One might extend that idea by suggesting that capital in the regime of flexible accumulation is finding ways to commodify what professionals do, too.

I have brought only three professions into view, here, and am not sure how well they can represent all the others. But they have been among the strongest, and there is no reason to think that those more weakly organized in the past, such as engineering and architecture, will find means to improve their position in current circumstances. Take accounting, which, like engineering, has had difficulty maintaining its independence from business. A little later than lawyers and professors, but in a decisive movement around 1900, accountants put together the apparatus of a profession. The American Association of Public Accountants, a small and primarily local group at first, took initiatives to get a licensing bill passed in New York (1896), establishing formal exams and the title "Certified Public Accountant." By 1910 the more industrial states all had such laws, and the AAPA was becoming a national organization. There were journals, textbooks, professional meetings. Large firms took shape. Although a high school education was enough to qualify accountants in most states, the discipline made its way into university programs, beginning with the Wharton School of Finance at Penn. It established a body of would-be-scientific knowledge, an ideal of objectivity, canons of ethics, and an apparatus of self-regulation. Like other modernizing professionals, accountants played a part in progressive era reform and regulation—of interstate commerce, of insurance, and of corporations themselves, which were under pressure to open their finances to inspection, and make externally audited annual reports to stockholders.

While accountants were thus involved in taming and rationalizing corporate capitalism, they were also, from the start of the Fordist era, servants of capital who helped create and rationalize the corporate form on behalf of its masters. They helped decide what profit was, how to measure it, who owned it, and, in time, how to make more of it and how to manage companies "scientifically." Many of them worked inside corporate walls, or served as consultants to business, with no obligation to the public good. From the outset, this double allegiance jeopardized accountancy's claims to the standard professional virtues of objectivity, scientific knowledge, public service, and autonomy, and made precarious its claim to self-regulation. Periodic scandals involved accountants who either overlooked corporate fraud or actively facilitated it, most memorably for the savings and loans in the 1980s. Arthur Andersen's role in the Enron debacle is nothing new. Nor are cries for external regulation of the profession: Congress looked suspiciously into it throughout the 1980s and passed a number of acts that defined or limited its work. Although such intrusions do—as with medicine—reduce professional autonomy, it remains to be seen whether Andersen's misdeeds will further weaken the whole profession. Nor is it clear that the rapid increase in the profession's size (from 9,500 members of the American Institute of Certified Public Accountants in 1945, to 95,000 in 1973, to 300,000 in 1994), though even faster than growth in medicine and law,[49] similarly affected the incomes of accountants. What is clear is that accountancy has, like law, decisively become a two-tiered profession. The old gap between Big Eight firms (now, through mergers and Arthur Andersen's collapse, the Big Four) and everyone else has widened. The large firms are as global and wealthy as the corporations they serve, while local accountants do small audits and compete with H&R Block and with popular, do-it-yourself software such as TurboTax.

To grasp the importance of the change, one must look not only at the separation of low- from high-end careers, but at the deprofessionalization, in effect, of the high end. Through the Fordist period, accountancy's defining practice was the audit: independent, dispassionate, principled, grounded in arcane knowledge and professional craft. Now, the part of big accounting firms' revenue that comes from audits has dropped to well less than half, and the part that comes from advising corporations on finance, management, tax, and so on has greatly increased. In short, the "commercial segment" of accounting has taken over from the sector that could plausibly claim to be serving the public by keeping capital and governments honest. Consulting accountants unequivocally adopt the interests of the managements they serve, helping them negotiate the complexities of flexible finance, track international flows of capital and profit, monitor and control labor, and present to capital markets and regulators the most favorable representation of corporate activities that is consistent with the law. Or, as in the case of Arthur Andersen, with not getting caught. That case has, as I write, made it a pious dogma among politicians that an accounting firm's performance of both auditing and consultancy for a single corporation is a grievous conflict of interest. Worse, the profession's capacity to regulate itself is now in doubt, and conflicts of interest threaten to discredit its regulating organization, the American Institute of Certified Public Accountants (successor group to the AAPA)—which has spun off a profit-making dot-com with a near monopoly on products that all accountants must use. These conflicts may be proscribed by law. But the transformation of big-league accounting into a business chasing profits on its own and its clients' behalf will proceed, while public service accounting becomes a low-prestige sideline. So accounting presents a special version of the argument I am advancing: the traditional part of the profession is routinized, while business absorbs the dynamic part for its own purposes. A happier outcome for the coopted, to be sure, than adjuncting at the University of Phoenix for peanuts; but the same process of professional subordination is deeply at work in the two cases, though apprentice accountants and TAs in English might otherwise appear to have little in common.

Managers

Managers as a group have perhaps still less in common with English instructors, and maybe not enough with professionals in general to make the category "professional-managerial class" seem socially real, despite the shared historical formation of groups within it. That, and similarities in their lives today—college, graduate study, the suburb or gentrified city neighborhood, intermarriage, high educational goals for their children, a complex relation to high culture, and so on—may seem overbalanced by differences or antagonisms in some areas of belief and practice. On the other hand, their working lives and relations have run a similar course. In the Fordist regime, managers, like salaried professionals, tended to enter their jobs with academic and social assets, not working up from office boy to president. Once hired by corporations, they expected to win the equivalent of tenure or a partnership after demonstrating their competence and loyalty. Many, in fact, remained with the same company for a working life punctuated by promotions: in short, a career. Companies held out job security as an attraction to managers and often made good on the claim; until two decades ago the IBM handbook boasted of no layoffs in forty years, as a matter of corporate policy.[50] Pay was better than for many professionals, though not outside the range. And managers had similar benefit packages: health plans, insurance, company-supported pension plans, as well as a variety of privileges and perks. A degree of autonomy on the job was standard, along with respect and a kind of fellowship.

By the 1980s all that was changing. Benefits froze or declined or required larger contributions from employees. "Defined benefit" pension plans gave way to riskier 401Ks and stock options. The workload intensified: fifty- and sixty-hour weeks became standard, with cell phones and beepers intruding on home and vacation time. Stern measurement of accountability shrinks the area of managerial independence on the job, with electronic surveillance augmenting traditional forms of supervision at most corporations. And of course layoffs accompanied and drove these other degradations. The likelihood of a dependable career at one company is now small, and the corporate reject resembles the Ph.D. castoff, at least in some ways: only about half of the former are landing new, full-time jobs within two years, and when they do, their compensation averages 15 percent less.[51] The slaughter of middle managers received much publicity in the 1980s, less since then; but in fact their "displacement" proceeded at a higher rate in the 1990s.[52]

These people have been challenged—more directly—by the same historical forces as professionals. As corporations have merged, downsized, and "reengineered" themselves in response to foreign competition, their unceasing effort to beat back workers has broadened to include managerial labor as well, in ways familiar to professionals. There has been a large increase in contingent labor within corporations, along with outsourcing and subcontracting. In addition, the franchise movement has put millions of service workers under the direction of low-level managers closely following a script drafted for them in corporate headquarters and rigorously enforced. Flexible accumulation and the agile corporation have been hard on Fordism's corporate bureaucrats, as on professionals. A further similarity: theirs has also become a two-tiered line of work, with CEOs and others in the upper tier winning riches that dwarf those of 1960s counterparts.

The phenomena I have selectively reviewed point to a clear enough trend in recent decades toward the degradation of professional and managerial work, and an erosion of their claim to privilege within market havens, grounded on their disinterested management and universally beneficial use of knowledge. I believe there is a compelling case—barely sketched out here —for understanding the setbacks of professionals and managers in these years as part of a single, broad, uneven historical process.

The Future of a Class?

If this generalization holds, will it support my broader hypothesis, that the conditions of possibility for a coherent and thriving professional managerial class are not a permanent feature of capitalism after 1890 but specific to a passing stage? Certainly the condition I have most emphasized—that is, the opening for groups of educated and expert workers to convert their knowledge into an asset for quasi-monopolistic use—a condition laid down a hundred years ago, has become precarious. In part that owes to the very success of the PMC: at its beginnings, for instance, about 2 percent of young people were going to college. In 1970, the moment I have posed as transitional, that figure had risen to over 40 percent, and it is close to 60 percent now, while the benefits of investment in a college degree recede. Even in a so-called knowledge society, can more than half the population escape from working-class conditions of labor by earning credentials and sharing in a guild's intellectual mysteries? However one answers that question in the abstract, the historical fact is that when global competition became a serious threat to American capital, capital not only terminated its unspoken compromise of 1945–70 with industrial workers but began in less obvious but equally effective ways to chip away at the autonomy and privilege of managers and professionals. Are we witnessing not just the death of the remaining "guilds," in Krause's term, but the etiolation of a social class?

It is easy enough to imagine a scenario for disintegration of the PMC, in which Marx and Engels will have turned out to be right after all, if we cut them 150 years or so of slack—not a lot, as prophesies go. On this scenario capitalism becomes, finally, a two-class world system, with the much heralded gap between rich and poor continuing to widen. The more vulnerable professions survive only as ghostly paradigms. The stronger ones proceed along the path they are already taking, in the view of observers like Krause and Hacker, toward disorganized, two-tiered groupings, with the eminences and the subalterns sharing less and less common ground. Managers, never well organized as a group, see their tacit, Fordist contract dissolved. The top brass prosper. The rest overwork in conditions of insecurity and disrespect, try to restart as entrepreneurs or consultants, retire early and meagerly, or become wage workers.

Comparable triage takes place among universities, with some marching on in good health, some dying, and some healing themselves by drastic surgery. Yale, Swarthmore, and their like, if wily and fortunate, maintain their prestige and privilege, serving as a base for elite professional remnants and the world's ruling class. Community colleges grow ever more serviceable to working students and local businesses. The University of Phoenix and its profit-making brethren (in real or cyberspace), along with corporate universities, become the most dynamic sector. For all other traditional universities and colleges, the going is tough. If the narrative goes forward in this way, it will make less sense than it does even now to speak of "the" university, because institutions of all the kinds surveyed above, as well as new ones not yet imagined, will divide up the postsecondary market into many niches. Only a few hundred of them will still offer customers a total, initiatory experience on the model of the traditional four years away at college, or even four years commuting to an urban institution for a hard-won B.A. or B.S. degree. Nontraditional degrees, certificates, and academic subjects will proliferate, as required by the agile corporations that deploy knowledge for profit. In this exfoliation of products and credentials, not only will "the" university cease to act as the sole incubator and repository of PMC knowledges; it will cease to act as a common portal through which the youth of a national class move in unity. In sum, there will no longer be a single, chief site of PMC reproduction.

Most of the young people who until recently would have passed through that portal will take one of several paths alternative to the settled careers that used to await them. A few will shoulder their way into the big bourgeoisie, capitalizing their knowledge on the Bill Gates model and becoming major exploiters of other people's labor. More will join the ever present petty bourgeoisie by setting up consultancies, partnerships, and individual practices of novel sorts,[53] selling knowledge and services to corporations until the successful ones are bought out by corporations. And a still larger group will slide into the working class, hustling their marginal and often part-time labor power wherever someone will pay for it. On this scenario the making and deployment of knowledge are at last fully absorbed into the universal market for commodities, whose scope even Marx may not have anticipated.

I note parenthetically that this script does not end in the immiseration of most people with PMC educations, skills, and social habits. Whatever the pain of exclusion from academic jobs, big law partnerships, or secure careers in upper management, such people are unlikely to find themselves in sweat-shops or on the streets. The dissolution of a class need not mean devastation of the families within it: consider slaveholders after emancipation. Rather, this scenario is one of recomposed social relations, with losers and winners, as in all epochal shifts. (And—a parenthesis within the parenthesis: though I speak myself from a lifetime in the PMC, I am not its transhistorical parti-san; my utopia, were I the sort of person who does utopias, would have no professions in it.)

Having pressed at some length my claim that a certain kind of historical frame can help us think about the future of a social class, I now put off the garb of prophet to conclude with a few thoughts about present circum-stances. Most would agree that whatever recuperative powers the PMC may be able to muster, individually and collectively it faces daunting challenges. What practical advantage, if any, might activists gain by framing them within this epochal narrative? In brief, the long historical perspective offers fans of the PMC little cause for optimism. Its solidarity as a class, for one thing, has never matched that of the big bourgeoisie or, in most capitalist so-cieties, the proletariat. It attained effective class consciousness and coherent agency only twice, I think: in the two decades before World War I and those right after World War II. If I am right about pressures brought to bear on it now, there is little chance for it to come forward again as a class-for-itself.

On the contrary, managers have little experience of or sympathy with sol-idarity, and professionals, for all their nurture in guild coziness, are not used to making alliances across disciplinary lines. So the commodification of knowledge and dispersal of intellectual assets will more likely drive PMC people toward strategies of individual survival and advancement. Further-more, 1960s radicalism left a legacy in the university that includes a sharp critique of mandarinism, of old-boy networks, of monopolies on knowl-edge, and of business culture, that has deepened antagonisms within the class. At best, something of a gap divided the literature professor from the engineer and both from the advertising agent, though all three might have been fraternity brothers in, say, 1950, and suburban neighbors in 1970. I intuit a further distancing since then, advanced not only by the feminization of the professions and the polarization created by social movements during and after the 1960s, but by the conservative backlash against those movements—from the defunding of public universities to attacks on multiculturalism and affirmative action. Professions do well when they are understood, and understand themselves, as politically neutral and acting in the interests of everyone. Such an understanding was widespread for much of this century. After the politicization of the last twenty-five years and the invasion of professional domains by business, what would it take to rebuild professional ideology and make it feel once again like common sense?

Nor are professionals (forget about managers!) effectively organized to combat public cynicism, ideological assault, and economic decline. Consider, in my own field, the sluggish, perhaps well-meaning, but inept efforts of the Modern Language Association to address the sorrows of its own graduate students, or even to calibrate supply with demand by trying to limit their numbers—until the students themselves took strong initiatives within the organization. Or consider the effort to unionize graduate students at Yale, not as professionals but as workers and in alliance with other nonprofessional workers at the University: all but a handful of Yale's tenured faculty members responded with indifference or hostility. Predictably, the now numerous campaigns to organize teaching assistants have won least support where the profession is most secure (e.g., New York University), and where there is little history of trade unionism. Or consider even the American Medical Association, once lord of all it surveyed, now an embattled and enfeebled organization in which (as I noted earlier) fewer than half of physicians vest their professional hopes and concerns. Only now does the AMA show belated support for the unionizing efforts of doctors. (In this it is far behind the American Association of University Professors; but membership in the latter includes only a small minority of all faculty members, and only a subset of those have the AAUP as their bargaining agent.) If the historical foundation of professionalism is cracking, the organizations that served it well enough in the old social order will have a hard time remaking themselves in the new. Their commitment to credentials and regulated meritocracy is a barrier to solidarity with less credentialed workers. It also entails a depoliticization of the public sphere, in deference to the ideal of disinterested public service.

It is unclear how the professional-managerial class could regain its lost power without political action, and at the same time laughable to imagine the sort of politics that would require: "Exempt People with Advanced Degrees from the Perils of the Market"?

A movement to end market perils for all workers, and stop capital's appropriation of human knowledge for profit, would be something else again.

TEACHING LITERACY
FOR CITIZENSHIP

◆

The next three essays look at how specific professional concerns fare in the university as agile capitalism has been revising it. In this essay I meditate on the supposition that higher education and schooling in general serve a democratic society by nourishing hearty citizenship. This claim has been a centerpiece of academic ideology for a hundred years and more. More specifically, I focus on the emergent subprofession of rhetoric and composition. In essay 6 ("Professionalizing Politics") I noted that as its practitioners organized their work into the forms of professionalism, they did not purge it of political commitments as most new professions do, perhaps in part because this group came together during the egalitarian sixties and their aftermath. Vigorous and critical citizenship was a commitment, along with useful skills and knowledge. How has the changing university abetted or subverted that commitment?

Democracy can't work unless citizens are literate and informed: that's the starting point of one familiar justification for universal schooling. College faculties and administrations may articulate it in ideological moments, or see it as too obvious to need articulation. Naturally, compositionists have taken encouragement from, and sought support by affiliating with, this amiably righteous principle.

A closely allied rationale for university education is that by building, preserving, and transmitting the national culture, it fortifies the nation itself. Bill Readings elaborated this idea in *The University in Ruins.*[1] Compositionists don't press this claim for their work so often as perhaps they did when usage and correctness were the coin of their professional realm.[2] But it is implicit in their offer to help immigrants and children of the working class enter a national conversation by first mastering conventions of academic discourse.

In my view, these ideas are better than some old ones we might recall (the university's task is to perfect the gentleman) and especially to others we hear now (education's task is to foster economic growth and American competitiveness). Still, the telos of democratic citizenship and that of national culture are themselves laced with contradiction and ideological trouble. In particular, for my purpose here—which is to wonder about the prospects for democratic literacy work in this time of privatized knowledge and education as a business—both rationales allow inequality to flourish, and to seem natural and inevitable.

Cultural studies after Raymond Williams have probably made it impossible, any longer, to think of culture as a realm cleansed of power or as homogeneous throughout a nation. If universities fostered nationhood, they did so by valuing the culture of some over that of others, by recovering (actually creating) selective traditions, by giving people unequal access to respectable culture, by helping some turn culture into cultural capital, by letting their children draw on that capital to extend privilege generationally, and so on. Not to say that culture is another name for snobbery or national culture just a ruling-class trick, only that the university can't stand apart from the class system of its society. The point is perhaps even more obvious for literacy, which, in spite of many compositionists' egalitarian hopes, is a birthright to some, a meritocratic attainment for others, a low-grade marketable skill for many, and a "remedial" insult to still others.

The trouble with citizenship is perhaps deeper—and more vexing, because citizenship is a relation of basic equality: you and I, however unlike in birth or circumstance, have theoretically the same rights and obligations before the law and the same weight in governance. Of course this has a hollow ring in the era of hundred-million-dollar campaign warchests, bought pardons, and Supreme Court sleight-of-hand. But there's reason to doubt that the ideal of equal citizenship could ever be realized in a society like ours, even if an army of John McCains were to banish such abuses.

T. H. Marshall posed the fundamental question fifty years ago: is citizenship —a relation of basic equality—compatible with capitalist class structure? Or, to point up the contradiction: since capitalism was the condition of possibility for both citizenship and class inequality, "How is it that these two opposing principles could grow and flourish side by side in the same soil?"[3] Marshall answered by showing that in fact capitalist inequality was *consequent upon* the principle of equal civil rights, which in turn was necessary to the free play of capitalist economic activities. Each man (later, person) had to have the right to enter contracts, pursue gain, seek advancement, and in general act as a free individual in the market. Free labor and free capital needed a relation like citizenship as their legal basis. So in effect, citizenship *was* the "soil" in which capitalist inequality flourished. Marshall particularly emphasized a universal right to education as critical for full citizenship: "The status acquired by education is carried out into the world bearing the stamp of legitimacy, because it has been conferred by an institution designed to give the citizen his just rights," and in this way, "citizenship operates as an instrument of social stratification" (110). In other words, equal opportunity and universal access to education are compatible with great inequality, and, because they make it seem the result of unequal merit and effort, they also make it seem both inevitable and just.

There is no way for egalitarian movements in composition or for education generally to escape this logic, though the reforms they promote may make teaching practices kinder and more effective.

To explicate the point, consider primary and secondary schooling, which, unlike attendance at college, is in the United States not only a universal right but a legal requirement. Access is universal. Yet even across the public schools, inequality is in Jonathan Kozol's word "savage." Attempts to level it out have always failed, and the currently popular strategies will surely also fail. About vouchers, and the privatization that would accompany them, I need not comment, to likely readers of this essay. Charter schools financed in the most common way take funds from the budgets of the regular schools that feed them, almost certainly making those schools worse, so that however bright and free the charter schools may be, the system as a whole remains as unequal as before, or more so. A third strategy—mandated statewide curricula with high-stakes testing—is spreading across the country, with its advocates stating always their intention of offering tough love to the weakest schools—that is state help with professional development for teachers and tutorial work for failing students, but no diplomas for students who nonetheless fail the tests, and various penalties for teachers and schools that don't make the grade. In Massachusetts, where I live, the first cohort of students to take the tests for real did so in spring of 2001, and, as was predictable, a majority of poor kids, kids in underfunded schools, kids with special needs, those for whom English is not the first language, and those in vocational schools, scored below the level they must eventually reach in order to graduate. The sorting by class, race, and (dis)ability that went on more subtly before will now proceed with stark clarity, as every student is measured on the same scale and either given or denied a diploma. This will amount to an ideological simplification, too, in that each eighteen-year-old's trajectory into college, career, dead-end job, or prison will now be explainable by reference to his or her numerically expressed merit. Unless, of course, as seems possible, the parents and students and teachers of Massachusetts rise up to defeat this unpleasant outcome.

The fourth strategy, just now gaining momentum, is to legislate or sue for much more equality[4] in public school funding, which has from the beginning depended on local property taxes and thus been a fluid transmitter of social class across generations. This kind of redistribution will disrupt privilege far more in most states than it has so far done in Vermont, so it seems unlikely to take place nationwide unless driven by a twenty-first-century equivalent of *Brown v. Board of Education.* Even if it did—and I certainly favor it wherever possible—I suppose that parents in Scarsdale and Oak Park and Beverly Hills would have little difficulty finding ways to preserve the advantage their children have over kids from Harlem and the Chicago projects and South Central Los Angeles. Universal and equal schooling will be a central policy of any truly democratic society, but the sad truth is that there can be no equal schooling in an unequal society. Nor, I think, can such schooling be the vanguard of egalitarian change. Aside from the unfairness of sending children to fight their elders' battles, as in Little Rock and South Boston years ago, democratic reform of the educational system does not make the rest of the society democratic.

Almost fifty years after *Brown,* public schools are at least as segregated as back then. If this holds for primary and secondary education, it holds more evidently for colleges and universities, where universal access has never been a reality, and where, should we somehow achieve it, access would be to Princeton and then Wall Street for some, and, for the rest, to the same array of less favored colleges and life trajectories that is available now, plus another tier at the "bottom" for new arrivals. After thirty-five years of *relatively* open admissions, the university system remains highly stratified and carries out its work in social reproduction quite efficiently. Good will and heroic efforts there by administrators, literary workers, and activist students and faculty members can make the institution more open and decent but cannot nourish citizenship in the basic sense, as a relation of equality. That will—to repeat—require a broader egalitarian movement.

What a good college education can and does achieve in the arena of citizenship is nearly the opposite: it helps some students refine and develop their literacy into a vehicle of self-advancement and maybe control over others. I don't refer to the economic advantage it will give them, though it will do that; I have in mind the leverage in public affairs. Citizens have obligations as well as rights, but the obligations are pretty slim in this country—paying taxes, obeying laws, providing census information, and the like. No law requires them to exercise the franchise, and most do not. Beyond that minimal and (for each individual person) inconsequential act, citizens as a whole must serve in elective office, take turns on the parent-teacher organization or zoning board, and so on. The tasks are required, but only a relative few citizens volunteer to do them. In addition, activists organize civic projects not mandated by any law: agitate to close down the nuclear power plant, set up a clinic for old people, get obscene books out of the library, establish favorable terms for businesses considering a move into the area, fight to keep them out (e.g., Wal-Mart), found a right-wing think tank or a ballet company, organize a teaching assistant union or a National Rifle Association chapter. Such work gives the society its texture and shapes its future.

Well before the days of "bowling alone," most people declined to join in. Those who do expand their citizenship in such ways help set the terms of social life for the rest. It is obvious that advanced literacy gives activists an edge in assuming such leadership and also, more tautologically, that those destined by birthright to be leaders will be offered advanced literacy along the way. Now that's no reason to deplore expanded citizenship (we couldn't do without it) or to give up on the project of offering it to working-class students. It is a reason, however, to dismiss claims that university education in general and composition in particular improve citizenship flat out, if that means putting all citizens on a more equal footing and helping them work well together. No, what American universities have done for a hundred years is prepare some youth to take up places in the professional-managerial class and, if they wish, exercise robust citizenship too—while preparing other youth for more technical work and narrower citizenship. Liberal and progressive composition instructors have worked within these limits of possibility, with more or less effectiveness depending on who their students were and what political winds were blowing in and outside of the university.

Why am I saying these abstract and gloomy things? I have meant to ground the question of citizenship and composition in terms and ideas that applied to the university system at least until recently. Today, however, our system of higher education is modulating from its mid-century form into something very different. The "managed university" names it well, and similar epithets such as the "corporate university" and "*Campus Inc.*" (Geoffrey White's title)[5] identify something that most observers from left to right and from the *Chronicle of Higher Education* to *Business Week* agree is happening. How does it change the conditions of postsecondary work in literacy? How does it bear on the question of citizenship?

Bill Readings's much-discussed book, *The University in Ruins* has pointed some toward a direct enough answer: that the new university has detached itself from service to the national culture.[6] In *College English* for January 2001, I come across this, by Daniel Green: "[T]he role established for the modern university over the past 200 years, to mold educated citizens who will take productive places in the nation-state, is no longer tenable," because—and he goes on to quote Readings—the university "is becoming a different kind of institution, one that is no longer linked to the destiny of the nation-state by virtue of its role as producer, protector, and inculcator of an idea of national culture."[7] The university is becoming a transnational corporation, Green says, and although I suppose you could argue that it now prepares the young for global citizenship, this doesn't help much, and certainly doesn't capture Readings's point. In my view, the concept of privatization gives us more analytic leverage than that of globalization in trying to grasp what is happening in postsecondary education.

To be sure, U.S. universities are selling their degrees and their knowledge "products" on a world market—attracting many thousands of international students, starting up branches abroad, and using the Internet to carry learning across global distances. Also, corporations shop worldwide for educated labor, and hence indirectly for education itself: if one of them sets up a facility in India to take advantage of engineers who earn a small fraction of what their American counterparts do, that company is also in effect buying specialized education that is cheap by comparison to engineering degrees in the United States. But then, capital has always sought cheap (and docile) labor in poor countries or colonies, just as it has sought or created markets abroad for its products. The international mobility of capital in recent decades is real and important; but to repeat, I think the idea of privatization works better to underline the gradual subsumption of higher education within markets and market-like processes, and thus explain lots of changes in our lives.

Those that involve academic labor are all too familiar. Part-timers doubling as a percentage of the workforce from 1970 to the 1990s; full-time, tenure track hires amounting to only about one-third of all hires, through the last decade; the consolidation of a two-tier labor market with the upper tier shrinking; the "oversupply" of credentialed workers and the disappearance of many from university work: such painful changes are familiar enough, and I want simply to mention two contexts for them. First, as I spell out elsewhere in this book (especially in essays 2, 9, and 12), similar changes have taken place throughout the economy since 1970, in this era of agile competition and flexible accumulation. Throughout the economy, steady, full-time jobs have given way to casual and ill-paid ones. Second, the conditions of academic (and other mental) labor increasingly approximate those of industrial labor, especially for professionals in the lower tier. And of course that has happened precisely because the academic profession is no longer functioning in the way successful professions do. It has failed to limit entry, regulate careers, restrict the practice of teaching to fully credentialed members and selected apprentices, control the definition and assessment of its work, and secure the high pay and prestige that people in strong professions enjoy.

But *are* there any strong professions these days, as medicine and law were strong a few decades ago? As I suggested in the previous essay, the forces of agile capitalism may be undermining most of the professions. Capital seeks to bring all areas of human activity into the market, and in doing so increasingly commodifies "information," including the kinds that we proudly but perhaps quaintly call "knowledge," and that professions have amassed as cultural capital, to ground their practices and justify their exclusiveness. This point may seem remote from what has happened to English studies and literacy work, compared, say, to the commodification of medical services by HMOs. But if you think about the various learning companies offering literary culture for sale; about provision of literacy skills on the Internet; about the fights over who owns and can profit from courseware; or about Rudolph Giuliani's threat to eliminate "remedial" work from the City University and subcontract it to private companies—if you think of such phenomena it will be evident that nothing intrinsic to the subject matter of our own profession will protect it from commercial exploitation, any more than the knowledge and skills of weavers protected their trade against the capitalists of Manchester.

Whether the emergent profession of rhetoric and composition is turned back by commodification remains to be seen, but there is no doubt that the corporate university is a less and less friendly home for it, as well as for the older professionalized disciplines. To be a little more precise: by "corporate university" I mean an institution that acts more like a profit-making business than like a public or philanthropic trust. Thus, we hear of universities applying productivity and performance measures to teaching, putting departments in competition with one another for resources, cutting faculty costs by replacing full-timers with part-timers and temps, and by subcontracting for everything from food services to the total management of physical plant, substituting various schemes of computerized instruction for classroom teaching, and so on, as spelled out in the previous essay.

Marketing the educational product becomes a far more self-conscious activity than it used to be: universities try to identify their niches, turn their names into brands, develop "signatures" and slogans. (The college where I used to teach paid consultants to invent a killer slogan for us; they came up with "the alternative Ivy," which students soon laughed out of court.) Universities have always prepared students in a general way for different job markets. Now, all but the fancier colleges tout specific training and offer credentials for specific kinds of work. Many now do what community colleges have long done: tailor course offerings to the just-in-time needs of students entering or returning to local job markets. They frankly imagine students as customers, not as citizens or as future leaders or as novices in a common culture. Universities also look around for other customers, in some cases selling their students *to* those customers, through large, long-term, exclusive contracts with such as Coke and Pepsi. Administrators scan the university for whatever resources they can take to market: research, patents, courseware, faculty reputations. They seek to "partner" with corporations in developing these products. Or they seek venture capital to help launch businesses that the university will partly own. Or they use their own venture capital to set up "incubators" for small, often local businesses, some of which will hit it big and bring fame or fortune to the university along the way.[8]

In the old days, administrators made pitches to trustees, regents, or legislators, seeking a mix of income sources (tax moneys, tuition, yield from the endowment) and staged their mainly traditional activities within the limits so established. In boom times such as the two postwar decades, they added new programs and expanded campuses. In lean times they trimmed costs. Now, like agile corporations, private and public universities look to develop new "products," enter new markets, preserve flexibility in labor and plant, and in general direct their efforts where they can generate income in excess of costs. They are not profit-making institutions as a whole, but they seek profit-like gains in whatever part of the operation such gains may be generated.

Elsewhere in this book I have explored several causes of this shift, including a decisive reduction in direct state funding of public universities following on the "fiscal crisis of the state" around 1970; the accountability movement that sprang up at the same moment, and the conservative reaction to social rebellions and educational reforms of the 1960s; competition from for-profit universities and programs; and a huge expansion in immediately practical training and education within corporations ("corporate universities"). These and other pressures have forced universities to think of themselves, too, as players in a vast *market* for postsecondary education. That is the most telling expression of privatization.

Along with this refiguring of education as a commodity, an ideology of education valued for the economic benefits it brings has become salient. I will allow myself to quote once more the elder Bush's rationale for his showcase bill, the Educational Excellence Act of 1989: "I believe," he said, "that greater educational achievement promotes sustained economic growth, enhances the Nation's competitive position in world markets, increases productivity, and leads to higher incomes for everyone." Most of the provisions in that act bore on K–12 education, but government increasingly demands that higher education, as well, repay expenditures on it within the same economic calculus. Critical intelligence? Historical consciousness? Appreciation of beauty? Spiritual growth? Ethical refinement? However loudly the Right may cheer when a Lynne Cheney or William Bennett or E. D. Hirsch or Allan Bloom condemns the politically correct as barbarians and calls for reestablishment of the Great Books, when it comes to federal support for education, market rationales take precedence.

Needless to say, although citizenship, like timeless works of art, gets a nod in pious moments, it has a smaller place now than before in official rationales for higher education and no place at all in the play of economic forces that are remaking the university. For students, citizenship is a recreational choice, an individual taste. For capital it is nearly irrelevant—of even less interest than other leisure activities because it cannot easily be commodified. In fact, robust citizenship is a downer for capital, a threat to its freedom of movement and its ability to mold the future society that best suits its needs. Those needs include quiet citizens and social calm, maintained by the police when necessary, not a vibrant public sphere where needs other than capital's can be asserted and dominance contested.

To return to the main question: how does literacy work fit into the corporate university and the commodification of knowledge? One might answer, only a bit sardonically, that it doesn't have to—that higher education as a whole has reconfigured itself on the model of literacy work, having learned from English 101 how to give the customer decent service while keeping costs down and the labor force contingent. The professionalization of composition, while installing the usual apparatus (journals, conferences, a professional society, graduate programs and degrees), bringing a great advance in theoretical sophistication, and winning job security and good compensation for advanced practitioners, has made little if any difference in who does the front line work, under what regimen, for what pay, and so on. Meanwhile English, the old professional home of literacy work, has itself fallen on hard times, along with most academic professions, losing much of its ability to maintain a market haven for its members. So the adjuncts and graduate students who teach composition instantiate well the floating, peripheral labor force of contemporary capitalism.

Nor is the service they provide the kind that can easily be packaged and sold as a job credential or career boost. It remains "basic" if not remedial, a foundation on which to build other marketable skills and capabilities. For that reason and because of the addictive arrangement whereby TAs staff first-year English, it seems likely that composition will go on being taught chiefly at the university, in a kind of sweatshop operation. Within the average literacy classroom, a dispossessed intellectual works at survival wages transmitting skills to people hoping they can trade these for more-than-survival wages. The instructor may be a graduate student TA, a part-time adjunct, a moonlighting high school teacher at a proprietary university, or a full-time teacher off the tenure track. Low pay, low status, and job insecurity level out differences across these groups, and make it nearly irrelevant that some have Ph.D.'s, some are A.B.D., some have M.A.'s, and some have no advanced degrees. In short, the academic profession as a whole is losing much of the ground it won a hundred years ago. Literacy workers within or outside of English departments have long been exploited and marginalized; nor has the professionalization of comp raised up most of those workers as it has their leaders.

In sum: the idea that universal education underwrites a polity of free and equal citizens was contradictory to begin with. But an illusion can serve well as a common goal, and the dream of a mutually responsible, educated citizenry probably did help open the gates to higher education in the United States, through the first twenty postwar years. In the present time of privatization and agile capital, the illusion shatters: education becomes a commodity among other commodities, with claims made for its contribution to the common good only on the basis of economic advantage. Meanwhile, the same forces of capitalist transformation and market imperialism have pressed the university to act like a business in many ways, including the casualization of its labor force and commodification of the knowledge it creates through research. All that is solid melts into air, yet again.

If this picture is even roughly accurate, what directions does it point for the progressives who, I think, make up a majority among literacy workers? Two thoughts come to mind. First, given the fading chances for strong professionalization among literacy workers, the present move to unionize and to ally with other groups of university workers is right and necessary. Further, adjuncts and grad students should continue to lean on professional and scholarly organizations to support unions and act more like unions, though they cannot *become* effective unions. The labor-related resolutions passed by the Delegate Assembly at the Modern Language Association meetings in 2000 show many members to be in agreement with the Graduate Student and Radical Caucuses, that struggle for better working conditions is now in the interest of both contingent and core academic labor forces, and in the interest of those professional values that are worth defending. We need solidarity, in short, pointing "out" toward a late capitalist extension of embattled citizenship, one that clarifies and builds upon class antagonisms. Of course a further extension—logical but famously difficult—would make common cause with workers everywhere and thus complete the ruin of national citizenship that capital has begun.

Second, if privatization is driving higher education into the market, to the point where even education presidents forget to include citizenship in official proclamations, deferring instead to gross domestic product and international competitiveness, could this be a time for literacy workers to take whatever high ground is available in public relations and in fights over budget and curriculum? If the Ph.D.-holding and tenured directors of writing programs work with those in the trenches to downplay the economic justification for composition, stressing instead historical, social, and critical thinking, . . . well, what? Not the revolution. Maybe the beginning of a fight to retake the university for education and to broaden citizenship within and outside it. This fight and the one for decent working conditions might enforce each other. Or not—we're in tough times.

9

HISTORICAL REFLECTIONS
ON ACCOUNTABILITY

◆

When "accountability" became a key political term around 1970, it some-times turned up in demands that actions of the powerful meet popular scru-tiny, as in Ralph Nader's phrase "corporate accountability," but this usage soon gave way to the one under consideration here. That is, "accountability" came to be about schools and other public institutions meeting requirements set by people with (or wanting) power over them. It's interesting that in the three years since I wrote the essay reproduced here, corporate scandals have brought on a revival of Nader's idea, from a quite different quarter. The presi-dent is now demanding "corporate accountability" and promising to back the demand with governmental power. Clearly he would not have done so except out of fear that popular forces would seize on the scandals to limit the free hand of business in less palatable ways. I take this as an illustration of how malleable such terms and such ideas are and as a hopeful omen of weakness in the present system of rule.

I imagine that almost all academics think of ourselves as *responsible* to oth-ers and, if pressed, might allow substitution of "accountable." Responsibility to our employers is contractual, and the professional ethos urges responsi-bility to students (our clients), to colleagues, and to vague but strong princi-ples of intellectual conduct that obtain in our disciplines. The professional idea calls for responsibility to society as well: we earn our privileges not just by guarding and augmenting our special bodies of knowledge but by under-taking to put those knowledges to work for the good of all.

"For the good of all" opens up a vast ideological space for disputes that are familiar enough, and a space for the antiprofessional cynicism that, as Stanley Fish has argued, festers endemically within professional groups, not just among the envious laity. Still, even cynics tend to think *they* serve the needs of important others; and except in times of deep conflict (such as the years around 1970), professionals with different allegiances live more or less comfortably together, under the capacious roof of that "all."

To speak of professors: most believe that open inquiry and free debate do in fact advance the interests of a democratic society. For liberals, that may be enough. Conservatives tend to identify the good of all with the good of the sovereign individual. People of the Left inflect it toward the good of those lacking wealth and power. At this level of abstraction, accountability is not especially controversial, nor is it exacting. Certainly it was not so for this person of the Left. Accountability to my students: plan the course, show up in class, keep it moving, comment thoughtfully on papers, mentor when asked, submit grades, write recommendations—the usual packet of services. To my departmental colleagues: take on my share of core courses and administrative duties. To the administration and trustees: just don't make scenes, I guess; the thought rarely crossed my mind. To society as a whole: I cheerfully held myself accountable to the wretched of the earth, the workers, the women, the racially cheated and despised, the queers, the reds, all the disempowered. And aside from the enmity of a very few colleagues and students, this noble commitment was virtually risk-free at Wesleyan University, as were the commitments of faculty conservatives and liberals. I know that accountability imposes itself more obstinately in the working lives of teachers at less privileged institutions, and teachers without tenure at all institutions. Still, when faculty members have been able to define our own obligations to society, we have charted a high road—the good of all—that practitioners can travel easily together in spite of different values and allegiances, and without much fuss about ways in which our specific work meets those obligations, or doesn't.

This mild regime of self-policing has been under pressure for some time. It articulated well enough with such concepts as responsibility and obligation. But accountability, the more salient concept in recent decades, is different, and in major ways. First, as its root suggests, accountability means keeping score, Not sufficient, in the new regime, to invoke free inquiry, critical thinking, socially beneficial knowledge, and other such ideals, however wide their appeal to the public. Accountability entails being able to show that the efforts of an instructor or department or institution actually did move toward the desired end. That in turn requires framing the goal precisely enough to permit agreement on the state of affairs that would constitute its fulfillment, and on the amount of progress made in its direction at any point. Measurement, in short. And while the measure of success may be crude (e.g., Wesleyan set its sights for a while on reaching at least a certain spot in the *U.S. News and World Report* rankings), it must be quantifiable. Academic resistance to accountability owes in part just to that fact: how can the complex things we most highly value be reduced to numbers? we ask.

Quantification of aims and accomplishments may seem less rebarbative to scientists than to humanists. All in the arts and sciences, however, are likely to be put off by the ideas and language of business that have trailed along with accountability in its migration into the university. A 1994 book on *Measuring Institutional Performance in Higher Education* (edited by Joel W. Meyerson and William F. Massy) works in a semantic medium of "client feedback," "stakeholders," "make or buy options," "output" (of departments), "use synergy," and the like, and carefully recommends to educators common business practices such as TQM (total quality management), BPR (business practice reengineering,) and benchmarking (comparing your performance by quantifiable measures to "best practices" at other institutions).[1] A brochure for administrators from Johnson Controls offers "open system architecture," "system integration," "cost control," "project management," and "performance guarantees." Speakers at an October 1999 conference entitled "Market-Driven Higher Education" sponsored by *University Business*[2] used a lexicon of "markets" (e.g., students), "product," "brand" (your university's name and aura), "value added" (including, I guess, to students as labor power), "marginal cost," "deals," and "resource base" (the faculty, chiefly). They taught why to want and how to get "customization," "knowledge management," "just-in-time learning," "strategic partners," "faculty management," good "assessment models" (though some said no good ones exist), "policy convergence" (I took this to mean something like consistency, and the left hand's awareness of what the right hand is doing), and—my favorite—the "Hollywood model" (i.e., the sort of contract put together by agents, actors, producers, and so on, in contrast to the antiquated and feckless arrangements we now have in higher education for owning and selling knowledge).

Administrators are becoming fluent in this language. It feels alien to many faculty members, and not centrally because of academic distaste for business. Some are hostile to business, some not; but I think all can see that

the discourse of books on accountability and of the *University Business* conference is one for managers, not the managed. And while it is no secret that
universities have ever expanding administrations, many faculty members
cherish the hope that their administrators are managing on behalf of us and
the students, taking care of the business side so we can teach and students
can learn. But accountability for administrators means managing *us,* not
just physical plant and endowment. The literature on the subject may urge
them to enlist faculty members in the setting of goals and devising of meas-
urements, but we are not within earshot of these prescriptions, not part of
the intended audience. In short, when politicians or businessmen or trustees
or university presidents call for accountability in higher education, they are
asking administrators to plan, oversee, and assess our labor.

Well, isn't that what managers do? Exactly so, and the accountability
movement would be of little interest except that it brings managerial logic
into the area of self-management to which all professions aspire, and which
the stronger ones were able to stake out in an uneven and conflicted historical process beginning more than a hundred years ago. Accountability, when
achieved, turns back that process. Its advocates stigmatize the foot dragging
of professors as whiny and selfish (which it may sometimes be), but more
pertinently as retrograde. And that it always is—in just the way that Luddite
resistance was retrograde in its time and the resistance of doctors is retrograde now. These were and are defenses against new relations of production,
imposed from without, to reduce or eliminate the control that groups of
workers have exercised over their labor.

That brings me to the last major way in which accountability differs from
obligation or responsibility. In the utopian regime of my employment at
Wesleyan, or at least in my fantasies about it, I could hold myself responsible
to the disempowered and identify my work with democracy and equality
(just as my colleague on the right could identify his with individual freedom). After all, most people here and abroad *are* disempowered. When Lynne
Cheney or William Bennett occasionally took hostile notice of my work, that
only proved I was doing something right. I and my comrades were on the side
of the general public; Cheney and Bennett spoke for an usurping coterie. We
wanted to try democracy, for the first time in history; the Right wanted to
maintain the rule of the few and call *that* democracy.

But of course there was an obvious problem with this comfortable position: the wretched of the earth do not organize militantly to support aca-

demic progressives, or the politics latent in much of our scholarship and pedagogy since the 1960s. Business and the Right organize effectively against the academic Left. Many of the general public see the world more as Cheney and Bennett do than as we do. That's ideology. That's hegemony. Accountability, in short, is not to the disempowered but to the powerful. There would be no agonizing among professors on this subject, except that boards of regents and trustees, legislative bodies, conservative foundations and interest groups, corporations, and so on want to make teachers and knowledge workers in general more responsive to their purposes, and they have power enough to advance that project.

Thirty-five or fifty or eighty years ago, they not only lacked such power, but had not even hit on the project. Why not? Why now? In answer, I will put two skeletal narratives to work. The first can be seen as more or less internal to education. In it, the years 1945–70 brought rapid expansion of the university system. Prosperity and a growing cohort of young people were in part responsible. In addition, the U.S. economy grew fastest in industries such as communications and petrochemicals that required both highly trained knowledge workers and an enlarged research apparatus. Meanwhile, cold war leaders mobilized the university to do combat against the Soviet Union and its allies, funding science and technology, weapons research, artificial intelligence, basic computer development, area studies, economics, and parts of other fields thought critical to the dominance of capitalism and Western democracy. These new tasks required no dramatic change in the university's procedures or its structure of relatively autonomous departments and research units, though the change in scale brought talk of, and worry about, the "megaversity." The academic professions flourished through this period, buoyed by proliferation of graduate programs, full employment for new entrants, and public demand for higher education.

Around 1970 the party tired. Public funding became less certain. Graduate programs in many fields were turning out more Ph.D.'s than there were jobs: in English and foreign languages the crisis was evident at the 1969 MLA convention, where a caucus of angry job seekers abruptly formed, to the surprise both of the leadership and of dissidents who had come to protest other things. Those other causes also disrupted the postwar complacency of the university and its constituent professions. Civil rights, black power, women's liberation, and antiwar militancy came in from the streets along with open admissions and new student populations. A student power movement germinated within the now alienating and "irrelevant" megaversity itself. This is a familiar part of the story, abbreviated here in cliché phrases to arrive at the following suggestion: that in the late sixties, dissenters within the university both put themselves in opposition to systems of domination outside it and staged a critique of its relations to those systems ("Who Rules Columbia?" etc.). The professions came under assault by many young aspirants and some established members. Secure old knowledges were challenged, new canons proposed. The curriculum, in the broadest sense, changed.

Conservatives, readying to launch their offensive against the liberal welfare state and alarmed at what seemed the rule of liberals and worse in universities, took countermeasures. Some of the new right-wing foundations zeroed in on education and intellectual life, building and circulating ideology and attacking the versions of democracy that had grown out of sixties movements. Their work on one front led in time to the culture wars of the 1990s and the attack on "political correctness" and multiculturalism. On another, it produced schemes of privatization. On a third, mainstream conservatives and neoliberals mounted a critique of U.S. education in general (including especially K–12) through commissions and reports that proclaimed our "nation at risk" because of inferior schooling, and called for "excellence." These official reports harmonized with media events like the "literacy crisis" of the mid-1970s and movements such as "back to basics" a bit later. Schooling became and remains as reliable a public concern—a *media* concern—as welfare or the British royals. Candidates run for high office on school reform platforms; both Bushes and Clinton have aspired to be "education presidents." It was in this context that calls for accountability became ubiquitous. Framed by this narrative, they can be grasped as part of a complex reaction against social movements of the sixties and seventies, and as sallies in culture wars that are often explicitly political.

The other narrative is economic and embraces far more than the university and the educational system. It too begins with the postwar boom, seen as the cresting both of corporate, Fordist capitalism in the United States and of our dominance in the world economic order. Around 1970 those arrangements began to unravel in an accumulation of economic snags, involving world trade, slow growth, declining productivity, debt, wages, and so on—as chronicled elsewhere in this volume (see essays 2, 7, and 12). Briefly put, the world became a far less secure place for American capital's project of development.

Capital responded with strategies, familiar enough by now, that are perhaps creating a new economic order: rapid movement around the globe; a proliferation of new products and services; elaboration of financial instruments; corporate downsizing and waves of mergers; dismantling of the old core labor force; and so on. This "regime of flexible accumulation"[3] has also been labeled "knowledge society," and that term may be critical for grasping the place of higher education in the new order. For if knowledge is now not only an accomplice in the making of other goods but itself the most dynamic sector of production, we could expect intense efforts on the part of business to guide its development, control its uses, and profit from its creation and sale. That has implications for universities and faculty members to which I will return.

First, however, I want to suggest a way of locating accountability in these two narratives. For both of them, the years right around 1970 are pivotal. And it was precisely then that accountability exploded into the language and politics of debate about education. In June 1970 "accountability" first showed up in the *Education Index*, with reference to teaching. The Library of Congress introduced "educational accountability" as a subject heading two years later.[4] To be sure, the word was in use much earlier, and its first *Oxford English Dictionary* citation is from 1794. But for nearly two hundred years "accountability" carried a broad meaning: the state of being liable, responsible, held to account for one's actions; and it had no special link to education. A keyword search at the library I use (University of Massachusetts, Amherst) turned up 585 book titles, only 6 of them predating 1970, and none of those 6 about education. In 1970 appeared professor of education Leon M. Lessinger's *Every Kid a Winner*,[5] soon to be characterized as the "bible of accountability." In the next five years, dozens of books were published with titles such as *Accountability and Reading Instruction, Accountability and the Community College, Accountability for Educational Results, Accountability for Teachers and School Administrators, Accountability in a Federal Education Program, Accountability in American Education, Accountability in Education, Accountability in the Elementary School Curriculum, Accountability: Systems Planning in Education,* and *Accountability, Program Budgeting, and the California Educational Information System*—to mention only those with "accountability" as the first word. Accountability had suddenly become an established idea joined at the hip to education, a recognized field of study, a movement, and a battleground.[6]

By no means did Lessinger's book inaugurate the movement. A 1972 anthology of articles and talks on the subject includes a number from 1969, and suggests that accountability, "one of the most rapidly growing and wide-spread movements in education today," began "as a flickering spark in the twilight of the 60s".[7] Writers seeking origins tend to mention the Elementary and Secondary Education Act of 1965, later amendments that required pro-gram audits, the beginning of the National Assessment Program in 1969, a 1970 speech by President Nixon, and so on. Frank Sciara and Richard Jantz thought the origins of the movement hard to isolate, and I agree. The inter-esting thing is that abruptly in 1970 it *was* a movement, felt as historically momentous, powerful, and, depending on one's point of view, either tonic or dangerous.

Beyond specific acts, speeches, and books, or vague and timeless agents such as "the federal government," "concerned taxpayers," and "alarmed ad-ministrators," it is clear that three main forces drove the movement. One was an intense fiscal crisis of the state, brought on in part by war spending, but ex-pressed chiefly as disillusionment with Great Society programs. In a speech of 1970, Terrel H. Bell (then a deputy commissioner in the Office of Education, later Reagan's secretary of education) noted that his department's budget had increased from $500 million to $4 billion a year through the sixties, and that Congress had poured "literally billions of dollars" into the schools, often into "crash programs" for which the schools were "comically unprepared." Money alone would not buy good education (does this sound familiar?). Washington now wanted "*results*," wanted "to be sure that every dollar in-vested in an educational program will produce a payoff . . . that can be meas-ured and that can be proved."[8] Nixon's man did not specify which "expensive will-o'-the-wisps" Washington had now rejected, but it is evident from the early literature that accountability was in part a counterthrust against libera-tory ideas and experiments in "open education": that is, against the critique of schooling mounted by sixties visionaries and radicals. That reaction was the second force. The third—more specific to higher education—was a reaction against "turmoil and disruption on the campuses" and "political action by students and faculty members," which had produced a "mounting distrust of higher education by the public" and an "increasing demand for colleges and universities to justify what they are doing and to disclose the effectiveness and efficiency of their operations."[9] In short, it is no coincidence (as Marxists like to say) that accountability emerged and gained strength as a coherent movement exactly when the postwar U.S. economy was tearing at the seams, and when the Right began to organize itself against sixties movements and build what Ira Shor has called the "conservative restoration."[10]

Origins do not set meanings permanently in place. Accountability has been and is a contested field of meaning and a terrain of conflict. But I believe the historical conjunction that birthed it continues to inflect and propel it. To put the case (somewhat too) bluntly: accountability is most deeply about the right's project of containing sixties movements and about capital's project of recomposing itself internationally, marketizing whatever areas of life had previously eluded that process, and dominating workers of all sorts in ways more pervasive but less confrontational than those that marked Fordism. For this reason, I do not think it will be easy to peel away accountability from "accounting," reclaiming the former as our professional way of taking responsibility for our actions, as Bill Readings hoped we might do.[11]

At this point, several hundred pages might ensue, arguing that the hypothesis organizes a variety of seemingly discrete events and situations into its tidy gestalt. I cannot supply those pages here (and hope I will not be the one to write them anywhere). But in shorthand, here is the sort of thing I have in mind.

1. The thirty-year job "crisis" for Ph.D.'s, the campaigns against tenure and for posttenure review, the heavy reliance on part-timers and adjuncts, the outsourcing and subcontracting of many academic and support tasks— these events and practices respond of course to local pressures on administrators and trustees, and (one must admit) to self-destructive inertia among the leaders of academic disciplines. But beyond that, one can see in the casualization of academic labor the same process of dispersal and degradation that capital initiated against the core workforce in almost every industry around 1970. The regime of flexible accumulation brings accountability to us in this guise, whatever the designs or motives of its local agents.

2. These labor practices nest within a far more encompassing set of tendencies. The list could be long, but just let me mention distance learning, burgeoning adult education, the buying and selling of courseware, the intensive marketing of academic research, "partnering" between corporations and universities for the purpose, the effort of administrations (and legislators) to assess and compare programs by bottom-line accounting, the rapid growth of for-profit universities (such as the University of Phoenix) selling job-related training and credits, the proliferation of learning companies (to

the great interest of Wall Street), and the existence today of 1,800 "corporate universities" (GE started the first in 1955). All of these, clearly, support the widespread observation that the university has become more and more like a business—an idea voiced not only by academic critics of the change such as Bill Readings, Lawrence Soley, Cary Nelson, and David Noble, but by advocates, including many speakers at the *University Business* conference and writers for *Business Week*.[12] My second narrative, above, suggests a more encompassing generalization: that capitalism in its new phase extends the logic of the market to encompass areas of production not previously within its scope, and, in particular, seeks to commodify knowledge wherever possible.

3. Which brings me to a nice "clipping" in *University Business* of January/ February 1999: "In 1955, not a single health care company appeared on the list of the top 50 U.S. Corporations as measured by market capitalization. Today, seven of America's richest companies are in the health care industry. Where the health care market was 40 years ago, the education-and-training market is right now."[13] What I want to comment on here is how the reorganization and extension of capital's work challenges the professions. Our self-managed intellectual capital (our specific bodies of knowledge), along with our creed of public service, legitimized our partial autonomy for a hundred years. The commodification of knowledge and the marketization of professional services are in direct conflict with that autonomy. If medicine, with all its prestige and power, has given up big chunks of its domain, why expect professors to do better in the new regime? In fact, most professions (worldwide) are losing ground.[14] Accountability, viewed on the broad canvas painted here, is not just an extra demand on professions. It erodes their historical conditions of possibility.

4. Primary and secondary education are caught up in the same economic transformation. Channel One, advertising in school corridors, contracts with Coke and Nike are but symptoms: the sale of children's attention to corporations, in an effort to ameliorate the fiscal crisis of the state. Marketization works more deeply through the project of companies (like Edison) that seek profit by contracting with school districts to manage learning. Voucher systems, if they gain ground against hot opposition, will be a further step. Whether or not the charter school movement tends in the same direction remains to be seen, but in any case, it is one sign of a tectonic shift in the way public schooling sorts children out—that is, reproduces the economic and

social system, by guaranteeing that there will in the next generation be much the same distribution of wealth and power as in this, and that inequality will be widely seen as just (i.e., based on merit), or at least inevitable.

Let me mention another sign, perhaps less noted as yet: high-stakes testing. More than half the states now have or are developing standard curricula linked to tests that will decide which students can graduate. In Massachusetts (where I serve on a local school board), the first trial run of the tests, in 1998, placed 39 percent of tenth graders in the bottom category, "failing," and a total of 72 percent in the bottom two categories, out of four, prompting the thought that in the Commonwealth, unlike Lake Wobegon, three-quarters of our children are below average. Predictably, students in vocational schools, special education, and inner city schools where English is for many a second language, failed in droves. The professed aim of educational reform in the Bay State is to guarantee all students a good education, but unless something bends, it will instead guarantee a much higher dropout rate five years from now. Why block the different paths toward a diploma that have been open to various kinds of students and push them all along this single track? Without guessing at "real" motives, I think it clear that high-stakes testing schemes will make for more surgical channeling into the job market and the class system—and under the banner of accountability, needless to say. The official ideology of public education now is that of the market. Recall George Bush the elder's reasoning when he sent Congress his Educational Excellence Act of 1989 and cited just four benefits of "educational achievement": it "promotes sustained economic growth, enhances the Nation's competitive position in world markets, increases productivity, and leads to higher incomes for everyone."

5. Finally, the Culture Wars. The attack on multiculturalism and political correctness this past decade explicitly took on 1960s movements, seen as having all but won the battle for higher education. Furthermore, the germination of this strategy in centers of conservative thought and policy, from the 1970s on, is well documented. So there is no need to flog the obvious point that it carries forward the *political* project embedded in the accountability movement right at the outset. What I want to suggest, also, is that between the lines of their crusade for traditional values and great books and free speech, the culture warriors have provided a rationale for defunding the public university and putting it in the custody of market forces.[15] This is a large hypothesis deserving careful analysis that I cannot offer. Let it stand as

a gesture toward the unity of understanding one might achieve by historicizing accountability in the way proposed here. Although big narratives can
shade into paranoia, courses of action pursued without the (tentative) understanding they provide are likely to be scattered, contradictory, and at
worst self-defeating. So I offer these large, pear-shaped thoughts to those en-
meshed in a thousand local skirmishes over accountability.

Among many others, that large group includes people working to revise
English, to make it work for or against (or both) the corporate university
in which some of these skirmishes take place. To such people I offer a few
thoughts about how they might imagine their future and plan their strategies, should they agree with my analysis.

First, it proposes a broad understanding of the whole educational system,
under the concept of privatization. But battles and futures will differ greatly
across the many kinds of institutions that make up that system. Even if, for
this book about universities, we limit the scope of the discussion to postsecondary institutions, there are complexities enough. Community colleges, for
instance, have always had a relatively direct and simple relation to the market for education and training. Yes, they have provided a liberal arts core for
some students heading toward B.A.'s; but for most, the community college is
a place to take courses for career-related needs, applying an economic calculus to the purchase of credits, knowledge, and skills. The University of Phoenix, DeVry, and many other for-profit suppliers of immediately useful knowledge will give the community colleges stiff competition, but not oust them
from the market, because they are local, handy, effective, and cheap.

At the other end of a familiar spectrum, Princeton, Swarthmore, and the
like will continue to experience accountability in only the most genteel and
indirect forms. Endowments and loyal alumni will fortify them against
harsh competition. But mainly, they will continue to offer an intrinsically
scarce good, incapable of mass production: cultural capital—made up of selectivity, name recognition, the right contacts, an education with relatively
broad horizons, access to the most prestigious graduate schools and Wall
Street firms, and so on. To be sure, the Ivies and the leading public universities are becoming more like corporations, "partnering" with businesses, setting up venture capital offices, subcontracting and outsourcing, selling their
curricula by distance learning, and finding other sources of extra income.
But the University of Phoenix will not be elbowing into their primary market any time soon, and they will be able to afford the useless liberal arts,

semiautonomous departments, and other paraphernalia of the old professional order.

Between these two locations, life will be strenuous. That is to say, most public and private universities will be scrambling to meet standards of accountability imposed either by hard-nosed trustees and legislators or by the market itself.[16] Such institutions will look to the bottom line as businesses do, and will decide by that criterion what their English departments are contributing to survival or to profitability. So will community colleges, of course. English departments in all these institutions are gradually shrinking, if we count only the tenure-tracked.

The educational and political choices available to people in English studies will differ, depending on how much of their time they spend in uncommodified spaces. For full- as well as part-timers at rapidly marketizing institutions, I see two main choices: obey the market or fight back—and you can do a little of both. The former entails seeking to give students the kinds of practical learning they might otherwise purchase in bits from proprietary schools or be offered within the corporations where they work. For people in English, this strategy will obviously mean an emphasis on writing, not just the basic composition courses, but training in more specialized and saleable skills. I was until just recently pessimistic about the second strategy —fight back. The forces arrayed on the other side were powerful, and the sixties movements that had been our allies in reforming the university are frayed or fragmented. Now, a movement grounded in workplace issues and professional concerns has sprung up from grassroots. I refer to the organizing of graduate students, TAs, and adjuncts of all sorts, which has won stunning victories at campus after campus, and, in modern language fields, built national momentum and successfully commandeered the support of MLA. This is a fascinating and explosive moment, I think, since scholarly organizations have in the past stayed as far away as possible from disputes over labor and work conditions. Should the politicizing of such groups move them in this direction, that could point the way toward a reconstitution of the academic profession on more militant lines. Short of such an (unlikely) outcome, unionization among those who otherwise will constitute the cheap labor pool for privatizing education could put up serious resistance to that process. Again, these choices are not exclusive: people teaching English in commodified circumstances can offer courses that respond to job or career needs and also resist the casualization of academic labor. In fact, as writing programs offer more practical, job-oriented course work, they had *better* fight against casualization, because the easiest way for the university to supply "demand" in this area is to hire part-timers, either for classroom teaching or for instruction in cyberspace. Ironically, the professionalization and partial autonomy of composition will serve this very, proletarianizing trend, unless people in the field imagine their professionalism in a new way.[17] On the other hand, working alliances of writing instructors with students as well as with other campus workers become more plausible in the present situation, since all these groups occupy similar, vulnerable positions in the regime of flexible accumulation.

For those who work at least some of the time in uncommodified spaces, and especially for those in colleges and universities able to preserve a liberal arts curriculum and privilege critical thinking, a third main choice (also fully compatible with the fight against casualization) is to continue and advance the ideological critique of oppressive social relations that gained a university beachhead in the sixties and has come to undergird the curriculum in English since—to the disgust of culture warriors on the right. I have in mind the critique of white and male supremacy, the multicultural critique of canons, history from below, a sour view of American triumphalism, an understanding of culture as a power-laden field of conflict, and so on. By extending this work, particularly into a critique of the university and its role in flexible accumulation, and by mobilizing it in battles over academic and nonacademic labor, practitioners of English may begin—have indeed begun—to disrupt the rules of accountability and open them out to . . . well, the people?

ACADEMIC FREEDOM, 2000 AND AFTER

◆

The attacks of September 2001 might seem to have altered the conventions of academic freedom rather abruptly and thus called for a revision of or long appendix to this essay. In fact, I believe my argument holds up pretty well, as did academic freedom itself through the aftermath of 9/11. At first, campus dissenters from the views of the president and of, apparently, an overwhelming majority of citizens encountered harassment by students, harsh rebukes in the press, and in a few cases repression by university administrations. But within a couple of months these reactions softened, criticism of the government's policies regained legitimacy, teach-ins and antiwar rallies took place on campuses, and faculty members voiced dissident opinions in the media with relative impunity. In November the American Council of Trustees and Alumni (a group founded a few years earlier by Lynne Cheney and like-minded conservatives to champion traditional Western culture and fight multiculturalism) put out a pamphlet called "Defending Civilization." It cited well over a hundred statements by faculty members, administrators,[1] and students to show that universities were uniquely unpatriotic in time of war. The pamphlet was laughed out of court in academic and most mainstream venues, for alarmism, witch-hunting, high-handed use of quotations, and so on. A different kind of threat came from the Department of Justice, the president, and the Congress (the "USA Patriot Act"), all evidently determined to scrap about half the Bill of Rights. Repressive strategies include asking university administrations to keep track of foreign students, punish those without proper visas, and so on. Such measures will hurt many innocent students and a few faculty members, but it would be wrong to think of them as

violations of academic freedom, rather than as part of a broader extension of
police power. The content and strength of academic freedom may well shift
once again if the "war on terror" persists, but not in ways that escape the
main point of this essay.

◆

What is the present condition of academic freedom? I say it's pretty vigorous,
and will later explain why. Critics of "political correctness," whose voices are
louder than such as mine, have for a decade shouted that academic freedom
is weak: that it has been subverted by doctrinaire leftists and feminists who in-
timidate conservative or maverick scholars, disrupt their classes, persuade
administrations to adopt repressive speech codes, and so on.[2] There are such
events; the 1990s brought us books stuffed with them. But if you scan the
news in an even-handed way, you will not see such a pattern. In roughly
the first six months of 2000, for example, the *Chronicle of Higher Education*
ran about twenty stories of professors under fire.[3] Three match the stereotype
of politically correct repression: a San Diego State professor denied tenure in
African American studies because, by her account, she was not "black enough"
(but she won a settlement in court); vigorous protests at Princeton against
Peter Singer's position on euthanasia; and the burning of an agricultural facility at Michigan State for its supposed work in foisting biotechnology on the
Third World. Three others would be a stretch, for PC sleuths: a scholar at California State–Long Beach accused of holding Jews responsible for the Holo-
caust; a Columbia law professor criticized by students and then the school's
dean for using offensive examples (e.g., fetus murder) in an exam; and a faculty member at Florida Atlantic who sued over a sexual harassment charge
(she lost in court).

And then, for symmetry, three stories raise questions about pressure from
the right: a gay faculty member fired by a Catholic college (it claimed that was
not the reason); George Mason University's conservative Board of Visitors
(i.e., trustees) intervening to insert two traditional courses in a new curriculum; and Michael Sperber of Indiana University taking unscheduled leave
because of intense heat, including death threats, from alumni and others
loyal to the egregious basketball coach, Bobby Knight, whom Sperber had
criticized.

The remainder of the stories are about faculty members fired or sus-
pended or denied reappointment for alleged offenses of one kind or another.
The list includes two bizarre cases (one professor charged with using grant

money to buy heroin for his subjects; another fired after pleading guilty to a child pornography charge—I take no position on the validity of such accusations, which are of course often vague or loaded with ideology). The other cases are humdrum, sad, and not very instructive: eccentric or rebellious professors in trouble with their bosses for . . . what? Typically the administration or department says unprofessional conduct or inadequate performance on the job; the professor says, being critical of the administration or department.

This sampling does not support the fears of the Right, as expressed for instance in the Republican platform ("At many institutions of higher learning, the ideal of academic freedom is threatened by intolerance"). In fact, the sampling doesn't clearly warrant any conclusion about academic freedom, 2000. My opening question calls not for a snapshot but for a narrative reply: that's how it was then, this is how it is now, these are the forces that changed it. Such a narrative might be converted into a prediction: the same play of forces will take academic freedom farther along the same (dismal/hopeful) path; or those forces are changing, and with them the course of academic freedom.

Well, a number of stories in that form are now circulating. For example, "In the late 1960s and after, leftists, feminists, and other dogmatic groups eroded academic freedom, which is frail now and will continue to sicken." Or, "Staunch defenders of academic freedom have put down the assaults that weakened it for two decades, and its prospects are now good." Or, "The Culture Wars had little effect on academic freedom, which is and will be healthy enough, unless the Right is allowed to create a new McCarthyism." Or, closest to the story I would myself tell, "1960s movements greatly expanded academic freedom, but the Right's counteroffensive has been telling and will, along with cutbacks, probably reverse the gains of recent decades." A listener to these contending stories, and more, will suspect not just that the tellers see recent history through different political lenses but that they mean different things by "academic freedom."

And certainly a contest has gone forward over the scope of that idea, as well as over who's trampling on whose rights and sensibilities. Daphne Patai speaks for many when she complains that "[t]he battle cry of 'academic freedom' is still aimed at assaults from outside the academy—no longer McCarthyism, but now corporatization and privatization. Yet encroachments on academic freedom from inside—speech codes and antiharassment policies, for example—are tolerated, indeed welcomed." In this way, she thinks, the concept of academic freedom has in this way been thoroughly debased.[4] Critics of higher education from well to the right of Patai have for a decade seen violations of academic freedom not just in speech codes and harassment policies, which are formally adopted by the university, but in attacks by students on the incorrect views of their instructors and in occasional disruptions of classes. From another political quarter, many students and faculty members have argued that academic freedom does not protect a right to demean or insult any group, certainly not one represented among an instructor's students, whose right to speak and learn freely is impaired by racism, homophobia, and other hostilities emanating from behind the lectern.

The battles of the last ten years have centered on policies and practices such as those just mentioned. It is worth noting that none of them (not even McCarthyism, except when enforced by university administrations and trustees) was among the threats against which the American Association of University Professors (AAUP) sought to guard academic freedom in its "1940 Statement of Principles," the document that, along with various commentaries and supplements, has guided case law in this area for sixty years. The "1940 Statement" postulated that "[i]nstitutions of higher learning are conducted for the common good," which "depends upon the free search for truth and its free expression." It went on to enumerate with elegant simplicity the activities of professors that were to be protected in this high cause: "full freedom in research and in the publication of the results," "freedom in the classroom," and freedom "from institutional censorship or discipline" when instructors "speak or write as citizens." All three freedoms are, like that last one, couched in terms making it plain against *what danger* the drafters meant to protect freedom: "censorship or discipline" by the university that employed the instructor. The second part of this document, "Academic Tenure," is devoted to procedural safeguards of academic freedom before and during personnel decisions. In short, the explicit working idea of academic freedom for many years concerned a faculty member's right to do research, to write, to teach, and to speak out as a citizen without being fired as punishment for unorthodox or irritating views. The AAUP proposed, advocated for, and, with what weapons it had, enforced this principle. The overwhelming majority of colleges and universities accepted it as a guide to routine practice, and still do.

So what stretched the idea of academic freedom to cover fights having little to do with the arbitrary dismissal by universities of intellectually and politically wayward faculty members? This is no place for a history, but consider just a few moments of conflict and adjustment. Calls for help from professors targeted by McCarthyism forced universities and the AAUP to think whether they meant academic freedom to protect not just the speech and writing of citizen-professors, but their membership in a party widely held to be both treasonous and a destroyer of free speech. (Could a Communist possibly be doing research in "full freedom" or practicing "freedom in the classroom," while following the Party line?) There were also battles in the 1950s over a faculty member's right not to speak at all, when under subpoena or the threat of it—that is, to commit principled civil disobedience, or maybe just save his or her own skin. Faced with this expansion of the work that the idea of "academic freedom" was asked to perform by those under anticommunist assault, and with considerably higher stakes, few universities acted bravely on behalf of free speech and free silence. The AAUP itself failed to meet the challenge, hiding its head in the sand for several critical years (see Ellen Schrecker's *No Ivory Tower* for the best account).[5]

The AAUP and the academic profession partially recovered from this humiliating encounter, helped by a boom and a labor shortage that made colleges ask fewer questions about the politics of qualified faculty members. Then, in the late 1960s, academic freedom came under new and far more complex pressures, toward which I cannot do more than gesture. Professors joined antiwar protests and sometimes disruptions, attacked the policies ("cooptation" and "complicity" were favorite terms) of their universities, agitated for new programs in black studies, and in many other ways gave offense to their employers. Some colleges and universities took disciplinary measures against such dissidents. Did academic freedom protect teachers who obstructed on-campus recruiters for the navy or Dow Chemical? Who committed crimes in the course of civil disobedience off campus? The "1940 Statement" did not say, and the profession wrestled with such questions.

In a closely related development, academic participants in sixties movements intensely rethought race, power, war, U.S. foreign policy, a bit later gender and sexuality—and the work of the supposedly neutral disciplines and the university in all these areas. This revaluation led to research that sharply challenged dominant views and methods and that opened new fields of inquiry (black studies and women's studies were the boldest projects, but there were many others). Radicals carried the same questions and ideas into their classrooms, taught about previously excluded groups, read forgotten texts, introduced students to critiques of power both in and out of the academy. Most of these rebels were graduate students and junior faculty members. In time, many failed to achieve reappointment or tenure. Had their employers dismissed them for courageously exercising "full freedom" in the pursuit of truth, or for falling short of established intellectual standards? Since the radicals often regarded those very standards as major obstacles to the pursuit of truth, the answer could be "both." Accepted procedures for awarding and denying tenure seemed inadequate in such cases, especially when a candidate's chief opponents were not deans, presidents, or trustees, but senior members of his or her own department and distinguished outside referees in the discipline.

As that last point suggests, political conflicts in this period created or deepened rifts among faculty members themselves, both within and across fields. (For instance, leftists in the humanities and the less mathematical social sciences were highly critical of mainstream economics and political science for ignoring class, gender, and race, and for close links between important practitioners and power elites.) There was a good deal of energetic debate and some name calling, over such questions as opening the university to previously excluded groups, and especially between opponents and supporters of the Vietnam War. Although the latter held more real-world power, the former became numerous and outspoken within the university, so that many conservatives and not a few liberals felt silenced or intimidated by colleagues. When they cried "foul," invoking academic freedom, they sought to appropriate that ideal in still another way unanticipated by the "1940 Statement." And of course, that document had nothing to say about how students' anger and student rebellions might deter faculty members from freely expressing their beliefs in class, or even from pursuing certain lines of research. Was it to be extrapolated in such a way? If so, who was responsible for punishing and silencing rude students in the name of academic freedom?

The AAUP recognized some of these difficulties at the time, and in a 1970 statement, "Freedom and Responsibility" (approved by the AAUP Council, not the whole membership), wondered whether the "customary procedures" it had long endorsed for promoting and dismissing faculty members "are sufficient in the present context." Not quite, the Council thought. It recommended some precautions against campus disorder, and, more interestingly for my purpose, laid down a new framework and rationale for academic freedom: "Membership in the academic community imposes on students, faculty members, administrators, and trustees an obligation to respect the dignity of others, to acknowledge their right to express differing opinions, and to foster and defend intellectual honesty, freedom of inquiry and instruction, and free expression on and off the campus." What had in 1940 been chiefly a relationship between employer and employee was now expanded into a set of mutual obligations among groups in disparate contractual relations to the university, but imagined as sharing "membership" in a "community." The authors of the 1970 statement were explicit about the reasons for this rather vague and confusing change: to wit, the "tactics of intimidation and harassment," "harsh responses and counter-responses," and generally "repressive atmosphere" that had come to campuses in this time of protest and rebellion. Clear, too, were the intent and primary audience of the change: it urged upon *faculty members* more respectful treatment of one another, of students, and of university officials, whereas the "1940 Statement" had sought to regulate the conduct of administrators and trustees.

One might interpret and explain this shift variously, depending on one's politics and memories. I note merely that the official guardians of academic freedom responded to *some* of the pressures mentioned above, by amending the concept in a way that favored some professors and implicitly censured others (including yours truly, in case anyone was wondering). The change in emphasis also made the sanctioned idea of academic freedom more available than it would have been in its 1940 version to the culture warriors (from the right) against "political correctness" in the late 1980s and after. For although some of the conduct cited as outrageous by Dinesh D'Souza, Roger Kimball, David Horowitz, and the rest has provoked administrative investigation or discipline of faculty members, it has rarely if ever led to dismissal or denial of tenure. Many of the conflicts have been about alleged misbehavior of colleagues toward colleagues, including severe criticism of supposedly retrograde attitudes and ideas about such topics as affirmative action and sexual harassment, sometimes via epithets such as "racist" and "fascist." And most of the juicier incidents cycled and recycled through the media have had to do with students intimidating faculty members or other students. Thus, the 1970 recasting of academic freedom as a relation of respect for disagreement and unfashionable ideas *among campus constituencies* not only answered to the concerns at that time of those who thought antiracist and antiwar protest had become too unruly; it met ideological and strategic needs of the conservative restoration two decades later.

Some see these developments as a perversion of academic freedom; some, like Daphne Patai, think them necessary in order to complete a weak and limited practice of academic freedom. I want to make a different kind of point: the working idea of academic freedom at any moment is the temporary, unstable outcome of competing historical projects and differential powers of agency. Before 1915, when the AAUP organized, there was no universal idea of academic freedom in the United States, only aspirations unevenly granted from college to college. Skirmishes continued after that, leading to the "1940 Statement" and (more important) its gradual acceptance at almost all universities and colleges—so that, for instance, most administrations accused of violating the AAUP principles try hard to justify their conduct; if found guilty, most correct their procedures to lift censure; and over the years only a few dozen have gotten in that kind of trouble—even though AAUP censure entails no penalty beyond the ill opinion of professors and of others who respect that opinion.

Academic freedom kept changing after that time, in response to events and political pressures. I have focused on just one amendment. Many are recorded in successive AAUP documents and in university practice. Academic freedom won't sit still. As Louis Menand writes, in his introduction to a useful collection of essays on the subject, freedoms, including this one, "are in effect manufactured by civil societies in order to further some conception of the good life."[6] This jibes with Stanley Fish's notorious and perfectly sensible argument that "abstract concepts like free speech do not have any 'natural' content but are filled with whatever content and direction one can manage to put into them."[7] Transcendence of politics is impossible. Individuals and groups claiming the shelter of academic freedom win or lose because they can or cannot "manage" to persuade others that the idea suits their case.

How they manage is complicated: neither just by mobilizing the best arguments nor—at the other end of an explanatory spectrum—just by having the most clout. We can best imagine this complexity, I think, through the idea of an hegemonic process, layered with multiple forces and agents. Thus, when corporate capitalists came to dominate U.S. society a hundred years ago, they held control less by direct force than had the robber barons that preceded them and more through the work of other social groups that found ways to advance their own interests while also advancing the project of industrial capital. Those groups included retailers, advertising agents, publishers and other founders of the modern culture industry, scientists, engineers, city planners, and all those who were organizing the professions as we now know them—including of course professors themselves, whose authority both supported and was sustained by the new research universities that were making a place for themselves in the corporate order.[8] The knowledge work of some professors (e.g., scientists) had great economic value to capital, and the work of others to reproduce, justify, and sometimes help repair the social order had great political value. For these reasons professors were able to win some benefits and privileges, including a measure of autonomy from big capital itself—including even the right to be *critical* of big capital and the social arrangements over which it presided, without automatically getting sacked by employers who had close ties to it. As Thomas L. Haskell nicely shows, the founding document of the AAUP, its 1915 "Report on Academic Freedom," was precisely an argument for such autonomy, to be justified by the social benefits of free inquiry within "communities of the competent."[9] In short, professors gained assent to the idea and practices of academic freedom (not without many battles and setbacks) just as the hegemonic arrangements of the twentieth century were settling into place. An important instance of those arrangements was the university's subservience to—but partial independence from—capital's project of development.

A helpful narrative of academic freedom up to now must begin that long ago and be understood as a subplot in the story of professionalization,[10] which itself is a subplot in the story of corporate domination and crisis. Fights over academic freedom participate in both those larger narratives. Let me suggest how, by revisiting briefly the moments of contestation mentioned earlier. When the academic profession struggled, not that boldly, to keep McCarthy and his allies from shredding the 1940 principles, the timid defense succeeded partly because McCarthy was distasteful even to mainstream capitalists and politicians, but chiefly because capital and its cold war champions needed to enlist the university in developing technologies for economic expansion, economic and social control, and possible war against the Soviet Union. Sometimes, as in the late 1950s and early 1960s, professionalization sings in harmony with capitalist development.

And sometimes not. The peace of 1955–65 began to collapse when large numbers of faculty members and graduate students joined undergraduates in critique of and rebellion against domestic inequalities and imperial ventures that seemed at first aberrations, then earmarks of "the system." Dissidents not only researched and wrote and spoke up as freely inquiring individuals—that was the sort of thing the "1940 Statement" meant to protect; they also formed caucuses and alliances and parties, held teach-ins and sit-ins, protested the war and the university's involvement, agitated for admission of minority students and hiring of minority faculty, challenged the authority of academic disciplines and their leaders, started programs in African American and women's studies, demanded more say in university governance, and so on and on. In short, these faculty members were active in *movements* (optimistically felt for a brief time to be a single, revolutionary movement). They went well beyond academic critique of power, and they attacked administrators and colleagues as well as generals and senators. It was not clear how or if the 1940 principles were to shelter such activities. Yet on the whole they did—better than for Communists fifteen years earlier. Of the thousands of faculty members who defied their employers or broke local and federal laws, few were punitively fired from even nontenured jobs, and hardly any lost tenure. I think the main reason that academic freedom in the 1940 sense held up well through the late sixties is clear. Universities were still growing, supported by the last wave of the postwar boom. Faculty jobs were plentiful, and professors had the power that comes, in such a market, to claim benefits and guard professional privilege.

But soon after 1970 the two narratives fell out of step. On the one hand, professional solidarity weakened because of the political rifts mentioned earlier, and because sixties movements were changing the university. Activists got Ph.D.'s, faculty jobs, often tenure. They found natural allies in previously excluded groups of students brought in by open admission and affirmative action, and in new movements of women, gays, and lesbians. They democratized and opened up the curriculum, as well as the political culture of the campus. And many of them staged a critique of professional conventions and privilege.[11] Faculty members (often liberals) who felt cornered by leftists and feminists sought to regain the academic preeminence they had enjoyed in the good, old, white, male days. One of their tactics was to charge colleagues (and of course students) with violating academic freedom by bullying the "incorrect," and administrations by instituting speech codes and the like.

While these rifts weakened professional cohesion, a more organized movement was pressing for a similar revision of academic freedom. This was the newly awakened Right, which undertook to reclaim the university from the

barbarians who, in its view, had taken control there. Working through conservative think tanks and foundations, the Right generated an ideological
offensive, portraying universities (the humanities in particular) as traitors to
Western civilization and democratic principles, and attacking the diverse
groups it corralled together as "the Left" for intolerance and intimidation.
This well-funded movement not only sponsored right-wing campus newspapers and groups such as the National Association of Scholars but also
influenced federal policy on education, most notably at the National Endowment for the Humanities during the Bennett and Cheney years. These
rightists made common cause with disgruntled professors in the battles over
multiculturalism and political correctness, from the late 1980s on. And it was
this unprecedented interaction of intramural, professional politics and capitalism's ideological counteroffensive against sixties movements that brought
forward the new and rather bizarre appeals to academic freedom I mentioned earlier. Professionalizing academics had for decades shaped it as a
bulwark against the rich and powerful. Now, it was being deployed by academics and some strange allies as a bulwark against the power of women,
queers, workers, people of color, reds, and deconstructionists—and was in-
voked in the Republican platform to protect not just conservative *professors*,
but editors of right-wing student newspapers and conservative students
protesting against fees that would support someone else's "political agenda."

Meanwhile, beginning also around 1970, the narrative of capital took another turn of great moment, as recounted at some length elsewhere in this
book. American business ran into an *economic* crisis more threatening than
the political and social movements of the time, and certainly far more threatening than their partisans on campus. Japan and Europe challenged U.S.
dominance of the First World economy, profits fell, debt of all sorts rose, the
balance of trade went sour, the U.S. dollar softened—and in sum, the postwar
party came to an abrupt end. American capital tried a number of strategies
against tough rivals and tough times; the overarching one was to take away
what labor had gained through the boom times: high pay, benefits, job
security, some control over the workplace and labor process (see William
Greider's popular book of 1997, *One World, Ready or Not,* or Robert Brenner's more technical and densely argued *The Economics of Global Turbulence,*
which takes up the whole May/June 1998 issue of *New Left Review,* among
hundreds of recent sources).[12] This, corporations have accomplished by
downsizing and decentralizing, shifting production to where labor is cheap

and docile, subcontracting and outsourcing, getting rid of the old core labor force wherever possible and replacing them by casual workers. This offensive went forward against knowledge workers, too, including those in universities. There, too, downsizing and subcontracting became standard practice, along with bottom-line rethinking of the university's operations and an effort to market its resources and products. The PC wars, by trivializing liberal arts education, made cuts in public funding seem justified as well as necessary. Finally, a host of companies jumped into the education market with everything from online courses to entire, for-profit universities.

This development is reversing the hundred-year-old process of professionalization, and will surely reconstitute academic freedom as well. On the first point I need say little, to likely readers of this essay. You are painfully familiar with the bad job market for Ph.D.'s (but may not know it dates back precisely to 1970); the proliferation of low-paid, part-time, insecure jobs; the loss of control over curriculum and, in some fields, of the research agenda; the shrinkage of departmental power and of departments themselves; and the near helplessness of professional associations. The academic profession is not alone in its post-1970 decline (even medicine and law have taken serious hits), but it has perhaps led the way.

Whither academic freedom, in such a time? It should be clear by now that the question cannot be drained of politics or separated from one or another group's values and wishes. I tie the following conjectures to the differing and conflicting wishes of three groups identified in the exposition so far.

1. To those (neoliberals, apolitical centrists, conservatives) who felt silenced or intimidated by members and inheritors of sixties movements, and who with some success have redesigned academic freedom to define a polite university "community," privatization will bring a blessedly quieter and less overtly political arena of debate in most colleges and universities—and also a narrower one. As business calibrates higher education more precisely to its needs, students will be pushed along highly pragmatic trajectories: get the knowledge that will translate into job credentials, and forget about changing the world. But of course this trend is not determined, either by corporate wishes or by the dialectic. The protests against globalization in Seattle (1999) and elsewhere could portend something else.

2. For those liberals and leftists and unionists who still think of the administration and trustees as academic freedom's chief enemies, and adhere to the ideals of 1940, the privatizing of education and the commodifying of

knowledge will bring a reduction in politically driven firings, yet at the same time a contraction of the safe area in which tenure protects fearless, disinterested inquiry. That contraction will happen partly through *economically* driven firings. These often become AAUP cases and turn up in the pages of *Academe*. In the last ten years, one institution after another has terminated faculty members, sometimes in bargain lots, for reasons of "financial exigency" or "institutional need" (an allowable cause, by AAUP rules, if it can be substantiated and if there is a semblance of due process). Thus the MCP Hahnemann School of Medicine[13] set out to fire thirteen professors while in bankruptcy court. Clarkson College (Nebraska) retrenched by firing six. The University of Bridgeport, plagued by debt and declining enrollment, tried to "restructure" by firing fifty, mostly tenured, professors. In like circumstances, Bennington College eliminated tenure in 1995 and has since declined to renew contracts for what some take to be retributive reasons. The Savannah College of Art and Design, Benedict College, Alaska Pacific University, Lawrence Technical University, St. Bonaventure University, and others have in the last ten years fired individuals or closed down programs and departments, claiming financial exigency. San Diego State University terminated 111 in a 1991–92 budgetary crisis, and the University of the District of Columbia set the record, so far, by firing 125. Several of these wholesale retrenchments were successfully opposed, locally and with AAUP help, but they strongly suggest that AAUP battles in future will pit traditional academic freedom against administrations claiming to make politically neutral, bottom-line decisions—fighting the next war with the last war's weapon? (Interestingly, sex and gender "offenses" account for most other cases in which the AAUP intervened this past decade. Does my admittedly cursory overview suggest that rebellion or perceived weirdness in this area of conduct and expression is today's equivalent of belonging to the Communist Party?)

But universities can eliminate positions or programs without attracting the attention of AAUP investigators, and the last war's weapons and tactics will be less than useless against the quiet shifting of resources to areas of high student demand, the elimination of full-time positions as their occupants retire, the substitution of part-timers, the staffing of basic courses with full-time instructors off the tenure track, the turn to distance learning programs that exploit the "courseware" of a few tenured professors and recruit adjunct or piecework help (not even physically at the university) to "interface" with students, and so on. Less than useless, because while the tenured professoriate shrinks and loses ever more control of higher education, academic freedom of the 1940 sort will win enough victories to seem inviolate.

3. For people like me, who identify with the Left in general and the academic inheritors of 1960s movements in particular, the post-1970 transformation of capital heightens the contradiction just explored: academic freedom has never been so robust/academic freedom has its back against the wall. I approach this contradiction through Menand's and Fish's point that the content of academic freedom is what people manage to put into it, and mine that the putting-in and taking-out are phases of a hegemonic process.

What I think we want to put into it—in *addition* to the familiar safeguards of competent and open inquiry—is full freedom for a critique of power, for the thought and perception and feeling of those excluded from power, and for imagining how to make the world peaceful, equal, and able to sustain decent life. As for hegemony: we do fight with one another, and also with regents and trustees and presidents, over the legitimacy of ideas, as groups 1 and 2 insist. Clearly, such contests also play out in job searches and tenure decisions, in admissions to graduate programs and the award of fellowships, in departments and curriculum committees, in caucuses and elections within scholarly organizations, in the channeling of money to right-wing foundations and campus newspapers, in the media spasms they are sometimes able to provoke (as with PC), in battles over public funding that are sometimes influenced by such publicity, in decisions at journals and presses on what will see print, in the whole apparatus of judging merit and allocating celebrity—and in many other, overlapping fields of contestation. In such venues, the movements against war and imperialism and the "military-industrial complex" and for racial equality, women's rights, gay liberation, and ecological sanity have fought for recognition, legitimacy, and sometimes power.

They do not run or terrorize the university, as the Right would have it. Yet in the arts, humanities, and social sciences they have established a counter-hegemonic presence of some weight. Think of it in terms of programs and courses and faculty positions, of journals and university press series, of lectures and seminars and research centers, unimaginable in, say, 1962. We can study and write and teach now about Jewett, Chopin, Chesnutt, Yezierska, and many other terrific, forgotten writers—to mention just a handful from the period about which I most recently taught. We can debate the sexuality of "Boston marriages" and the historical construction of race. The non-European world turns out to have cultures worth the attention of more than anthropologists and worth theorizing (as postcolonial, subaltern, Third World . . .). Historians can work "from below." Scholars from many fields can think from many angles about commercial culture and commodities. Science now has a social and institutional history, not entirely separate from domination. In fact, power, once a well-kept secret, is now discernable and subject to critique in all areas of public and personal life. And so on—not to mention that traditional academic topics and problems look entirely different now than they did in 1962, largely because of perspectives and urgencies brought to the university by those democratic movements. This paragraph could be expanded to a book. Indeed, the Right has produced many books on the subject, lamenting such developments as intellectual foolishness or a new, tyrannical orthodoxy. I say: academic freedom has in forty years grown beyond all expectation, and as a result, we understand the world better.

Now, the Right, sensibly worried that students will be taught a better understanding of the world than is conveyed by the media or the old liberal arts curriculum, has gone to battle against these advances, in many familiar ways, but hasn't put the genie back in the bottle, and won't. The main threat to the genie comes from the post-1970 dynamic of relentless privatization. As knowledge is increasingly made and organized to sell in tidy packages, where will the market be for feminist or queer or Marxist critique? These are not among the intellectual properties that the university's venture capital team will see as foundations of spin-off enterprises. Nor will it find corporations ready to "partner" with it in developing and selling the ideas of Joan Scott or Judith Butler. Nor will corporations themselves look to the university as a subcontractor that can efficiently supply their needs for Gramscian or Foucauldian critique. Students will still want bell hooks and Noam Chomsky, at least as celebrity speakers. But how many students will jeopardize their economic futures by majoring in the fields where post-sixties critique is the center of intellectual excitement? The likely answer is: quite a few at elite campuses, where having been admitted in the first place is a ticket into the professional-managerial class; not so many at major public universities; a handful at the branch universities and state colleges; very few at community colleges; and none at the strictly-for-credentials University of Phoenix and its drive-through clones. There will doubtless be a niche market on-line for "Revolutionary Thought" as an elective, but it is hard to imagine most students who pursue their degrees by distance learning—students short on capital and with adult responsibilities—straying far or for long from the subjects that promise (however falsely) to pay off in lifelong earning power. In the dystopia toward which this paragraph squints, academic freedom is a mighty fortress, quite empty because no one can afford to live in it.

Well, that's an answer to the question that launched these reflections. It's an answer that completes my own narrative, in this way: "1960s movements greatly expanded academic freedom; their academic inheritors withstood an ideological counteroffensive from the Right, but were eventually exiled from the curriculum by strategies capital had adopted around 1970 to beat down industrial labor, and then extended to the production and circulation of knowledge, the professions, and the university." Strong energies drive the story in this direction, but something is wrong with the story, aside from its unpleasant ending. For one thing, it reifies academic freedom in just the way I have opposed doing: why should academic freedom circa 2000 be preserved in amber, any more than academic freedom circa 1940? People will be fighting over the content of the idea until it ceases to be worth fighting over.

A related flaw is my story's assumption that the present lineup and balance of contending forces will remain unaltered. True, globalizing capital has momentum. The academic Left is weak in spite of its freedom to say critical things about capital, and even if strong would be to capital as a mouse to a lion. But globalizing capital's dominance will not last forever. Opposition is out there. Resistance happens now; it will become smarter and more organized. Many will join it because many are harmed by globalization. They are potential allies of academic progressives, especially as labor is casualized and the profession undermined. What will save academic freedom from obsolescence will be actual alliances of teachers with other workers in the university and with knowledge workers of all kinds, here and abroad. Such alliances, if and when they form, will also change, once again, the idea of academic freedom and the terrain defended in its name.

BOOK AND MAGAZINE
PUBLISHING THROUGH THE PERIOD
OF CORPORATE REVOLUTION

◆

This essay is my contribution to a large, collaborative history-in-progress of the book and print culture in the United States. Along with my next essay it argues that the book and magazine industries fell out of step around 1900 and back into step after about 1965, and that their uneven development may be neatly explained by seeing them in context of the larger changes in American capitalism and its social relations at those two times. Thus, apart from whatever interest the particular topics of these essays command, I offer them as further support for the epochal idea that informs much of this book. That the university, the academic profession, and the professional-managerial class went through major shifts in step with commercial print culture begs for a comprehensive explanation. I hope to have made a start in that direction, building of course on basic work by many scholars.

Around 1900, magazine publishers radically transformed the economics of their business, which then expanded at a rate far more robust than that of book publishing. The story is well known,[1] and I will abstract it very briefly here before turning to the main task of this chapter, which is to consider relations between the two businesses and the two forms of print culture, especially from 1880 to about 1910, when their differentiation was most intense. My focus is on monthly magazines, which initially stood in close relationship to books.

In 1880, prestigious monthlies such as *Harper's* and the *Atlantic* sold for twenty-five or thirty-five cents an issue and attained modest circulations—

probably no higher than 150,000—among cultivated and relatively well-to-do readers. Neither they nor the most successful women's monthlies (*Godey's Ladies' Book, Peterson's Magazine, The Delineator*) carried much advertising; revenue came chiefly from subscriptions.

This landscape shifted suddenly in and after 1893, when a price war developed among three newcomers to the field of general monthlies: *McClure's, Cosmopolitan,* and *Munsey's.* The latter was first to set a newsstand price of ten cents, with a subscription rate of a dollar a year. Its circulation rose from 40,000 in October of 1893 to 200,000 the following February to 500,000 in April, with a steadier increase after that. *Cosmopolitan* and *McClure's,* selling now at the same price, reached similar figures a bit later. The *Ladies' Home Journal,* not seen as in direct competition with these "general" magazines, had already established a ten-cent price. By 1900, as it grew more like the others in content, it became the first ever to attain a circulation of one million copies.

At the *Journal,* publisher Cyrus Curtis and editor Edward Bok had gradually worked up a business practice that S. S. McClure, Frank Munsey, and John Brisben Walker (*Cosmopolitan*) more abruptly and somewhat desperately adopted during the panic and recession of 1893: find and organize an audience of middle-class people not well served by the elite monthlies but with money enough to spend on brand-name commodities; meet and shape the cultural needs of that audience; build unprecedented circulations across the United States; sell advertising space to makers of brand-name commodities at rates based on circulation; sell the magazine at a price below its actual cost of production; and make advertising the source of profit. In this way, magazine publishers actually changed their business: now their main "product" was not the physical magazine itself but the interested attention of readers, sold en bloc through ad agencies to manufacturers, who were now the main customers.[2]

The change was timely (indeed, almost historically necessary, as I will suggest later), and the results striking: total U.S. circulation of monthly magazines rose from about 18 million in 1890 to 64 million in 1905, far more rapidly than did that of weeklies, newspapers, or books. This amounted to nearly four magazines per month per American household. Magazine advertising revenues burgeoned at a comparable rate through the same years, and the industry sustained vigorous growth on through the 1920s.

To approach a discussion of how this dramatic expansion of the magazine industry culture changed its relation to book publishing, I turn first to the way that relation had developed *before* the 1890s; for most of the new magazines' direct antecedents were periodicals founded by book publishers. As early as 1842, the New York publisher Appleton started a house periodical called *The Home Book Circular*, free to booksellers, announcing new Appleton books each quarter. A year later it was replaced by a monthly, *Appleton's Literary Bulletin*, which reported on new books from many publishers in the United States and Europe.[3] Perhaps catalogue-like trade journals such as this led other publishers toward the idea of the house monthly. In any case, Harper & Brothers launched the most successful of these, *Harper's New Monthly Magazine* in 1850. An obscure Boston publisher founded the *Atlantic Monthly* in 1857; Ticknor & Fields acquired it in 1859, and by 1873 it had come to Hurd & Houghton (later Houghton Mifflin), where it remained until 1908, never much exceeding fifty thousand in circulation but wielding enormous cultural authority. The other monthly that stood on the same plane in the 1880s was *The Century*, which had also begun as a house journal, *Scribner's Monthly*, in 1870. It passed on to the Century Company in 1881, along with the premier children's monthly, *St. Nicholas*, and the Century Company also went into book publishing. In 1886 Charles Scribner's Sons started a second house journal, *Scribner's Magazine*, which rivaled the other elite monthlies until its demise in 1937. In the same group were *Putnam's Monthly*, *Lippincott's Magazine*, *Appleton's Journal*, and some others that bore the names of prominent publishing houses, as well as many that did not (*St. Nicholas*, *Popular Science*, *House Beautiful*, and so on). In short, the "general" monthly magazine was essentially a creation of book publishers. Even the venerable *North American Review*, founded in 1815 (though not a monthly until 1879), and perennially a money loser, was taken on by Ticknor & Fields, then James R. Osgood Company, then Appleton, through the post–Civil War period.

Several aims led book publishers to start or acquire magazines. Most obviously, as with Appleton's effort of 1842, they used the monthlies as an advertising medium, rather abundantly. Representative single issues of the *Atlantic* and *Harper's*, at five-year intervals contain many pages of ads for Houghton Mifflin and Harper books, respectively. To wit:

	1880	1885	1890
Atlantic	9	25	12
Harper's	16	10	15

In each, approximately one hundred books are listed, priced, described, praised, sampled for illustrations, promoted as gifts, commended as well-crafted material objects, touted as cultural capital. Layout emphasized that last point: book advertisements were generally segregated not only from editorial material but from ads for toothpaste, cleaning powder, and so on, when these crept into the magazines—and, by 1890, claimed more than half the ad space there. Publishers also advertised through newspapers, billboards, posters, and otherwise, but their own journals were cheap and reliable channels to groups already assembled by reading taste.

The cultural values advanced in the magazine found embodiment in the publisher's book list for two closely related reasons. First, many texts and authors appeared both in the magazines and on the publisher's list of books. From the outset, house magazines serialized or excerpted novels, memoirs, travel narratives, and journalism of all sorts before book publication, on the premise that doing so would create a demand for these texts when they appeared in book form. So thought Appleton when it founded the *Journal* in 1869. Charles Scribner and others agreed. Houghton Mifflin's experience, on the other hand, "indicated that periodical publication was far from essential for commercial success," and George Harrison Mifflin wrote to one novelist, "The truth is, strictly between us, that few people read serials in the magazines." *Atlantic* editor Horace Scudder had low regard for serialized novels but continued to print them in the nineties as "an essential feature." His successor, Bliss Perry had similar views, and in 1906 tried omitting this "feature"; not a single reader registered an objection. For all the uncertainty, most publishers did regard serialization as essential, and it was a rare issue of a monthly that lacked even one installment; for a while in 1885 *Century* gave all its fiction pages to *Huckleberry Finn* (excerpted) and *The Bostonians* and *The Rise of Silas Lapham* (each serialized in toto). Double publication was entirely conventional. Authors bargained for it; publishers such as James R. Osgood with no magazines found serial outlets elsewhere for their authors; the *Atlantic* in its period of skepticism about the practice shunted serial rights to Houghton Mifflin books off to *McClure's* and the *Ladies' Home Journal*.[4] In short, literary monthlies and respectable book publishers organized a cultural space around the same values (those of the genteel classes in the Northeast) to promote the same texts.

Second, publishers from the outset subordinated magazines to the exigencies of the book business. If a monthly turned a profit on its own, fine;

but few of them regularly did, and many, like the *North American Review,* almost always lost money. The *Atlantic* usually did, but Mifflin kept it going in the nineties for its prestige and its ability to attract new authors to the house, often by accepting short stories or sketches early in a young writer's career. Scribner's subsidized its money-losing magazine in the nineties for similar reasons—many authors found the magazine "a vestibule to the House." Although some editors were granted a fair amount of independence, it was usually clear in a pinch that journals were to serve the purposes of their parent houses. Bookmen founded the magazines, bought and sold them, paid for them out of book profits, hired and fired editors. In the ideology of print culture as in its business relations, the book was dominant. Long before he became editor of the *Atlantic,* Horace Scudder interpreted the relationship thus: "[T]he magazine carries [the publisher's] name like a flag everywhere it goes, and accustoms people to associating certain qualities with it; for the magazine rarely fails to symbolize the house from which it issues. . . . It is indeed much more likely to reflect the character and taste of the house than of its editor."[5]

Scudder's terms are revealing: he sees the magazine as a *signifier,* not only of the house whose "character and taste" it reflects, but of "certain qualities" that I imagine Scudder identified with a general range of culture as much as with any single house. That was book culture; as Janice Radway and Carl Kaestle argue in an unpublished essay, the bound book has generally been the form of print culture with "the highest authority and permanence." But not all books, even bound books, have at any time shared the claim to cultural dominance. In the United States after the Civil War the ones that did were primarily those (including of course many by English writers) associated with the old reputable publishing names—Harper, Appleton, Putnam, Scribner, Dodd, Mead, Dutton, Houghton, Mifflin, Osgood, Lippincott, and so on—who purported to act like gentlemen, more in the interest of literature than of profit. A subset of these sponsored general monthlies that reflected the "character" of the houses and the "qualities" of elite book culture. By and large the very genre of the monthly connoted gentility, class prestige, Anglo-American roots, intellectual seriousness, high culture. Those were the connotations McClure, Walker, Munsey, Bok, and others sought to appropriate around 1890, shifting them downscale a bit by trumpeting the vigor and worldliness of their new productions in contrast to the ascribed effeteness of the elite monthlies. Theirs was a business revolution, a cultural modulation. The mass circulation magazine descended from the old book via the elite monthly. Now to complicate that tidy thought for a while on the way to a second main hypothesis.

Admittedly, magazines of many other sorts existed from the eighteenth century onward, and some influenced the founders of the new monthlies. I subordinate them, in the genealogy offered here, for the following reasons. Older "general" monthly magazines not connected to publishing houses were frail enterprises, most of which died in the 1840s and 1850s; the most famous of them, *The Knickerbocker,* lasted only to 1865. By the time others appeared (e.g., *The Galaxy* in 1866 and the *Overland Monthly* in 1868), they entered a genre shaped by *Harper's,* a great success from the beginning, and then by its imitators from other houses. The hundreds of religious and political journals were disqualified as models by their sectarianism and partisanship: the project of the popular monthlies was to identify their own work with the interests of society as a whole and to build readerships assembled around middle-class views and ways of living. Nor did advertisers wish to associate their products with sectarian polemics. Women's magazines achieved a suitable tone of middle-class respectability, but had to broaden out from narrowly "feminine" concerns—as the *Journal* gradually did—in order to appeal to advertisers as family magazines. And the cheap or free "story papers," while they helped show the way to advertising-based profits, were too rude, and read by too many poor people. McClure and the others knew (or intuited) their business when they sought to imitate but popularize the cultural form established by genteel book publishers.

The new entrepreneurs challenged and changed that form but by no means seceded from book culture: they worked it into the new editorial mix. Book chat was a standard genre of cultural instruction; authors were profiled as celebrities alongside actresses and statesmen; halftones of them and their homes appeared as part of the new visual display. Magazine entrepreneurs also energetically carried on the practice of serializing novels and other texts before book publication, making deals with book houses and, incidentally, driving up authors' earnings. Walker (*Cosmopolitan*) and Munsey issued books from their own presses. Frank Leslie and his widow (who changed her name to "Frank Leslie" after his death) had long published books alongside their string of popular magazines. McClure, eager to compete with editors who could offer writers book *and* magazine publication, joined with Frank Doubleday to found Doubleday, McClure & Company in 1897, and took over Harper & Brothers (at the request of J. P. Morgan, its new owner) when it failed in 1899, though both ventures were short lived.

Expanding in the other direction, the new book company Frank Doubleday started with Walter Hines Page founded magazines (*The World's Work* and *Country Life in America*), not to "symbolize the house" but to make money. Book publishers also contributed to the subfield of magazines *about* book culture. Most significantly, Dodd, Mead inaugurated an American edition of the *Bookman* in 1894, and printed the first bestseller lists there in 1895. Appleton put out the *Book Buyer* for forty years. Funk & Wagnalls founded the *Literary Digest*.

So there was a good deal of commutation across these print genres, at the turn of the century. A few additional instances: pictorial dust jackets on books became common in the 1890s and almost universal after 1900, intensifying the visual appeal of books as commodities at newsstands, in department stores, and on bookstore shelves, just when the new magazines were first attracting the attention of shoppers by changing their often pictorial cover designs each month. Halftone illustrations proliferated in books, hinting at affinities with illustrated monthlies. Some publishers of cheap books even tried running ads in them for a while. "Libraries" and series from the fiction "factories" (dime novels, Alger stories, Frank Merriwell, the Rover Boys) approximated magazines in periodicity and formulaic repetition.[6] Later, book clubs intervened to build a new kind of periodicity and cultural continuity.

Business practices, too, tended to blur boundaries in print culture, even more than indicated by the discussion of serialization and other crossovers. Through the 1890s a new group of workers—*literary agents*—established a need for their services between author and editor. Seeking the most profitable outlets for their clients, they further emphasized the commodity status of text (indeed, of talent) and thus its amenability to different venues of realization. It could become book, magazine material, newspaper fodder, or any combination, depending on what deal the agent could consummate. Newspapers, growing toward their twentieth-century formats through the 1880s and 1890s, were becoming a medium for some of the same material (especially fiction) that made its way into books and magazines. A business practice that hastened the process was syndication, which had earlier worked mainly with cheap filler texts. In the mid-1880s, several entrepreneurs began syndicating newspaper publication of stories and novels in a big way. S. S. McClure became the runaway leader in this field; his syndicate, predecessor and partial foundation of *McClure's Magazine*, brought the work of Stevenson, Kipling, Hardy, Twain, Howells, and Garland, of poets Morris, Tennyson, and Swinburne, and many other less-well-known writers to the rapidly forming mass readership of big-city newspapers.[7] Like literary agentry, syndication intervened between author and editors. A similar amalgamation of print forms had already taken place in *distribution*. The American News Company, formed in 1864, had by the 1890s virtually monopolized magazine distribution and taken over a large share of the wholesale book market. These two print formats jostled with newspapers at thousands of newsstands and other outlets, proclaiming the unity of the cultural field. Meanwhile a much older practice, subscription publishing of books, continued to flourish, encompassing almost the whole process of production by ensuring sales (through orders gathered by drummers), usually in advance of publication, or even before the text was written.[8]

Finally, book and magazine publishers were both taking aggressive roles in the actual generation of text. It is a familiar story that the new magazine entrepreneurs declined to wait decorously for manuscripts, then choose from among those offered. Instead, they chased after authors, sometimes put them on assignment, suggested ideas for articles, and planned series of articles to run over several issues before becoming books. This was "magazining," in McClure's term. Organizers of fiction factories had long generated cheap books even more imperiously, reducing the writer's part to that of a pseudonymous hired hack fleshing out the editor's outline, and producing formula text for repeat readers seeking dependable pleasures. Reputable publishers rarely gave orders in that way. For one thing, their product depended for its appeal on the ideology of an individual author and his or her artistic originality. But by the first decade of this century these publishers, too, had moved well along toward the initiation of book ideas and the management of talent. In sum, magazine publishing strongly influenced its parent industry through the early decades of this century.

Thus to the second hypothesis: the magazine and book businesses, and to a lesser extent the newspaper business, collaborated in a rather long historical process, the commodification of writing and the fluid circulation of text through product categories that were in this way like different kinds of packaging. Janice Radway makes the point for the new "commercial book," which was less like the old "unified volume conceived, penned, and edited by a single writer" than "like an ephemeral apparition, that is, a temporary embodiment of cultural material in wide circulation at the time in other formats."[9] Mass circulation magazines occupied a more economically dominant position in this system than did their predecessors. In addition, they probably helped diffuse reading habits associated with what Radway calls the "commercial book" (she is referring to dime novels and other such productions) across a wider social spectrum. Without doubt, turn-of-the-century observers felt a privileged, older style of reading—the leisured, "gentlemanly exchange" implied by the elite monthlies and the high literary culture they led—to be under assault. The new editors favored a brisker, more personal, and more muscular style. They encouraged reading to *keep up*—with the new, the timely, the edge of progress. Through advance publicity for future issues they shaped anticipation, to make magazine reading a kind of eager consumption not entirely different from that promoted by advertisers of household goods.[10] One may conjecture that, as book publishers entered bidding wars for celebrity authors, promoted their wares with enlarged advertising campaigns, published material already "boomed" by magazines, and in general imitated the methods of the new editors, middle-class book reading tended more toward the hurried pace and social urgency fostered by magazines.

For all that, *within* print culture the book and magazine industries remained distinct, and in some ways antagonistic. They competed for readers. However great the synergy across forms, leisure is finite and people must make cultural choices. Even before the magazine revolution, Henry Holt worried that monthly magazines would "kill off" books, and indeed, through the 1890s magazine readership grew far more rapidly—with most of the gains posted by the new monthlies, not their old elite models, which were of course economically tied to the book industry. These rival business groups competed for authors as well, driving up the price for serial rights, and leading authors to think of magazines as their primary source of income. The old book-and-magazine publishers found it hard to keep writers who appealed to wide audiences: Horace Scudder of *The Atlantic* wrote Sarah Orne Jewett that he could no longer afford to be her regular publisher, now that the "illustrated magazines . . . are like buyers in an auction room bidding hard against each other." The bidding wars became more intense with the advent of the new monthlies, which turned even the Harper magazines into money-losers, and thus hastened the bankruptcy of the venerable house.[11] *McClure's, Munsey's,* and their cohort were besting the older book publishers and their magazine subsidiaries in traditional industry practices: buying and packaging text and selling the package to as many readers as possible.

To conceptualize the relationship thus, however, is to overlook the more profound change in print culture and in the whole economic system, of

BOOK AND MAGAZINE PUBLISHING 175

which magazines' ascendance was an effect. A brief discussion of that change will help explain the ascendancy of magazines in commercial print culture. As noted earlier, the new magazine publishers had not simply outdone their genteel predecessors in the making and distribution of a familiar commodity, the "general" monthly magazine. They had in effect joined with newspaper publishers in inventing a new commodity, the audience's attention, and making it available to those with very different kinds of products to sell: breakfast cereals, crackers, cleansers, toothpastes, soaps, canned goods, baby foods, bottled beers, soft drinks, chewing gum, cigarettes, bicycles, typewriters, cameras, ready-made clothing, safety razors, kitchen appliances, household conveniences, and beautifications of all sorts. These commodities were themselves novel, not for the most part in their basic qualities and uses, but in the way they were put on the market.

Crucially, all came with brand names: Mellin's, Ivory, Uneeda Biscuit, Cream of Wheat, Quaker Oats, Campbell's, Welch's, Wrigley's, Coca-Cola, Swift, Armour, Gillette, Kodak, Arrow, 1847 Rogers Brothers: these and many others, still in use or long forgotten, date from the time in question. It is hard to imagine advertising in national magazines without brand names and the trademarks that usually accompanied them. The intense and successful campaign that launched the National Biscuit Company's "Uneeda" in 1899 distinguished the product sharply—and historically—from the anonymous pound of crackers scooped by the grocer out of his cracker barrel. So did the uniform packaging, the trademark, the slogans, the copy, and the iconography that marked display ads in this period. Though a few products had long been given identities in this way, the cluster of practices just mentioned became normative only toward the end of the nineteenth century, as is perhaps suggested by the increase in registered trademarks from 121 in 1870 to over 10,000 in 1906. This was a revolution in selling, generated by rather broad economic forces.

To encapsulate the argument of my book *Selling Culture,* through the second half of the century American manufacturers had greatly expanded industrial production, put factory and city in the center of economic life, and come to dominate the social formation they were creating. But their *control* of the world they had made was weak and disjointed. In spite of varied strategies for stabilizing their environment (trusts, pools, gentlemen's agreements on pricing, and so on), individual enterprises remained volatile, bankruptcies abounded, profits gradually declined, and the boom-and-bust cycle spun along by a logic of its own, bringing a severe depression in each decade from 1870 to 1900. These economic upheavals led to social disorder, with intense labor conflict especially in 1877, 1885–86, 1892, and 1894. Many observers feared anarchy or revolution. Populist movements and parties did in fact gain momentum and, in 1892 and 1896, electoral force.

Leading capitalists gradually converged in a structural economic response to this compound crisis: the large, vertically integrated corporation.[12] These new giants organized the entire process of production and distribution, from extraction of raw materials to final sales, thus removing many uncertainties from their project of accumulation. Most to the point of the present discussion, they brought within their own compass the work of getting products to consumers. Previously, firms had concentrated on making the goods and relied on jobbers, wholesalers, and other middlemen to place them in stores. The new corporations sought to eliminate from distribution the power of such unreliable agents. They built elaborate sales organizations within the corporate structure and adopted the strategies of brand-naming, uniform packaging, and extensive advertising in order to ensure that demand would be there for what they produced. They wanted a customer who shopped for Ivory Soap or Quaker Oats, not one with generic needs who would rely on the storekeeper's advice.

To give the customer these specific desires was the work of advertising agencies, which assumed their modern form in the 1890s, and in fact often took the lead in showing backward or uncertain corporations how to do business in the new way. Before, agents were essentially brokers, selling space, primarily in newspapers, to local advertisers such as department stores. That practice continued, but modernizing agencies such as N. W. Ayer and J. Walter Thompson quickly developed a full line of services from market research to copywriting, art, and design, suitable to the creation of meanings around brand-named commodities. News of these items, "sold at grocers everywhere," required a medium that would bring together a large, national audience made up chiefly of people with the desire and the means to live efficient, modern lives, in which the new commodities would play both a practical and a symbolic role.

Such a medium was—or would soon be—the illustrated monthly magazine. Bok, McClure, Walker, Munsey, and others had differing goals and ideologies, but each assembled a journalistic mix that flattered readers for their progressive ideas and worldly leadership, gave them cultural instruction, charted for them the social world in which they would meet their equals (face to face and through the pages of the magazine), dazzled them with art and photography made available in this format through the new halftone process, fed their dreams of individuality and merit through fiction—*and* put before them, often in more than a hundred pages of advertisements in a single issue, a stunning array of commodities given significance and allure by the techniques of the ad man. In my view, the monthly magazine was an important site—along with the suburb, the university, and the emerging network of professional, civic, and social organizations—for the actual formation and growing self-awareness of the professional-managerial class. It played a significant part through the Progressive era and afterward in politically tempering and legitimizing corporate capitalism, while it consolidated itself economically.

Like advertising agents, and like the mail order and department store merchandisers I have left out of this already overcrowded cast of social transformers, magazine editors and publishers were far more than compliant errand boys for the captains of industry. They invented a business for purposes of their own, including but not limited to profit. In their vision, advertising was a means to the establishment of a cultural form, and for most of them, to the establishment of more than that: a fresh configuration of social and domestic life, even a renewal of the nation, on sensible, forward-looking principles. However one sorts out the complexities of historical agency in the transformation of American society, magazine publishers were integral to it.

The older elite monthlies took part in it only marginally, and, for reasons that should now be clear, book publishers hardly at all. The latter continued to make and sell the same commodities as always, in much the same ways. Nor *could* books easily have become vehicles for advertising about soap and cereal, even had that possibility been thinkable to publishers. For in spite of series and cheap "libraries" and the apparatus of best-sellers, most books continued to arrive on the market as thousands of discrete commodities each year that readers would buy or not, with little carry-over from previous purchases. "Brand loyalty" to authors was unsteady, to publishers almost nonexistent. (One failed advertising slogan, "When in doubt, buy Scribner's," showed that publishers understood the problem.) Lacking secure and continuous control of an audience's attention, book publishers had nothing to sell to the new corporations.

Nor did publishers themselves adopt the new corporate forms. Take vertical integration, for example. It was no fresh idea, and some publishers had long tried to control their own raw materials (authors and texts), manufacturing plants, and sites of distribution (bookstores). But if anything, these efforts faltered just when other businesses were making their imperial move. The older firms had professed "trade courtesy," meaning they would not try to buy away one another's authors, but the principle was erratically observed at best, as were the contract clauses giving a publisher first option on an author's next book. A few reputable publishers tried holding on to prized authors by contracting for all their output, as Harper & Brothers did with William Dean Howells in 1885 (at the enormous sum of $10,000 a year). But the bidding wars of century's end, with popular monthlies heating up the competition, defeated most such attempts at control. Publishers' ownership of production facilities was an equally venerable arrangement; in fact, many publishers had begun as printers. But the trend around 1900 was toward separation of printing from publishing, and in 1914 just 18 percent of publishers ran their own presses.[13]

As for distribution: book publishers generally declined or failed to adapt to the new merchandising environment. Many, for example, still favored subscription and mail order business over sales in retail stores. Most strikingly, they banded together in the American Publishers' Association in 1900 in an attempt to enforce standard markups, then fought Macy's discounting practices for years, until stopped for restraint of trade in 1914.[14] In short, they now undertook to fix prices and regulate their market just at the time when manufacturers generally were abandoning such tactics in favor of the new corporate structure and the effort to ensure large sales by associating images of respectable living with products such as gelatin and toothpaste, in the minds of consumers.

To be sure, publishers did also boost their investments in advertising, from apparently negligible amounts in the 1860s to perhaps $5 million annually by the end of the century, and more in the next decade, which was known then and remembered later as the era of the "boomed book." As that phrase suggests, extravagant ad campaigns sought to create a sensation around an individual book and propel it into best-sellerdom. A publisher might spend $10,000 on newspaper, magazine, direct mail, billboard, and streetcar advertising for such a book, in addition to money spent by local dealers. Results were highly erratic. It was a commonplace among publishers to admit that they had no idea how to entice the public or make a book popular; they lamented that pressure from authors and competitors drove them to imperil profits in the attempt. After Houghton Mifflin had increased its advertising budget from $30,000 in 1881 to $67,000 in 1895 to nearly $100,000 in 1900, Mifflin set out to study the effectiveness of such expenditures. His colleague Francis Garrison concluded that "there seems to be no relation between" either ad costs and sales of a single book, or the whole budget and gross Houghton Mifflin sales for a given year, and that the firm had "wasted" tens of thousands on advertising "for many years past." A $23,000 cutback followed this research, and 1900 remained the peak year for a long while.[15] One way or another, many houses drew similar conclusions, and before 1914 the whole industry seems to have backed off a bit from its commitment to publicity.

A key principle of the advertising that manifestly worked for safety razors, oatmeal, and so on was repetition over months, years, decades. With rare exceptions a book catches on in its first few weeks if at all, and since name recognition does not carry over to the *next* book, advertising cannot insistently accrete meaning around the book-as-commodity. Ads in the elite monthlies in 1900 tended to strive for such continuity by positioning the new book in a high cultural narrative: "the most important book he has written," "remind one strongly of Poe's tales," has the "qualities that made 'Q' famous," and so on. Ads in the mass circulation magazines were chiefly about middle-brow books and were likely to promote them as similar in value to other kinds of domestic accessory. Encyclopedias, definitive biographies of Napoleon, nine-volume histories of the world, would offer practical knowledge and give an impressive look to your living room, at an astonishing bargain. Most tellingly, I think, while the *Atlantic* and its peers continued to carry clumps of book ads from ten to thirty pages long (and separate from soap and cereal ads), book advertising nearly vanished from the popular monthlies, as if book publishers at some level understood that they were in an entirely different kind of business from Procter and Gamble, and would be pouring money down the drain by paying *Ladies' Home Journal* rates to boost their ephemeral commodities. The P&G idea was to guarantee that a customer would go into the grocery store and ask for Ivory Soap. Book advertising failed any such test: according to a 1901 survey, book retailers unanimously believed that the average customer came into the store not knowing what he or she intended to buy.[16]

Magazine entrepreneurs facilitated and fed on the corporate transformation of the U.S. economy; some, like Curtis, themselves became large corporations. Book publishers continued to grapple with nineteenth-century uncertainties, including basic ones about the nature of their product, who owned it (copyright laws remained confusing until 1909), who would pay for its production, and how the profits from it might be divided. Hustling, piracy, and cutthroat competition went forward alongside the genteel procedures of the old houses, with their reliance on the loyalty of authors and their quaint idea that literary culture was not really part of the capitalist market. Above all, dependable sales eluded the publishers, for reasons mainly beyond their control, and they continued to lose money on perhaps four out of five new books.

Until the middle of the twentieth century, the old-fashioned family firm remained the norm in book publishing. It is interesting to note that two of the major houses, Harper and Appleton, failed in 1899–1900, at exactly the moment of frenetic mergers and corporate reorganization in other industries, and of the new magazines' triumph. J. P. Morgan took a hand in the rehabilitation of Harper & Brothers (to which he had lent money as the business went deep into trouble), but even his magic could not bring publishing into conformity with the new capitalist arrangements. The industry stayed remarkably unconcentrated. In 1914 Harper, still among its leaders, had less than 2 percent of total book sales, and a Bureau of the Census report listed 819 publishers in all. The same report showed that the book industry accounted for one-fourth of 1 percent of all manufacturing value, down from 1 percent in 1850.[17] Magazines had long since passed books by this measure. Doubtless their success cut into the market for books. But the most compelling truth about the two is that magazines played a leading role in the corporate revolution, and books neither did nor could have. They became in effect a niche product until, in the 1960s and after, still another transformation brought them within the compass of the multinational corporation and the pursuit of media synergy—along *with* magazines, which by then had become a niche product, too, pushed aside by radio and television.

EPOCHAL CHANGE:
PRINT CULTURE AND ECONOMICS

◆

In the introduction and elsewhere, I have warned the reader (and, really, myself) against surrounding the arrangements of the passing era with a halo of sentiment. Those arrangements were chiefly the ones that obtained in higher education. I think the warning equally apt with respect to the book industry. Niche publishing and marketing by media conglomerates may make successes like that of Rachel Carson's Silent Spring *or James Baldwin's* The Fire Next Time *less frequent than forty years ago, but they will still happen, and books for niche audiences can sustain a critical or subversive conversation in dark times. In any case, high-cultural disdain for mass publishing should not be mistaken for progressive politics.*

This essay is an expanded version of the eighteenth annual James Russell Wiggins Lecture on the History of the Book, which I gave at the American Antiquarian Society in 2000.

In 1980, Thomas Whiteside published a series of articles in *The New Yorker* on "startling changes" in book publishing through the previous two decades. Until the early 1960s, he began, trade book publishing "was believed to offer its practitioners a rather select and gentlemanly way of life. . . . [It] was a business in which publishers and editors could feel sustained not only by their love of books but also by their sense of professional independence . . . and by a diversity of relatively stable relationships with authors, agents, and booksellers."

On Whiteside's account, a series of mergers and takeovers had all but ended the autonomy of trade publishers, leaving intact only a handful of the independent, family-owned firms that had dominated the industry through its entire history. Along with corporate ownership came a more rigorous profit discipline than had prevailed; an emphasis on paperback and movie rights and complex deals from the earliest contract talks on; enormous payments for these; correspondingly large advances to celebrity authors, often following auctions in which publishers were invited to bid against one another; and intense and expensive publicity for new books—ad blitzes, author tours, talk show appearances, and so on. The best-seller became publishing's holy grail. Whiteside called his book *The Blockbuster Complex: Conglomerates, Show Business, and Book Publishing.*[1] The title projects a sense of cultural decline or contamination, one voiced to Whiteside by many of his informants from the old houses, and publicly by such writers as Archibald MacLeish, who, when Western Pacific Industries eyed Houghton Mifflin as a takeover possibility, decried the practice by which certain corporations, having no connection with literature, no knowledge of it, no interest in it, have acquired publishing houses not to enter publishing but to diversify their investments.[2]

Whiteside reports that the chairman of Western Pacific reasonably asked another defender of the old Boston house, "Are you under the impression that Houghton Mifflin is not a profit-motivated business?" (131). The question's rhetoric was lost on those who saw the bottom line as literature's enemy, and who, like Felix Rohatyn, said that the industry now catered to a limitless "appetite for vulgarity" and turned everything into "show business" (198)—thus supplying Whiteside with part of his subtitle. Whiteside generally remained calm, but did permit himself the judgment that with all books seen as undifferentiated "product," the hype that then pervades the industry is "in its very essence anti-art, and even anti-thought" (193).

The annals of cultural history resonate with such laments. Art repeatedly comes under threat from hustling commerce and its parasitism on the vulgar appetites. One earlier example will help establish a parallel, and launch the speculative argument of this essay. A hundred years ago, some observers of the literary scene were deploring what Gerald Stanley Lee called *The Lost Art of Reading.* He saw "literature" in 1902 as a "mere headlong, helpless literary rush." The product now of commercialized print culture, it was "getting to be the filling of orders—time-limited orders."[3] Christopher P. Wilson nicely describes that concern in a 1983 article on "the Demise of the Gentle

Reader" and attributes it more to the rise of the "cheap" magazine than to the yellow press or the new "frenzy" over best-sellers.[4]

That seems right. Lee deplored the acceleration of periodicity from annual to quarterly to monthly to weekly; but it was the mass circulation monthlies that arose in the 1890s that made most evident, through hundreds of bold advertisements printed in each issue, the commercial basis of the form. One had of course known that highbrow monthlies such as *Harper's* and *The Century* sought profits, just as one knew in 1978 that Houghton Mifflin was a business. The record $3.2 million bid at auction for Judith Krantz's *Princess Daisy* in 1979 made it harder to think of trade book publishing as the literary pastime of gentlemen. Similarly, the ads that by 1895 had bulked up *Munsey's, McClure's,* and the *Ladies' Home Journal,* along with boosterish editorial voices, plainly announced a new era in magazine publishing, and demanded a new art of reading.

I don't dismiss the recoil of gentle folk at commercialism in either instance—no more than Hawthorne's contempt for the "scribbling women" who outsold him, or Pope's for Grub Street dunces, or that of university-educated gentlemen such as Robert Greene for the "rude grooms" of Elizabethan popular theater, including the "upstart crow," Shakespeare. Yes, culture seems always to be in vulgar decline, just as the middle classes are always arising. But the perception of decline or contamination may signal a deeper and less repetitious change (perhaps a structural one), and so reward a closer look.

Certainly the "magazine revolution" took part in such a change. A brief price war in 1893 lowered the newsstand price of the new monthlies to ten cents each, less than the cost of their production. Within a few years this strategy not only yielded unprecedented circulations (a million for the *Ladies' Home Journal* by 1900) among, presumably, new demographic groups: it reconstituted the industry on a new foundation. As I have argued at length,[5] the publisher's main product was no longer the physical magazine, but the attention of its readers. The customers who bought that commodity, at rates pegged to circulation, were manufacturers of household goods such as breakfast cereals and cleansers. And they generally made their purchase through the intermediary of a new commercial institution: the full-service advertising agency, which prepared copy and graphics to put before the eyes of the consuming reader. This, of course, is the set of arrangements that has since grounded the magazine, newspaper, and then radio and television industries.

Did the "startling changes" deplored by Whiteside not only create mega-best-sellers with unprecedented payments to authors and hardback publishers but reconfigure the trade book industry itself?[6] I would say yes, though not in so tidy and sweeping a transformation as happened with magazines just before 1900. For some publishers there was a comparable shift in "product": no longer primarily the hardback books sold individually to ten thousand or a hundred thousand customers, but the right to do various things with the text, such as print a mass market paperback edition of it, offer it as a book club selection, turn it into a movie script, or license makers of dolls, clothing, china, greeting cards, and so on to use its images, words, and characters in their products. Licensing became not just an ancillary source of income, but "a way to market the product," where "the product" seems to be not even precisely the text, so much as an underlying or abstract intellectual property.[7] As revenue from subsidiary rights outran revenue from sales through bookstores, the most important customers for a publisher of such books became the Hollywood studio or television network or paperback house, or book club. Another homology: just as the modern advertising agency had come forward to advance the magazine by articulating it with the project of corporate makers of consumer goods, a new kind of agent came forward in the 1960s and after: the deal maker who articulated book publishing with other enterprises by orchestrating tie-ins and subsidiary rights and marketing strategies from the outset.

The change in social relationships was in fact more extensive and messier than that because, in many important cases, negotiations began not with a completed manuscript or sample chapter or prospectus, but with a promoter's concept. Whiteside relates a nice story to illustrate the buoyant high-handedness of deal-makers. One of them, David Obst, was sitting with producer Peter Guber outside the latter's Mulholland Drive house, overlooking Los Angeles. Guber said, "What would happen if all this burned down?" Obst replied, "There would be a terrible L.A. fire. Let's do the terrible L.A. fire as a book and a movie." They developed a "concept," found a writer to turn it into a book and sold it to Simon & Schuster, sold the movie rights to Columbia pictures for ten times what they had paid the author, then got a six-figure advance from Fawcett for the paperback rights on the strength of the movie sale. As Obst said, "This is an example of almost-no-risk publishing."[8] Or the book might not exist even as a concept until the success of a movie led to its "novelization." In such deals, the book is less a piece of intellectual property than one component of a marketing plan.

Of course a lot of trade book publishing went on through the time of these changes that had little in common with the promotion of *Princess Daisy* or the "spontaneous generation" of *The Great Los Angeles Fire.* Perhaps a more pervasive shift was the one with which Whiteside began: the mergers and takeovers that from the late 1960s on brought consolidation to an industry that had kept its unsystematic and entrepreneurial (not to say mom-and-pop) character through the era of the great corporation. To be sure, mergers and changes of ownership had been common long before 1965, as is evident in old industry names such as Houghton Mifflin, Harcourt Brace, and Little, Brown. So although more recent acquisitions such as Random House's of Knopf, Dell's of Dial Press, and Penguin's of Viking sometimes created strange bedfellows, they were nonetheless transactions of a familiar type. Some deals in the late 1960s were not. When CBS absorbed Holt, Rinehart & Winston; Gulf & Western acquired Pocket Books; ITT bought Howard Sams; Litton Industries swallowed the American Book Company and others; National General acquired Bantam; RCA, Random House; and Xerox, Ginn & Company, book publishers became subsidiaries of companies in other lines of production.[9] So not only were publishing mergers occurring at a furious pace, three or four times as fast as in all other areas of manufacturing and mining;[10] most companies buying trade houses were strangers to the publishing business, and some (Litton Industries, ITT), were in fields remote indeed from literature.

There were a few more such takeovers in the 1970s, and at least three attempts failed when the publisher fought off a culturally alien suitor: there was Western Pacific's courtship of Houghton Mifflin, already mentioned; Mattel's of Macmillan; and Western Union's of McGraw-Hill, which was a bit like Fitzwilliam Darcy's first offer to Elizabeth Bennett in *Pride and Prejudice* —the condescending suitor astonished at the ingratitude of his intended. However, as mergers proceeded briskly through tough economic times in the seventies and eighties (more than fifteen a year from 1974 to 1978), a different pattern came clear. The paradigmatic merger now brought a trade book publisher under the roof of an already huge entertainment or media corporation. The bought included Chilton Books, Simon & Schuster, Putnam, Ballantine, Book-of-the-Month Club, William Morrow, Bantam, Random

House, Viking, Wadsworth, Dell, Doubleday, Harper & Row. Buyers included ABC (later part of Capital Cities, then Disney), MCA, RCA, Gulf & Western (later, Paramount Communications, then part of Viacom), Time Inc. (to become Time Warner), Hearst, Advance Publications (the Newhouse empire), Westinghouse, and Times-Mirror. Another group of buyers deserves separate mention, because they acquired U.S. publishers from their bases in other countries. I have in mind German-based Holtzbrinck and Bertelsmann AG, the Dutch and English Reed Elsevier, the United Kingdom's Penguin Books and Pearson Longman, the Canadian International Thomson, and News Corporation, run and largely owned by Rupert Murdoch of Australia.

It is time to sift this pile of facts for some initial thoughts about changes in the structure and relations of trade book publishing from the late 1960s to the present time. First, the old New York hometown business is now thoroughly international. Not only do U.S. conglomerates sell entertainment and information to the rest of the world; major foreign corporations do the same here, and control a significant part of U.S. book production and sales. It is almost arbitrary to identify some of these corporations with a homeland, so dispersed are their activities.

Second, this used to be largely a freestanding industry. Now most of the chief American publishers are subsidiaries of media conglomerates. No one company can exactly typify that group, or stand as a model for the rest. But a look at the holdings of Time Warner (in 1997 the biggest of these giants, with $25 billion in sales) will suggest the comprehensiveness of their operations. Unsurprisingly, Time Warner owned the Warner Brothers film studio and the magazines of Henry Luce's old company (*Time, Fortune, Life, Sports Illustrated, People*). It also owned twenty other magazines, Castle Rock Entertainment, and New Line Cinema, plus a thousand movie screens outside this country and a library of six thousand films. Beyond its original base in magazines and movies, it embraced WB, a new television network; a dozen or so TV programing and production companies; the largest cable and satellite system in the United States as well as several global channels (owing largely to the acquisition of the Turner Broadcasting System in 1994); three music labels accounting for over 20 percent of U.S. music sales; CNN Radio; two of Atlanta's major league sports teams as well as the Goodwill Games; a 49 percent interest in the Six Flags theme and amusement parks; and some even more miscellaneous enterprises. It is tempting to include Time Warner's book business among the latter, since it brought in less than 5 percent of the company's revenue, through Warner Books and Little, Brown, among seven publishers, and four mail order houses, including Book-of-the-Month Club and Time-Life Books. But the activities carried on in this negligible corner of the corporation ranked it fourth in sales among American book publishing companies and accounted for 6 percent of all U.S. book revenues.[11]

That brings me to a third point. Although media conglomerates dominate trade book publishing—for example, three of the four largest ones own the three largest book publishers—the biggest conglomerates are not now and were not originally book publishers, with the partial exception of Bertelsmann, whose book clubs were foundational to its growth. At the historical cores of these companies were movies, newspapers, magazines, broadcasting, cable, music, and—beyond the border of media "content"—xerography, electrical equipment, communications networks, and so on. Not books. It's interesting to note, in this connection, that several book publishers, perhaps deciphering the "mene, mene, tekel, upharsin" that appeared one day on their paneled walls, branched out into other entertainment fields: Harcourt Brace Jovanovich into marine parks; Doubleday, the New York Mets; and Macmillan, band instruments, for instance. None of these eclectic moves laid the foundation of a media empire.

And fourth, trade book publishing grew more concentrated. At the time of the Great War, no publisher accounted for much more than 2 percent of book sales, and concentration proceeded only gradually until the wave of mergers gathered after 1965. By 1993 the largest publisher, Simon & Schuster, brought in close to 10 percent of book revenues, and the ten leaders, just over 60 percent.[12] While this was a significant change, it hardly amounted to oligopoly, nor matched the degree of centralization in other media, or, indeed, in textbook publishing, which is in some ways almost a separate industry, and which will now vanish from the already cluttered radar screen of this essay. Furthermore, the point about concentration needs qualifying in two other ways. But, for the tidiness of my argument, I will defer that part of the exposition until later—stopping now, only to remark in passing the much more intense concentration in book*selling* over the last thirty years. To wit, in 1972, the four largest bookstore chains took in less than 12 percent of revenue from trade books, but in 1994, just the big two accounted for 43 percent, while sales at independent book stores declined from 72 percent of the total in 1958 to 25 percent in 1994[13]—and those figures, of course, antedate the rise of Amazon.com.

I have meant to persuade you that trade book publishing has in recent decades passed through a transformation quite different in its parameters from that of the magazine industry a hundred years ago, but at least as sweeping in its rearrangement of basic elements and economic relations. It would be only a modest hyperbole to say, for instance, that large-scale trade book publishing no longer exists as a separate enterprise. Of the old majors, only a handful, such as Houghton Mifflin and Norton, remain independent. What might such a change tell us about the movement of history? A modest question, to whose complexities I will devote the remainder of this essay.

The magazine revolution both responded to and helped bring about the shift from nineteenth-century entrepreneurial capitalism to the kind of corporate capitalism that prevailed through most of the twentieth century. Having told my version of that story at length in *Selling Culture* and reprised parts of it in essays 7 and 11, I will compress it ruthlessly here. In the post–Civil War decades, captains of American industry remade society to their purposes, yet failed to stabilize or securely manage it. To defend against declining profits, ruthless competition, high risk of bankruptcy, system-wide volatility, and the threat of class warfare, they had pursued various strategies to secure their project of development, but nothing worked for long. What did work—not as a cooperative venture, of course—was the establishment of the big, vertically integrated corporation, which sought with much success to control production all the way from the gathering of raw materials to the marketing of final goods. Its work included careful management of the sales process itself, which had previously been left to chance, and to a variety of middlemen with interests different from those of the manufacturers.

That is where magazine publishers and advertising agencies came into the picture. Pursuing *their* own interests, they helped corporations develop a way of marketing that made the realization of profit less chancy. Specifically, crackers and toothpaste and soap were now uniformly packaged, brand-named, and advertised directly to consumers around the country, thus ensuring a demand not contingent on the whim of the jobber or storekeeper. Ad agencies sent the message out via newspapers, billboards, streetcar posters, trading cards, direct mail, and so on. But the best *national* carriers were the ten-cent general and women's magazines, once the new editors and publishers had established their respectability and pushed their combined circulations well up into the millions. To repeat, then, a dramatic reorganization of print culture around 1900 both enabled and was driven by a still deeper transformation of the whole economic system.

Is it possible that the changes in book publishing itemized in the first part of this essay participated in another epochal shift? Let me postpone my address to that question while I turn briefly to a logically prior one: *are* there historical epochs? (And how can we tell, and what difference does it make?) In ordinary talk, we freely parcel out historical time in handy units. There is the much-controverted millennium that ended either December 31, 1999, or a year later. There are the centuries (though historians may amend their arbitrary boundaries—the "long eighteenth century," for instance, or the hundred years between Waterloo and the assassination at Sarajevo, or the "short twentieth century (1914–89)—in efforts to reconcile them with big events or changes). Decades seem to have a special appeal as filing systems for the relatively recent past. We all know what we mean by the twenties, the thirties, the fifties, and the sixties. Maybe the seventies or eighties will in time acquire that sort of reputation. I thrice taught a course that I called "The American 1890s" (after an excellent book by Larzer Ziff, the third Wiggins lecturer) and eventually persuaded myself that everything of significance took place in that decade—thus exemplifying (Stuart M.) Blumin's Law: "It happened in my period." But whenever one of these decimal conventions does segment the historical process in a conceptually useful way, that is purely accidental. So historians have generally preferred less metronomic divisions, such as the Middle Ages, the Renaissance, early modern Europe, the Age of Empire, and many more—each with its polemical freight, and each endlessly contested.

In a broad Marxist tradition, I think of historical periods as times between fundamental changes in economic and social relations. Capitalism is the epoch during which labor power is a commodity, when factory owners push aside the nobility and gentry and dominate the social order, when social surplus appears in the form of profit, and so on. Is it fruitful to divided the history of capitalism itself into smaller periods? I will not pursue this difficult question beyond repeating my suggestion that around 1900 corporate capitalism became dominant and adding that it decisively altered the ways people lived and connected to one another—from the development of domesticity organized around brand-named commodities, to the explosion of mass entertainments and national advertising, to the emergence of the modern research university, the suburbs, the automobile, a new professional-managerial class, and much else. Just this capacity to connect seemingly disparate phenomena, and so invite explanation and theory, makes periodization worth attempting.

Let me emphasize the point: historical periods are constructions. They are not real, in the way that, perhaps, a real meteor hit the Yucatan some eons ago and periodized the evolutionary process to the great advantage of us mammals. The tidal wave of corporate mergers that recombined one-third of all manufacturing assets from 1898 to 1902 was real and is recognized by historians of every persuasion, as was the wave of mergers in the cultural industries that began in the 1960s and gave us today's media giants. But the epoch of corporate capitalism—or Fordism, or monopoly capital, to mention just some of its proposed names—which lasted through roughly the first three-quarters of the twentieth century, is not real in the same way. It merits a place in our historical understanding only if it can bring things together in fresh and illuminating and (in my view) explanatory ways—for I am not sure what else historical explanation might be.

That said, I will now briefly consider the usefulness, as a speculative instrument, of the idea that American capitalism has recently experienced a metamorphosis comparable in significance to the one that occurred a hundred years ago. This is by no means a new idea; many scholars and journalists have advanced one or another version of it.[14] Evidence of a shift abounds and is familiar to anyone who keeps up with the economic news. The difficulty is to make a brief selection of evidence, here, that will allow a judgment as to the depth of the change and ease the way back to books and print culture. Let me begin by summarizing again the economic troubles that beset American capitalism around thirty years ago.[15]

Profits as a proportion of national income declined (as they had in the late nineteenth century). So did productivity. Inflation soon threatened to end the postwar boom. The federal debt began its notorious rise in the late seventies, along with personal debt, and, a bit later, corporate debt. Meanwhile, competition from Japan and Europe put U.S. capitalism on the defensive. The balance of trade turned negative in 1975, and has worsened spectacularly since then. The dollar began to fade against stronger currencies; then, after the Bretton Woods agreement fell apart in 1971, exchange rates fluctuated wildly. (All these difficulties were aggravated by the oil price crisis of 1973.) Unemployment, which was below 4 percent in 1969, rose rapidly and hovered near a figure twice that high for more than two decades. And finally, real wages, which had risen steadily since 1940 (and, except for the depression years, pretty much throughout the whole era of corporate capitalism), stalled for a few years after 1970 and then dropped about 10 percent.

Now, if we pull the last two items (wages and unemployment) out of that flat list of setbacks, and consider them more dynamically, they can reappear as intended results of a corporate strategy: that is, to reduce the gains made by workers in the U.S. throughout the Fordist regime, in order to improve productivity and competitiveness, and so fend off the assault of Japanese and European capital. Whatever degree of consciousness or intent one posits, there is no question about the outcome. The core labor force of the Fordist period has in the U.S. shrunk back to around 10 percent of the workers in manufacturing. Companies reduce labor costs and increase flexibility by subcontracting and outsourcing to smaller, ununionized shops, by replacing core workers with temporary and part-time labor, and above all by moving production facilities to places where labor is cheap and docile and under severe governmental discipline. Of course capital has always sought to outflank labor, but the number and variety of schemes for doing so now are unprecedented—from building state-of-the-art factories in South Asia to be staffed by young girls, to encouraging maquiladoras along the Mexican border, to reinventing the sweatshop in Los Angeles as well as in El Salvador. That these changes have at least eroded or subverted Fordism is plain. For just one telling example: in the 1950s and sixties, the number of people employed by the Fortune 500 biggest companies doubled, but after 1970 it actually declined. Another: the largest employer in the United States is now a temp agency.

This change invites thought about downsizing and the "lean and mean" company so highly valued these days. In sharp contrast to the Fordist corporation with its steady production flows, stable workforce, and concentrated effort to market what it made and make what it could sell in a mass market, a new kind of business organization characterizes the present economic order. A helpful analysis from the Iacocca Institute at Lehigh University calls it the "agile company," and its strategies "agile competition." The company tends to make knowledge-based products or sell knowledge itself, accompanied by services to customers. Although it mass-produces goods, it can turn them out in arbitrary lot sizes, and customize them along the way to meet the needs of individual customers. Thus, at an extreme, John Deere now makes seeders only to match individual orders, They come off a single production line, but can be configured in more than two million ways, on eighty-one chassis types.[16]

As this suggests, there now exists an astonishing proliferation of goods and segmentation of markets, with advertisers targeting narrower and narrower groups, defined by taste, ethnicity, age, ability to pay, and so on.[17] Quaker Oats, Ivory Soap, the Gillette razor, and many other products from the corporate revolution have held steady in the market for a hundred years, changing little from one year or decade to the next. Today, new products enter (and leave) the market in very different ways. A brand name like Seiko might compare to these in recognition or market share, but Seiko is not one watch or several: it is more than three thousand models. Revo, a Bausch & Lomb subsidiary, markets sunglasses in eighty frame styles with four choices of lens, at prices of up to two hundred dollars a pair.[18] Sunglasses used to be utilitarian, almost anonymous, and cheap. Now the customer can purchase several pairs at fancy prices to proclaim distinction, accent this morning's outfit, or express today's mood. In the world of agile competition this process is aptly called "sneakerization."

It is not limited to areas of fashion and personal display; high-tech companies also feverishly develop new products to stay even with rivals. David Harvey estimated that the half-life of a product in the Fordist regime had been five to seven years, and just eighteen months for entertainment and information goods in the 1980s. It is surely less than that now. At Panasonic, the "product cycle time" for consumer electronic goods is about ninety days: when a new product reaches the market, its successor generation is already in development. I own shares, as part of a mutual fund, in a company called Maxim, whose annual report announces that it brought out 383 new products in 1999, compared to 284 in 1998 and 250 in 1997. (It makes "linear and mixed-signal integrated circuits" to detect "real world" phenomena such as temperature and voice and convert them into digital form.) Linear Technology's annual report notes that in fiscal 2000 it "introduced over 100 new products addressing a broad cross section of analog functions and end market applications." Companies of this sort compete to achieve the "lowest concept-to-cash-flow time." The fact that rapid innovation characterizes the "hot" knowledge and service industries and also such lines of simple consumer goods as sneakers and sunglasses suggests that agile competition is becoming a prevalent strategy. It might make sense, then, to divide American capitalism's last 150 years into three periods, according to which business activity was site of the most intense competition and development: until 1900, mass production; from 1900 to 1970, the sales effort; since 1970, design, as an integrated part of the whole process, and in rapid response to the customer's wishes.

Needless to say, Fordist corporations could not step that lightly without refashioning themselves. Those that are healthy today have done so through "just-in-time" inventory management, lean production, draconian labor policies, subcontracting, and so on. (Toyota and other Japanese companies were among the pathbreakers, driving American companies, belatedly, to follow their lead.) The change has gone well beyond such internal practices, to the incessant reconfiguration of whole companies. Mergers and acquisitions are now a staple of the daily business news. Corporations sell off divisions and whole businesses with almost equal frequency. They subdivide: ATT, having been broken up by the government, is as I write openly considering whether to break itself up, now, into four parts. Also in the news are agreements between Bertelsmann and Napster and between Universal and MP3—that is, between large record companies and the Internet music services they have been accusing of piracy. If they happen, these will be in a sense forced marriages, but otherwise typical of many collaborations and truces in the high-tech areas. Most surprisingly, pairs or groups of competing corporations often enter into temporary partnerships, forming what theorists of agility call "virtual corporations," with no geographical headquarters or factories, to seek profits in ventures that none of them could pursue on its own. To be sure, Fordist corporations struck unwritten agreements (and occasionally secret written ones) not to enter into price competition with one another, but the aim of such practices was to sustain the market share and autonomy of each firm. Now, firms combine in order to create or enter new markets. The agile corporation is a shape-changer. It may herald a paradigm shift for capitalism.

In sketching it, I have barely mentioned globalization, which many consider its distinctive feature. Others point out, however, that long before the industrial revolution, capitalism established itself as a global system with plantations, extraction of metals, the slave trade, and colonization—and that industrialism itself built upon global trade. Certainly the rise of the global corporation was under way well before 1970, when the top three hundred based in the United States gathered 40 percent of their profits abroad—one of the many signs read by Richard J. Barnet and Ronald E. Muller as already achieved transcendence of the nation state, in their book, *Global Reach: The Power of the Multinational Corporations*.[19] I do think that late twentieth-century globalization has departed qualitatively from earlier schemes. The dispersal of high-tech mass production, to Indonesia or the Philippines or wherever, may in time amount to a wholesale deindustrialization of First World countries and a dramatic shift in the international division of labor. Surely it differs in critical ways from shutting down a textile mill in Massachusetts and opening one in South Carolina.

Multinational companies now use their economic power to press advantageous deals upon Third World governments, often with avid assistance from our own government. The nation state is not, in my view, withering away, but corporations have encroached more and more upon its ability to set foreign policy—not to mention policy on labor and the environment. Or, in a semirandom list, think of the nearly half of U.S. imports and exports that take place within multinationals; the enormous increase in foreign investment (up fourfold in the 1980s alone, with much of it for the first time coming *into* the United States); the tripling of international loans in the same decade; the almost instantaneous movement of capital around the world in a dazzling array of speculative vehicles; or the challenge of foreign corporations, so that barely a third of the world's five hundred largest are now based in this country. These are major shifts, surveyed handily in William Greider's recent *One World, Ready or Not: The Manic Logic of Global Capitalism*,[20] which makes an interesting contrast to *Global Reach*. One could add the proliferation of organizations and agreements such as the World Trade Organization, GATT, and the North Atlantic Free Trade Agreement, to stitch together the new world system.

For all that, I suggest that the dismantling of the Fordist corporation and its refashioning as another kind of institution with a different relation to labor power is a more fundamental index of epochal change. In any case, my aim in rocketing through these stratospheric regions of thought is not to provide a decisive characterization but to see if even a roughly sketched hypothesis of epochal transition in the last thirty years helps understand the changes in book publishing with which I began. One reason I have for optimism is that in a parallel inquiry I have intermittently pursued for a while, I have convinced myself that the hypothesis does help explain, through the commodification of knowledge, a corresponding transformation of the university into something like a money-making business; its increasing reliance on temporary and part-time labor; the decline of most professions; and what I take to be the dispersal of the professional-managerial class that formed alongside and within the giant corporation a hundred years ago.[21] I do realize that the desire to lasso and corral diverse phenomena with a unified theory can signal paranoia. But then, if some paranoids in this vein become unabombers, there is also a quiet version of historical imperialism that my 1992 predecessor in the Wiggins lecture series, Ian Willison, expressed in his encouragingly commonsensical way: "the history of the book is part of general history."[22]

Even a quick glance inside the busy world of publishing makes it tempting to read the changes of the past thirty years as instancing the broader history about which I have been speculating. Publishing has become a more international business, especially within the English-speaking world. It is geographically far more mobile now than it was fifty years ago. Mergers proceed apace. In the first six months of 1995, *Publishers Weekly* reported Harper-Collins's acquisition of Westview, Holtzbrinck's of Macmillan (it already owned St. Martins and other important U.S. publishers), Pearson PLC's of Troll Associates (children's book fairs and school clubs), and Simon & Schuster's purchase of a 20 percent interest in Byron Preiss Multimedia (with the intent of selling its CD-ROMs through bookstores). And almost every issue of *Publishers Weekly* during those six months brought news of deals and partnerships between freestanding companies, for strategic marketing. Bertelsmann, for instance, combined with America Online to sell "interactive services" in Europe. Time-Life Books, wanting to be more visible in bookstores, arranged with Williams-Sonoma to publish books about gourmet cooking and with the Nature Company to publish outdoor books for kids. John Wiley joined with Adweek Magazines to create a new "Adweeks Books" imprint. Random House and Kiplinger set out to publish business books together. Random House had invested in or joined with no fewer than four electronic publishers in the previous year, and was one of many old-line publishers branching out into multimedia forms. Flexible accumulation was in effect *Publishers Weekly*'s headline story.

Although amalgamations and takeovers were a significant part of that story in 1995 and had amounted to the most obvious change in the industry since 1960 (consolidation), an interesting countertrend proceeded alongside the mergers. The number of book-publishing firms actually increased about 150 percent between 1960 and 1990, while the number of titles published annually in the United States more than tripled, to a surprising 55,000.[23] There are well over a million American titles in print. I interpret these numbers as evidence that in spite of intense economic concentration, and in spite of the best-seller's centrality for the big firms, publishing also became more segmented, eclectic, and nimble, both in the proliferation of specialty houses and in the profusion of books published for every taste and need. What looked like a belated move toward Fordism to observers such as Whiteside has actually resulted in an array of niche products perhaps not totally unlike sneakers and sunglasses and mixed-signal integrated circuits. Even a number of best sellers (campaign biographies, stories of famous recent crimes and trials and disasters) exemplify lightning-fast design to meet or shape a market need, with the concept-to-cash-flow interval reduced in extreme cases to a week or two.

I think the same point applies if we view book publishing in its main institutional context, that of the media conglomerate. Here, too, we find a steady and intensifying concentration of ownership, and hear with alarm that twelve or eight or maybe six corporations could soon command the apparatus that puts out what we read, see, and listen to for enlightenment and fun. It may be worth stating the obvious about them, however: that they have not divided up the territory medium by medium, with one or two firms owning the newspapers, another monopolizing cinema, a third in charge of big sports—as did the steel, oil, and car oligopolies of the Fordist epoch. Instead, each conglomerate holds a bouquet of cultural enterprises from various media. That's because the rationale for this mode of corporate expansion is not monopoly but agility and synergy.

At least so goes the insider talk, in *Publishers Weekly*. The theme of flexibility is pervasive there, but I will highlight just one story out of many pertinent ones from the first six months of 1995, in order to sample the prevailing ethos: "Newcomb Looking to Instill New Corporate Culture at Simon and Schuster," by Jim Milliot.[24] The impetus behind cultural change was Viacom's 1994 acquisition of Paramount, which already owned Simon & Schuster. This opened up the way to projects such as the use of Blockbuster Video's database to advance book sales directly to consumers; the use of Blockbuster locations "as the on-demand printing business grows"; and the collaboration of Simon & Schuster with Nickelodeon on a children's book imprint. (This pair of divisions soon initiated a "Beavis and Butthead" book series, as well.)[25] The book company also looked to increase sales in Latin America and Asia, in line with Viacom's plan for global expansion: specifically, according to another source, to earn 40 percent of its revenues outside the United States by 2000, and challenge News Corporation and Time-Warner for international leadership.[26]

Summing up, Jonathan Newcomb, president and CEO of Simon & Schuster, said, "The market is changing dramatically and we have to be able to react quickly." The publisher must exploit corporate investments in technology, and use its own "back office functions," to support teams of employees, and let them "succeed at a unit level." To facilitate such rapid response missions, Newcomb created a "venture fund," which divisions could tap for imaginative new projects. The next issue of *Publishers Weekly* reported on a new Simon & Schuster Web site, to help "market our intellectual properties in a broad range of distribution pathways, multiple-media formats, and emerging markets."[27] In short, the corporate culture that the venerable publisher is learning from its conglomerate parent is one of commando-like rapid response and global mobility, within the very un-Fordist, large corporation.

So evolved, in fifteen years, the principle of synergy Whiteside had remarked with something between distaste and horror. Although it was and is a misleading hyperbole to speak of books as software for the movies (one-third of movies do derive from or germinate along with books, but the fraction of books that become movies or TV series is infinitesimal), there is no doubt that the blockbuster phenomenon retains its momentum. Many synergistic practices that were new and seemed outlandish when Whiteside wrote are standard now, including the tie-in, the package deal, the novelization, and so on. Michael Ovitz, head of the Creative Artists Agency, told Whiteside that the agency business was changing beyond recognition: "[T]here are a myriad ways of putting projects together. . . . We represent authors *and* producers *and* directors. We basically develop material that we haven't actually bought. We can put together all the elements for a project, and, with the agreement of the principals, sell the result as a package."[28] A process of germination such as this puts the emphasis on design for specific market purposes; when it occurs inside a media conglomerate it perfectly instances agile competition, in which the book division can play an important role.

A more general point is that along with concentration in media and entertainment has come an elaboration and hybridization of channels, formats, and media, often now with digital assistance, comparable to the proliferation of sneakers, watches, and e-products mentioned earlier. In this abundance, culture seems almost indistinguishable from not-culture—from the multiplying services and products on offer to help us make and save money, stay fit, cure our ills, travel, communicate, and choose which to buy among the millions of things flexible capital puts before our eyes and at our fingertips. An ever finer segmentation of markets accompanies this cornu-copia. Before 1970, for instance, we tended to imagine the huge audience of prime-time TV as where all commercial culture was tending. Now, that au-dience is thinned out and redistributed over hundreds of cable channels, thousands of videos, millions of Web sites, just about all the music ever recorded, and so on. The mass market of the Fordist epoch exfoliates into a constantly shifting array of niche markets. Three thousand publishers and a million books in print are well adapted to niche production; from this per-spective it scarcely matters (though it does matter politically) that 2 percent of American publishers sell 75 percent of the books, and almost all the blockbusters.[29] Both the 2 percent and the remaining 98 percent are deeply committed to niche production and marketing.

Furthermore, when a relatively undifferentiated mass audience does come together, for a planned sensation like *Titanic* or the Olympics, or to partici-pate in a media spasm (such as occurs after the unexpected death of a John F. Kennedy Jr. or a Princess Diana, or during a scandal such as the O. J. Simpson trial or the Clinton-Lewinsky saga, or after an undecidable vote for presi-dent), books are always part of the mix, helping create the gee-whiz aura, or squeezing out the last profits when the spasm subsides.[30] Books are well suited to flexible accumulation because they can accommodate and advance agile design at various stages of the process and contribute both to the as-sembly of mass audiences and to the satisfaction of niche demand.

Before moving to my conclusion, I note that other media held separately during the Fordist regime and now incorporated in media empires have tended to converge in their practices. Magazines, already owned and man-aged in groups back then (Curtis, Hearst, and so on), are now increasingly part of conglomerate empires.[31] On the other hand, most magazines were always niche products, and since the demise of such "general" Fordist dino-saurs as *Look, Colliers,* the old *Life,* and the *Saturday Evening Post,* all maga-zines are more specifically targeted. The process goes on apace, with over four thousand consumer magazines and eight thousand trade magazines on the market today, and with such mass circulation periodicals as *Time* put-ting out regional and ever more finely customized editions. It seems likely that soon you will be able to have your own personalized versions of na-tional magazines, with digital help. Television, by contrast, was the most concentrated media industry before 1970, but on the Fordist model. Now it, too, swims in the conglomerate sea and it, too, multiplies channels and programs catering to every subgroup with enough disposable cash to be of interest.

One may, incidentally, discern an analogous shift in strategy even in businesses where products do not change or proliferate. Take Coca-Cola: it sells few brands, and sells the main one partly by celebrating its secret and historically invariant formula. The company has long been thoroughly global. According to Ira Herbert, who was involved in the marketing of Coca-Cola for many years, thirty years ago the company made its advertisements for the U.S. market and distributed them globally. In the late 1970s it developed "pattern advertising," which "could be adjusted to fit the local environment, . . . and could be changed or edited as long as the concept wasn't changed— as long as the feel wasn't changed." In the early 1990s the company adopted "a more fragmented approach, based on the assumption that the media today is fragmented and that each of those groups that are targeted by that media core should be communicated to in their own way with their own message, with their own sound, with their own visualization."[32] In short, the company now promoted its chemically unchanging soft drink as many different products, with the difference magically created by advertising. As the capitalist market expands into more and more areas of life—becomes "universal," in Marx's forecast—it apparently wants to offer each consumer his or her unique gratifications, achieving flexible accumulation through personally tailored consumption.

I have strayed far enough from books, and from my historical speculations. To resume the latter: I have asked you to consider a narrative of the past hundred and some years, divided into three tidy chapters with three main actors:

1. The Industrial Entrepreneur (–1900)
2. The Giant, Vertically Integrated Corporation (1900–1970)
3. The Agile Corporation (1970–)

In chapter 1, mass production is king, but profits, though often large, are also mercurial. Around 1900, and after a time of crisis, capital makes its world safer by concentrating on the sales effort and guaranteeing the realization of profit on its mass-produced goods. But after the postwar boom the creaky Fordist corporation itself becomes the problem, and in chapter 3, under hostile fire from Japanese and European competitors, it either modulates into a nimble, shape-changing outfit or gives way to leaner new entrants.

I propose that this scheme organizes a variety of events and processes in the conceptually satisfying way we expect from epochal periodization. During the first of the three epochs, for instance, we find raw exploitation of labor and outbreaks of class warfare. By the end of the second, labor and capital achieve a benefit-sharing truce—from which capital defects under pressure, seeking and largely achieving in the third epoch a downsized, more flexible, less unionized, global workforce. Closer to the initial subject of this essay: in the first chapter there is no regularized, national, commercial culture. The culture industry emerges along with brand-named commodities and national advertising around 1900, helping the new corporation achieve stability and market control. A good deal of concentration takes place across the culture industry, too—radio and television, movies, magazines, newspapers— but within discrete media. Before 1970, culture-making companies (along with their partners in other sectors) once again take the lead in reorganizing the economic order. They form conglomerates that seek agility through strategic niche marketing and the synergy of media spasms and blockbusters. The culture they sell spans the globe and serves as a vehicle for agile marketing of other goods, knowledges, and services.

I have broadly sketched the evolution of trade book publishing from the Fordist to the flexible regime but have ignored an obvious question about this industry in the earlier transition from entrepreneurial to corporate capitalism: why did it not participate in *that* change? My answer is that books had nothing to offer the new corporations of 1900: they could not, like magazines, serve as a dependable medium through which to sell the attention of audiences to makers of toothpaste and canned soup; nor could books themselves be turned into brand named products for repeat purchase. They could not become Fordist commodities.[33] They could, however, figure in the combinatory possibilities sought by flexible media corporations, which partially solved the brand name difficulty by turning a few authors' names (James Michener, Barbara Cartland, Stephen King, and so on) into brands, or by letting the book's fame sell the movie, and vice versa. And the niche appeal of the overwhelming majority of books, a drawback for the Fordist corporation, became an attraction for the agile company skilled in strategic marketing. Although media conglomerates have not always been able to digest publishers without heartburn, I do not see a reversal of the general trend.

Where in fact is the industry headed next? This essay has already exceeded the limits of my competence and of my capacity for precision. But two recent articles by Jason Epstein in the *New York Review of Books*[34] provoke me to an afterword. Epstein predicts that electronic means will soon allow producers to bypass the centralized, physical production of books, creating texts in various forms, available at many sites, to satisfy the wants of individuals, and thus bring an end to the "hit or miss distribution" that still bedevils the industry. If so, it will have attained the farthest horizon of niche marketing.[35] Epstein also thinks that in the face of such developments, media conglomerates "face certain extinction." Reorganization, maybe; but I hope to have shown that there is no contradiction, in the epoch of flexible accumulation, between great corporate size and rapid response to shifting market challenges.

I3

THE PERSONAL AS HISTORY

◆

David Bleich asked me in 1998 to write on this topic for a book he planned to edit with Deborah Holdstein. I agreed, more in a spirit of friendly obligation than out of enthusiasm for the project. It was, in fact, at best uncomfortable for me to write this essay, and at worst a felt violation of professional ethics. As I dragged myself through the task I warmed to it, and in the end was (am) pleased with the result. I thank David for the stimulus to think more than I had done about what it means to be a person in a profession, in addition to what professions are and where they came from, about which I had been thinking for twenty-five years.

When I summon up remembrance of my early teaching years, lively courses and fine students swim to the surface, but chiefly a feeling of inadequacy bordering on desperation. A twenty-three-year-old standing in coat and tie before privileged eighteen-year-olds, I took attendance with gravity, carefully announced that papers would be due or would be returned at the end of the hour, passed around a list of conference times, said, "OK, please turn to Orwell's essay," and withal sought to prolong the safe time during which there could be no question who was in charge. I knew the script. They knew the script.

"Mr. So-and-so" (no first names in those days; students were "Mr.," I was "Mr.," our famous professors were "Mr.," this was Harvard), "Mr. So-and-so, what is the assumption behind that first sentence?" My lesson plan spoke through me, but would it speak through Mr. So-and-so? If yes, back to the script, but suppose he got it wrong? Should I put the same question to Mr. Such-and-such and keep going until someone hit the answer that matched my plan? Kindergarten stuff. Come back to Mr. So-and- so? Try to figure out the nature of his mistake? Tease the right answer out of him? Suppose he didn't know what an assumption was? Suppose he hadn't read that part of the assignment? A bad breakdown in the script. Do I reprimand him? By what authority? Suppose he wasn't listening? Doesn't care what an assumption is? Can't see why he should be studying logic and rhetoric instead of writing like Thomas Wolfe or playing squash? A worse breakdown, especially if he should through an intonation or a gesture or glance at his friend in the next seat open up such vistas of indifference. Suppose, worse still, that he is unhappy, homesick, afraid, needs me to be something other than a nervous teaching fellow, trying to make it through this difficult hour, on script?

The hour might—usually did, I guess—include moments when learning happened. Certainly there were times I thought I had something to teach: how to explicate "The Unknown Citizen," or which introductory paragraphs on a dittoed sheet from students' essays were stilted or superfluous, and which purposely taut. I remember one or two times (doubtless there were more) when students talked with animation to one another and to me, and the class felt more like a conversation among smart people about matters of serious interest than like a test of my skill at impersonating a professor. But the high point of the hour was that of its cresting toward a close—of astonished realization that I could once again surf onto the beach with my hoax intact. Then the low-stakes busyness of giving out the next assignment, returning or collecting papers, perhaps sympathetically granting an extension, assuring a dutiful student that his missing next Wednesday's class would not leave him in too deep a hole. Human exchanges. Then out the door and the rest of the way back to a life I could recognize as my own. Buoyantly if the class had gone "well," with shame or relief if not. Two days or five days or a week before I had to stare down humiliation again.

How I spent those intervals: reading for orals, working on my dissertation, drinking with friends, being domestic. Work or play—at first with ease of mind, with teaching anxiety at a distance. It came nearer each day. Procrastination, then panic. Grading papers helped. A practical step, a manageable duty. But it, too, could let the specter into my study if I relaxed my guard. Sure, I was way ahead of most freshmen (but not of a precocious few) in my command of grammar, usage, diction—the comp teacher's trade secrets. On the other hand, why did I seem to be spattering as many "dics" and "grs" and "trs" and "awks" on each batch of themes as on the batch before? "Work harder on organization," I would write, but hadn't I said that last time? And when I peeked at my grade book before settling on a judicious C+, depressing to see that I had given him C+ last week, too, and every week except for the beginning-of-semester D–, which had terrorized him into paying attention. What was I teaching, really?

Back to panic, and a quick end to "the sad account of fore-bemoaned moan" allusively promised in the opening sentence of this essay. When panic got the better of avoidance, I began what I thought of as preparation for class—an activity so excessive and so poorly attuned to the challenge of helping students improve their reading and thinking and writing that there should be another term for it: depreparation? pedagogical disablement? I read tomorrow's text as if it were Talmud, amassing enough commentary to fill a semester's class hours and put the most rabbinical of students to sleep. A few years later, in my first regular job, the problem shifted: now I often taught about daunting Great Books (Homer, the New Testament, Dostoevsky), already encrusted with commentary I had no time to learn while trying to keep one chapter or book ahead of my students. Either way, nights-before developed along the same pattern. A gathering awareness that I could never build my teacherly fortress high enough; 1:00 A.M., 2:00 A.M., I'll finish in the morning, can't sleep, guzzle a quart (truly? so memory tells me) of cheap sherry, destroy consciousness; set the alarm for 5:30, shatter my coma with its ringing; waken consciousness again with a Molotov cocktail of coffee, shower, and fear; cobble together a disorderly sheaf of teaching notes; proceed grimly to class, do the opening rituals, and launch my professor act one more time.

To be sure, another part of my memory says it can't have been that dismal. Some students told me how much they thought they had learned from my classes. A few hung out in my office, seemed to value my conversation and even advice, became friends. The director of the freshman writing course, Harold C. Martin, visited my class, read my comments on papers,[1] said I was doing fine. Later he made me "head section man," then invited me to collaborate in the making of two textbooks.[2] I came to Wesleyan (my first and only regular job) trailing clouds of pedagogical glory. Tenure was quick and easy, though I wonder still if I would have made the grade had my judges paid even the most perfunctory attention to students' views of my teaching. There was no scheme of assessment in the early 1960s. Hearsay ruled. Wesleyan promoted those making a mark in scholarship and assumed their teaching to be commensurate. We were "scholar-teachers," with the teacher part in rhetorical boldface, but the scholar part dominant in tenure case law. No surprise, that, to anyone familiar with academic folkways and the economy of institutional prestige.

"Scholarship." The word resounds with dignity, implies solidity and permanence. ("Scholarship sublime," mocked Gilbert and Sullivan.) By contrast, "teaching" suggests interminable activity, pushing a boulder up the mountain, never reaching the top. The end of a course: respite, free time for scholarship. The end of a career: a fading hologram of Mr. Chips, while one's scholarship endures, in print, on one's curriculum vitae (a telling phrase), and in the edifice of knowledge—monuments of unaging intellect. These hyperboles seem to me to capture something powerful in the ethos I learned without being exactly taught. Scholarly writing was to be my real career. I was to pursue truth and get it into print when I found it. Fantasy whispered that I might become a hero of the intellect. Short of that, my fresh and yet solid contributions to knowledge would, along with the learning that grounded them, earn me repute and fund my authority.[3]

It is a common criticism of the academic institution that the privileging of research devalues teaching. I am after a related but different point: that one's authority as a teacher is supposed to *derive* from one's effort and achievement in research. That relation may hold pretty well in a research seminar for graduate students and post docs in biochemistry. And indeed it worked for me in similar settings: giving an MLA paper was a breeze compared to teaching an English 101 class. But universities house many renowned chemists who failed in introductory courses, and they at least "know" the whole field of chemistry, while for my generation (and to an extent still), advanced study and research in English added scarcely a tittle to one's authority as a composition teacher. In a liberal arts college such as Wesleyan, there were in fact very few settings where advanced training and research translated into classroom authority. I was, in the early 1960s, amassing scholarly credentials at a good pace, while floundering in my courses in spite and because of the extravagant labors I have described.

Now clearly, something was askew in the expectations we bright boys had for unity of academic being. The ideology of research as guarantor of good teaching collapses for the reason just stated, and for a still more obvious one: scholarship and teaching are very different social relations. Among many dimensions of difference I will stress two. Getting ahead in research and publication is a matter of pleasing, impressing, and often contending with one's peers and elders; teaching is chiefly a relation with less entitled juniors. And: scholarly intercourse takes place over spatial and temporal distances, through measured exchanges and with the personal element mediated by professional conventions and crafted styles; teaching, except in the mass-production format, happens live and on the wing, with the instructor's plan and persona open to a thousand unpredictable responses (including dreaded indifference) and needing constant adjustment. The teaching moment can yield ease and even exhilaration, but neither those pleasures nor the enlight-enment of students can be had by transposing relations of scholarship into the classroom.

To do so literally is impossible. Students are not journal referees or fel-low specialists. Students are right there with you; they talk back in the mid-dle of the exposition rather than framing a decorous response after it's over (and of course you need them to talk back). So no teacher tries to be an expert with students in the modes of authority and discourse he or she has painstakingly learned through apprentice scholarship. But since those are the modes that have *made* you an authority—earned you the right to *be* teaching—the impulse to rely on them is powerful. How else do you signify and enact that right?

On this account, it's not that teaching is personal and scholarship imper-sonal. No social practice can be entirely one or the other. But we screen and project ourselves differently in these two practices. Scholarly conventions—and I resume the past tense here—demanded the etiolation or bracketing or erasure of much that pertained uniquely to the individual presenting re-search. Out of bounds were, for example, the writer's gender (though we have learned since that it was unmarked and hence male), his age and physi-cal characteristics, his life history, the labor and conflict and perhaps uncer-tainty that went into production of the written or spoken text, how the writer was feeling at the moment (I'm cold and a bit edgy right now, but it's unseemly for you to know that), how the reception of his writing mattered to him beyond acceptance of its contribution to certified knowledge, and so forth. He might imply such information through style; probably he couldn't *help* conveying some of it to the canny reader. But the conventions largely forbade its explicit communication, restricting the scholarly persona to a disembodied fund of old and new knowledge, mobilized in accepted forms of argumentation and circulated among other such disembodied personae.

In class it was a struggle to wall out so much of the personal, but it also seemed both proper and safe. Physical appearance was ineradicable, but we did our best by wearing the professorial uniform. I, like most, flattened the social field by sharing "Mr." with my students. Although during my early teaching years the legal barriers against sexy literature were beginning to crumble (*Lolita, Tropic of Cancer, The Group, Naked Lunch,* etc.), and although a style of reading all texts as sexual (via phallic symbols and the like) was wildly and naughtily popular, silence was to shroud our own sexualities—and, needless to say, the erotics of teaching. Political conviction, autobiography, family? I thought it permissible to voice antifascist or anticommunist sentiments, speak of having met a poet whose work we were studying, or accept congratulations on a newborn child, but beyond such admissions of a life outside the classroom lay risky terrain.

A remembered incident: I was teaching about seventeenth-century poetry, which necessitated a good deal of annotation on everyday Christian theology. A student asked if *I* believed these things. With no pause to think through the implications of one or another reply, I said I couldn't talk about that, but would be glad to discuss it with him outside of class. In fact I disbelieved Christianity across a cool distance. Neither ambivalence nor sensitivity on the subject had anything to do with my reticence, which proceeded automatically, in response to a novel question, from the rules of impersonality as I had learned them.[4] Only my professional self, stripped down for intellectual work, was to be present in class. And of course I was tacitly asking students to abstain, reciprocally, from the personal. No sloppy revelations here, please; we're practicing objectivity together. Did I want their approval? Their affection? Certainly; but I could not be a person who wanted affection at the same time I was being a teacher.

It is embarrassing yet also therapeutic to write these things, to write personally.[5] Retrieving experience and posing its authenticity against the dissembling and the public half-truths we let pass in accommodating our individual lives to myths of professional solidity: these are by now common maneuvers. And when put forth in writing, such disclosures usually enable and are enabled by another common maneuver: my experience is *not* after all just personal. Maybe its idiosyncrasies, explored with a psychiatrist, would have come together in a healing story of neurosis. But read another way—almost always privileged—they tell a more social narrative, showing how the teller is like other people so situated, not distinct from them.

Earlier in this essay, as I recalled my experience of teaching, I found myself easing into the second mode, giving weight to the "so situated," providing social coordinates for my discomfort, intimating ways in which it might be understood as exemplary.[6] I referred it to the way academic authority was constructed, to the valuation of scholarship over teaching, and in general to professional ideology, which (especially then) muted the personal and charged experience with certain kinds of tension. Other elements of my social location surely helped constitute that experience. I will not explicate, just mention a few topoi for analysis. Maleness: the drive to be emotionally invulnerable. Middle-class upbringing: the importance of scripted self-presentation, the undesirability of surprises, the imperative never to make a scene. The 1950s: boom time, rapid expansion of the university system, professional aggrandizement, cold war ideology in the disciplinary form of literature freed from historical circumstance. I could go on,[7] but my aim is not to spin out such an analysis, only to remind readers how it conventionally goes. We evoke the personal, in venues like this one, to show how thoroughly social it was and is. The social may not exhaust the personal; there may be a residue of pure, individual difference; but we tell these stories to look *through* personal history at the ghosts of other, similarly situated people.

◆

But where did this convention come from? How did it establish itself in academic practice? I will approach these questions, too, through personal history: my own is perhaps both odd enough and commonplace enough to launch a discussion of more general interest.

Like most of my academic cohort, I maintained an easy skepticism toward the building of U.S. hegemony through the postwar years and the triumph of "business society." We took cold war pieties with a grain of salt, deplored McCarthyism, rooted for Stevenson, sniffed at commercialism and advertising—all from the platform of our allegiance to the best that had been thought and known. Needless to say, we also accepted the status and advantage afforded us by postwar economic arrangements. Some habitually but vaguely sided with workers and Negroes and poor people—for me, upbringing in a New Deal family had taught this affinity, which was then transmuted into parlor socialism by my immersion in G. B. Shaw's work, on the way to a dissertation. But until Michael Harrington rediscovered poverty, it could seem that the rising tide of the economy was lifting these groups, too, along with us happy humanistic few. We championed Culture in our daily work.

Politics, beyond voting liberal, seemed irrelevant. My one activist sally in the fifties, marching against the bomb, was in behalf of life on earth.

Oppositional politics moved closer in the early sixties. Two colleagues of mine at Wesleyan had been freedom riders; others flew down to march at Selma. I stayed on the sidelines, though with rising sympathy and anger. Vietnam pushed me by degrees into politics. Why was my government entering a civil war, backing the wrong (undemocratic, corrupt) side, using my taxes to slaughter peasants? I wrote in private rage to congressmen, signed a public letter to Lyndon Johnson ("Mr. President, please stop the bombing"), withheld the portion of my income tax that went for war, turned in my draft card. The latter two actions made me a criminal with an FBI file.[8]

The law and its institutions of enforcement, made and adjusted over centuries by white men of substance, constitute people like me as good citizens. They draw around us an invisible circle of respectability and allow us to conduct secure lives—except when exceeding the speed limit—in no conscious relation to police and the courts. When such a person steps outside the circle, everything that is taken for granted becomes problematic. I felt myself to be in a new and unstable relation not just to the state and the FBI but to other ordinary people (most of whom, in 1966, would have thought me unpatriotic or worse, had they known) and to the institutions of daily life. Its elements came unstuck.[9]

Mine were individual crimes, though of course not of my own invention. In 1965 I had heard that Noam Chomsky (whom I greatly admired) and others were refusing to pay taxes, and by 1966 many young men had burned or otherwise unburdened themselves of draft cards. But I did not act with them or belong to their groups, and when I did band with others in organized opposition, that was a sharper breach from apolitical habit. I phoned antiwar colleagues and asked them to sign a public statement of support for Wesleyan students who refused induction; this felt very different from politicking with them about, say, a change in graduation requirements. Prompted by a phone call from Mitch Goodman (see the beginning of Mailer's *Armies of the Night* for an amusing account of the call *he* received from Mitch), I joined an action at the Justice Department before the 1967 march on the Pentagon. At the end of the rally, a few dozen of us (beyond draft age) filed across the steps of Justice, announced our names, and dropped our draft cards (in my case, a classification card, since I no longer had the other) in a sack of a thousand or so cards collected from draft-age men around the country, and watched as the sack was carried inside and given in peaceful defiance to an official. My participation in this ritual brought me a predictable office visit the next Monday from two FBI agents, and some less predictable visibility. Walter Cronkite's evening news ran a five-minute clip of our civil disobedience, including my pass by the sack and my declaration that I was "Richard Ohmann, Wesleyan University." This cameo appearance led to puzzled inquiries from two of our trustees that weekend at the inauguration of a new president (I was by then associate provost), and a call from my mother asking if I was all right—meaning was I under arrest yet, and also, I surmise, how could I have so departed from her tutelage as to make a rude display of our family on national television?

Soon after, I helped found RESIST, an organization supporting various kinds of resistance to the war, legal and illegal. I signed its "Call to Resist Illegitimate Authority" and went to work on its board. We were all on the FBI's radar now (my mid-1970s file included many RESIST bulletins with every name on the masthead but mine blacked out), and some (the "Boston Five") were brought to trial for conspiracy. We encouraged civil disobedience and committed it. I found myself part of an informal network helping draft refusers and deserters leave the United States, among other felonies that the FBI apparently did *not* detect. But self-criminalization was by then as habitual as lawfulness had been just a few years earlier. The change I felt most keenly in my social activity and location was membership in a big, loose affiliation called the antiwar movement, and soon the larger and looser one called simply the Movement. In this heady, naive moment we saw it as embracing civil rights and black power, women's liberation, student power, youth liberation, then gay rights, environmentalism, and so on, with a penumbra of sex rebels, drop-out communards, drug advocates, left sectarians —everyone saying no to the tyrannies and complacencies of the old order. In spite of deep and ultimately insuperable rifts, around 1970 it was possible to see ourselves as millions of people not only joined in opposition to "illegitimate authority" but working together for a free and egalitarian society. The word "revolution" was in play.

New organizations came together, new forms of collectivity. In addition to RESIST, I belonged for a while to Students for a Democratic Society, worked in the New University Conference (left and feminist academics), helped form professional radical caucuses, checked out a couple of vanguard parties but couldn't accept democratic centralist discipline or adherence to "the line." We tried to live democracy, in New Left groups: the end would be our means. At the same time, many of us sought to subvert or reshape existing institutions such as the National Council of Teachers of English and the Modern Language Association—that they were malleable or even (in the case of NCTE) friendly shouldn't have been a surprise, since many of their members had passed through the same revulsions and illuminations as had activists from my quarter. Likewise the universities where we worked: clearly they were part of "the system" (a common term whose vagueness suggests the primitive nature of shared analysis at the time). They were complicit in war making, white supremacy, capitalist rule. Maybe we could remake them to serve peace, justice, and ordinary people.

Here's the part of my experience that was odd. While positioning myself with the disempowered and against "the system," I had landed in its middle echelons, propelled by the momentum of my early career. In 1966, just when anger was spilling into protest, I took the job of associate provost in my college's administration and became editor of *College English* as well as a member of the governing committee for NCTE's College Section, sponsor of the journal. I thought to facilitate reform at Wesleyan (reduced requirements, more interdepartmental studies, less autocratic tenure procedures, etc.) and a critique of the field of English (its aping of more scientific disciplines, amassing of endless New Critical explications, weakness in theory, inattention to its professional folkways). By 1970, when chaotic local events had elevated me to the post of interim chancellor,[10] I had passed through the estrangements described above. Not reform, but radical change was my agenda. Yet at work I was charged with holding things together *against* radicals like me, and as editor of *College English,* with sustaining the dignity of a profession whose structure and practices I now thought carceral.

At *College English* the contradiction was tolerable and often productive. Colleagues around the country were furiously rethinking literature, writing, culture, pedagogy, and professional ideals in a fluid mix with power, injustice and democracy, war and peace, soon gender and sexuality. Manuscripts tumbled in. I accepted many that more conservative editors would have found unmannerly or outlandish. I also contracted with guest editors for clusters of articles or whole issues on themes heretofore incompatible with a professional or scholarly context: feminism, Marxist criticism, the rebellion in MLA, emancipatory curricula in community colleges, gay liberation.

These projects made *College English* controversial and of course offensive to some; though I published conservative articles, too, the journal was hardly a model of "balance" through this period. But neither was it completely out of step with thought and action in the field or with the interests and concerns of NCTE's generally populist leadership, which at least tolerated and usually encouraged these editorial adventures.[11] I and my associate editor Bill Coley made a habit of transgression, but in the supportive company of very many readers and contributors, also caught up in "the Movement" or sympathetic to it.

At Wesleyan the contradiction was intense. Not that the trustees or my administrative superiors condemned my activism or made my tenure precarious: to the contrary, they seemed ready to boost me up a notch in the administrative hierarchy whenever campus tensions heightened. A few of them hated the war as much as I did; some demurred but sincerely endorsed the value of academic dissent and debate; perhaps some thought my presence a palliative to student and faculty radicals. (The word "coopt" came unpleasantly to mind.) The problem was one of structure, not antagonism. An academic administrator like me can put out a few ideas and rally support for them, but most of his or her time and energy go to negotiation and compromise. Collect the desires and demands of faculty members and students, try to reconcile them with one another, see what the budget will stand, patch together a proposal, see how it fares in committees, hope that the result will be at least an incremental improvement. Not much leverage in the process for one's own passions against the weight of custom, institutional constraint, and other people's entrenched interests. In daily work, I was a sort of conduit.

Worse, in those frenzied years I often did crisis management. Our administration would drop all routine when protest or disruption threatened and huddle in endless strategic sessions. How would we respond to the black students' occupation of a building? To the blockade of a military recruiter in the administration building? To a sit-in at the admissions office by Puerto Rican students demanding that more of their number be recruited? To a midnight assault by two black students on a white student who had written an insulting letter to the newspaper? To women faculty members and staff demanding that Wesleyan depart from its old-boys' club practices? I might be put on assignment to negotiate or control damage or write a bit of judicious administration-speak to faculty and students. Given my job, this made some sense, but always my sympathies were with the protesters, if not with a particular expression of their politics.

Sometimes the ambivalence of my position worked out all right, as when I sat with the black students' organization (after their takeover of a classroom building) to plan what eventually became our African American studies program; or negotiated with the women's group—among other things, for the hiring of a woman associate provost, who turned out to be the admirable Sheila Tobias.[12]

More often the dissonance was somewhere between comical and shattering. Toward the comical end: insisting that a Grateful Dead concert not be canceled for fear of riot; declining to host a national SDS conference (I knew that SDS was about to implode in revolutionary adventurism); missing a meeting of the Student Affairs Committee, which I chaired, while in jail after doing civil disobedience outside a Sikorsky helicopter plant; representing Wesleyan at the inauguration of a new president at Mt. Holyoke, and standing—red-gowned, back turned to him and the other platform dignitaries, in protest against a ceremonial address by the war criminal McGeorge Bundy; giving a talk in a rally at Southeastern Massachusetts University against its autocratic president, and seeing our own president, deluged with angry letters from alumni, respond to the effect that I was not representing Wesleyan, just exercising my right of free speech. Not a bad place to work.

Far from comical: having to decide in the middle of the night whether to accept or reverse the dean's decision (he reported to me) to expel, without due process, the black students who had beaten up the white student;[13] in the conflict that followed, being thrown out of Malcolm X house along with the president as we were trying to make peace; being sent to observe the blockade of the military recruiter and being mistaken by my antiwar friends there for a fellow blockader, with quite understandable recriminations to follow; going to negotiate with the Puerto Rican students in the admissions office and being held hostage there myself. I lived uncomfortably in two polarized milieus: the educational bureaucracy and the movement challenging its legitimacy, along with the legitimacy of almost everything else.

A prickly contradiction it seems, even today. But I think my two-world experience, though perhaps unusually intense, was deeply congruent with that of many other thousands caught in the same historical turbulence. Teaching assistants and instructors, only somewhat less than full professors and the occasional provost, had labored to win academic authority, to master professional decorum, to build the kind of invulnerability I have described. Teaching, we performed routines of talk, dress, gesture, and classroom order legitimated by the bodies of knowledge that grounded our disciplines. Researching, we enacted loyalty to those knowledges even when we sought distinction by contesting their received truths. Going to meetings, which is to say administering, we paid tribute to the dignity of the institution even when trying to modify it—however we might ironize its rigidities and chafe at its demands.

But by 1968 or so, those who had followed a trajectory from anger at racial injustice or protest against the war to a conviction that our society was laced together with bad power had come to question the solidities that underlay those routines of daily, working life. The knowledges we professed were honeycombed with pockets of inexcusable ignorance (e.g., of women and black people), or shaped to the needs of cold war ideology. They served technocratic domination or (worse) surveillance, terrorism, and war. The beloved institution—the university—appeared now to be complicit as well. "Who ruled Columbia?" and "Who ruled America?" turned out to be two forms of the same question. Our enclave of free inquiry and emancipatory culture looked instead like a conveyer of ideas that made Vietnam possible, and of students into predictable slots in the social hierarchy. I report these discoveries laconically but don't mean to patronize them. They proceeded from feverish investigation and analysis, driven by both political and intellectual need—a "ruthless critique of all things existing," in one of my favorite phrases from Marx—and they decisively altered scholarship and curriculum in all traditional fields except the sciences. That's what the culture wars of the eighties and nineties have been about.

Through the time of these revaluations, the unbearable tension I have described between academic rituals and the injustice in which they were embedded began to look systematic. At first it read something like this: how can I be seriously deliberating whether to put a B or a B+ on this student's paper while the government is napalming peasants in my name? As ruthless critique proceeded, however, the disjunction reconfigured itself into a perceived unity: my painstaking enactment of the rituals *enables* war making (or helps this student escape the draft and sends that one to Vietnam; or reinforces the whiteness of the university system; or perpetuates the habits of male supremacy; or greases the skids of class reproduction and makes it look fair—and so on). The caucuses and study groups and activist organizations and coalitions and professional insurgencies and consciousness-raising groups that were piecing together a dissident, holistic understanding of U.S. society and its imperial outreach turned the analysis, inevitably, back in on the institutions in which we worked, and on our own unexamined practices.

Of those, teaching came under the most careful scrutiny. For the first time in my experience groups of like-minded college teachers gathered outside the context of staff meetings to talk about pedagogy, because we saw it as political, in the broad sense of the term that was newly salient.[14] Every customary procedure that our professional training had naturalized now seemed laden with political relations, chiefly undemocratic: the lecture format, the inflexible syllabus, the canons it transmitted, the insularity of the disciplines, the exam, the unchallengeable paper topic, the gap between assignment and finished product wherein "process" later took up residence, the independence of each student's work, the grade meted out according to immutable standards. Classroom etiquette, too: last names, formal dress, discussion dominated by the more assertive, the absolute distinction between instructor and student. Architecture itself spoke hegemony. The form of the amphitheater, the lectern in front, ranks of desks bolted to the floor, all enforced the "banking concept" of education.

As we knocked down the walls that had set apart profession, pedagogy, and politics, a fourth "p" came forward: the personal. Famously, the women's movement legitimized public talk of the personal; in fact, insisted upon it. That talk was in part a refuge from and assault on domination of antiwar venues by, well, us: by male "heavies" with "correct" political lines. But it also joined with and fortified a critique of professional detachment and scholarly objectivity already under way. To tell one's own story and hear the stories of others, we were learning, was to restore differences hidden behind *the* instructor and *the* student and *the* reader. Provided with genders, class locations, and so on, these characters now garbled the professional script in which they had been asked to perform as universals. A pedagogy of the lyric poem, meant to open vistas of timeless unity, might instead work for a first-generation student at a state college as a class put-down—the "laying on of culture," in a phrase we took from John MacDermott. An actual female reader of *Lady Chatterley's Lover* might not willingly take up the part assigned to her by Lawrence or by the male instructor. *The* profession meant something different for an adjunct writing teacher in a community college than for an ivied professor. Such banalities were fresh in 1968 or so, and narratives of personal experience were as crucial to the interrogation of professional ideology as to the making visible of male supremacy in interstices of daily conduct.

I think it important that the personal turn of the late sixties happened in groups of people joined by common purposes and shared anger—for me, the MLA Radical Caucus, the New University Conference, various faculty and student groups at Wesleyan (including, later, the women's studies collective), like-minded colleagues in NCTE and around my work for *College English*. In David Bleich's term,[15] ours were *disclosures* of previously silenced experience that showed one person's discomfort or inadequacy or embarrassment or pleasure to be not after all unique, not inherently private. They expanded our affiliations and drove our activism as they deepened our understandings, and so helped "bring the subjective and the collective categories of experience together."[16] Sure, I recall explosions of runaway bitterness, indulgent confession, unusable ego—including my own. But the personal mode settled into movement process because it raised consciousness, and because it knit people together by clarifying the social relations in which we found ourselves and by hinting at how they might be changed.

Not that disclosure and political resolve automatically charted the way to worthwhile change. To speak only of teaching—my point of departure in this essay—the furious experimentation of the years around 1970 threw up a number of strategies that were largely stylistic. Wearing blue jeans to class instead of dresses or suits, using first names, meeting in informal spaces, sitting in circles or on the floor: these signaled eagerness to renegotiate authority in the classroom but did not forge new contracts, and by themselves led to "grooving in the grass"—structureless, feel-good pedagogy. Other strategies collided with invisible walls outside the classroom and the university itself. Take grading. Everyone saw that grades were invidious, poor incentives for learning, incompatible with serious collaboration, and (especially when linked to the military draft) consequential beyond anything intended by the award of a C rather than an A. So instructors tried no grades, pass-fail grades, giving all As, grading by lottery, self-grading, peer grading, and doubtless many other arrangements. All failed because students needed grades because in turn employers and graduate programs and draft boards required them. Our assignment was not just to teach and to generate certificates of learning but to rank students for purposes of social sorting—the "reproduction," as we later would say, of class and race and gender systems. No socialism in one classroom, then, and we had to find other fields of battle.

This aside, in my view the ferment around teaching yielded healthy and lasting results. A democratic revolution in the United States was not one of them, but more democratic relations of instruction and *better* pedagogies did ensue. Collaborative learning, small-group work, peer tutoring, flexible syllabi, responsiveness to the capabilities and needs and social positions that actual students bring with them to class, critical reflection on the learning process as it goes along, a humanizing of the instructor and demystifying of his or her authority (not abandonment of it), and many strategies to help students take responsibility for their own learning. The shift will seem old hat to likely readers of this volume because it has been most decisively achieved in women's studies, in writing instruction, and to a lesser extent in literature.

These pedagogical discoveries certainly transformed my own relation to teaching. Even the grooving-in-the-grass phase was therapeutic in loosening rigidities of authority that had earlier caused me such confusion and discomfort. Teaching became a field of innovation, not an inflexible heritage of conventions. I could try new formats, decenter my precious authority, let down defenses, rethink the ways learning might happen. This was possible because I now felt teaching must respond to political as well as professional urgencies—Vietnam cried out in every classroom—and paradoxically, those urgencies made it far more personal than before. Still more important, I believe, was the conviction that even in my own classes I was working daily with many student and faculty allies (and of course against powerful antagonists), not striving to meet some heroic standard of individual performance.

Teaching never became easy for me, but challenge, imagination, achievement, and sometimes joy flowed into it. Stress came now from feverish but cheerful overwork, not helpless repetition of my defensive professional routines. There were small collaborative victories, institutions were built,[17] pedagogies developed over time,[18] the irreversible movement by thousands of colleagues in English and American studies to demystify and remake the literary canon. All this amounted to a cumulative and cooperative project, very different from the desperate scramble to escape each semester and turn with relief to the "real" work of scholarship.

About which a word, now, because the upheavals of circa 1970 and the assumption of historical agency they provoked made for an entirely different relation between teaching and scholarship from the one I described earlier in this essay. Those on the left came to see research and writing as charged with political urgency. In caucuses and collectives we intensively reexamined scholarly practices, their theoretical underpinnings, their historical construction, and their institutional housing.[19] Many of us now took up research that aimed to question disciplinary givens and set new directions. Black studies, women's studies, working-class studies, and gay and lesbian studies were the most visible expressions of that project, which not only created new subjects and won reputability for them but changed what could reputably be thought and written about the traditional subjects, The engaged scholarship that ensued has of course been a scandal to the Right and a main battlefield of 1990s culture wars. It was an intellectual liberation for us and, in my view, for the disciplines.

Be that as it may, the transformation brought my own teaching and research together in a refreshing and unanticipated way. From about 1972 on, almost everything I wrote answered directly or indirectly to a felt political imperative. In my teaching (I was lucky to be at a flexible college), I transited from English literature to American culture, and from a formalist to a historical outlook, furiously learning about economic and social theory along the way. Politics informed my teaching, and my teaching now became the basis of new research and writing.[20] I left behind my specialized training in linguistics and literature, taught what I studied, and studied what I needed to know to teach.

What I knew always trailed my need to know. And what I knew was always provisional, always in formation. This meant that my authority in class—earlier so precariously and often irrelevantly derived from scholarly credentials—now rested more on the openness of an inquiry whose difficulties I could happily admit, and to which students could contribute questions and insights that taught me things, as well as secure knowledge of their own, especially when the subject was mass culture, about which they inevitably knew more than I, at least experientially. So the social relations of scholarship and teaching overlapped and grew closer. The authority generated as the class moved along was as much as I wanted and was the more satisfying because collaboratively built.[21]

Did these changes bring on a personal turn in my scholarship as well?

Certainly not of the sort that academic feminist writing took, in the early seventies. I did not "speak bitterness," as the phrase went, about indignities and slights and oppressions that invaded my daily life from systemic inequality: how could I, or anyone situated as I was on the privileged side of most social boundaries? But I did let anger flow into my writing from the place it now occupied in my political life: this was a departure from the scholarly conventions I had previously learned, which permitted no tone more personal than huffy indignation at the stupidity of an intellectual antagonist. *English in America* barely contained the rage that drove its composition—rage at war and oppression, of course, but also at what I took to be the complicity of my own discipline and its institutions. In criticizing these ("exposing" might better characterize what I thought I was doing), I did also give some authority to my own experience and admitted more personal anecdote than I would have thought permissible before. After that (1976), I adopted a rather conversational academic style that felt personal to me, at least in leaving behind the fortifications of tonal distance and disciplinary authority we had all used to guard our collective, professional capital. And more recently, taking advantage of the indulgence granted elderly folk, I have laced several articles with reminiscence. (Does experience somehow gather credibility and a claim on polite attention as it grows hoary?) This is by far my most personal essay,[22] and, since it unsettles me, I doubt I'll prowl farther along this path. In any case, the most important way in which I imagine my scholarship of the last twenty-five years to have been personal is by following imperatives of the movements in which I claimed membership. The personal is the political, yes, and I want to emphasize how *social* it has been for me, how saturated with affinities and alliances and conflicts both real and (no doubt) fanciful.

At the beginning of the last section I hoped that its first-person story would ground "a discussion of more general interest." That, I now attempt—with abundant reservations about what may be justly concluded from any such account, reservations, that is, about whether I've written anything of use to other people, these last many pages. What I've *meant* to do is historicize the personal turn. But by means of my own history as I choose to tell it, or maybe can't help telling it? What presumption lies in that strategy: that my experience has been paradigmatic, that I can in this way represent the many people assembled from time to time, without their consent, inside my "we"? I'm suspicious of the personal even as I practice it, about which more later.

But first, to draw out the inferences I want from this story: the rules of college teaching and academic writing began changing, around 1970, under pressure from activists in feminism and other movements, to admit a good deal more of personal experience and feeling than had been respectable or even tolerable before. The thinking behind this pressure was simple. Movement people identified rhetorics of impersonal authority with the lies our leaders told us about Vietnam, with the crackpot rationale for war, with the complicity of the corporate university, with cost-benefit analysis that left human suffering and harm to nature outside its equations, with social engineering that treated the lives of poor and nonwhite people as problems to be solved from above, with male assumptions of privilege, with the bromide that in America we had no social classes, with curricula and pedagogies driven by professional imperatives and thus abstractly "irrelevant" to students' needs, with scholarship that justified or took as natural the world as it was—in effect, with all that seemed ignorantly hierarchical and undemocratic in our supposedly egalitarian society. To recognize experience and speak from it was a step toward truth and decency. Furthermore, in the practice of dissident groups, especially feminist ones, the personal turn at its best delivered radical insight, strengthened sisterhood and solidarity, and helped build new institutions and ways of working together.

The specific conditions of historical possibility that enabled a liberatory personal turn three decades ago are attenuated or gone. The ferment of rage and opposition and experiment and discovery within which we learned to speak truth (personal and otherwise) to power has simmered down. "The Movement" that never quite was, but whose idea stirred millions to transformative action, looks naive in retrospect about how much and what kinds of power laced "the system" together, and about what would be required to replace it with something better. Not that the Movement disappeared: rather, it dispersed into more specialized campaigns, whose partial victories are everywhere embedded (sometimes precariously) in U.S. society now. Women become physicians, executives, secretaries of state. Abortion is a right, albeit an embattled one. Migrant farmworkers are powerfully organized. African Americans attend previously white colleges and law schools in large numbers, travel where and how they will, buy homes in suburbs, are heard from in national media (and constructed as avid consumers in TV commercials, right alongside white yuppies). Gay and lesbian people have at least some rights—meager ones, but such as were unimaginable before. Corporations cannot destroy the natural world with complete impunity. Vietnam is free of U.S. occupation, and what was known for a while as the "Vietnam syndrome" now apparently prevents us from invading countries (but allows us to bomb up to four per year). Anyone can add to this list, and although to do so is simultaneously to realize how incomplete and disconnected the advances have been, they are not nothing, either.

And my list omits the site where movement gains have taken root most deeply: the university—or rather, that part of it where we study the humanities and social sciences, and where we pursue and debate "personal effects." Here, the change is tectonic. Look around at the various "studies" programs that were unimaginable in 1965, each the academic sedimentation of a social movement. Look at how we have changed the subject within traditional fields—the texts that appear on syllabi, the questions that can be asked about them, the vast enlargement (in the humanities) of what we take culture to be, the intellectual seriousness and partial autonomy of rhetoric and composition studies, and the infusion of politics (broad sense) into all these studies. Look at the changes in teaching and scholarship that have been my topic in this essay. The liberal arts curriculum, understood most deeply as the texts and problematics and ways of thinking that we put on students' and our own agendas—the curriculum has become quite another thing in three decades, gradually transformed by the urgencies of circa 1970.

It's almost enough to cheer up a decaying Leftie. But as I was saying before this optimistic swerve, history has left behind the conditions that brought personal experience into fruitful play back then. First, the academic movement that changed our work has grown apart from the activism that initially inspired it. (With many commendable exceptions, but still.) We now enact and dispute the personal in a conversation chiefly among ourselves, on terms that have more to do with academic politics or even fashion than with changing the world.

Second, since "the" movement that didn't quite happen has fragmented into largely separate social movements, the academic "I"—when it does reach out beyond the academy—tends to make contact with identity politics, where who "I" am is most saliently female, or disabled, or Asian American, or gay, or . . . . In this situation the personal tends to imply that identities are given and fixed, to reify difference, to veer away from disclosures that might strengthen a universalist solidarity or even point toward coalitions.

Third, the gains of sixties movements provoked a reaction from the New

Right. By 1964, it had already come in from the fringe (the John Birch Society, and such) around Goldwater's candidacy, and it took new strength from its opposition to what the sixties came to mean for much of "middle America." Through the 1970s, it established right-wing foundations, organized among Christian fundamentalists, contested for power within the Republican Party, and gradually reconfigured American politics. It vigorously challenged the liberal hegemony of the postwar decades, and in the process demonized the social movements that had built momentum within that hegemony. The culture wars of the 1990s were one manifestation of that conservative reaction, and in them the Right took aim as much at positions won by radicals *in the university* as at those won in Congress and the courts. Whatever weight the personal may still carry in our internal conversations, it seems to me ill adapted to a defense of the university against charges of political correctness or of multiculturalism grounded in identities.

And finally: since 1970 our economic system and social formation have been passing through a fairly deep transformation. I have discussed it in some detail elsewhere in this book; here, let me simply gesture toward the rapid movement of capital (in a hundred new forms) around the world, the proliferation of new products and services, the repackaging and incessant commodification of knowledge, the breakup of the old Fordist work force, the casualization of labor, the application of market logic to institutions of all kinds, and so on. These forces have been at work in and on the university, needless to say, producing there a crisis whose dimensions—from the erosion of tenure and collapse of the old job market to the marketization of academic services and research—are woven into the texture of daily academic life. Our profession (along with medicine, law, and most of the others) is in decline. The personal turn was in part a challenge to its claims of authority, and those of the fat and complacent postwar university. Does it still have that meaning? Do we want it to, in our present circumstances?

Those circumstances are much on my mind: I imagine the tasks of and threats to a democratic Left at millennium's end to be starkly different from what they were in 1970. If I'm right, is that cause for those who share egalitarian and democratic goals to abandon the personal, to declare it mined out and anachronistic? It's hard to separate that question from my own uneasiness with disclosure—doubtless evident enough to the reader of this mixed essay, so determined to become an argument or a master narrative, so uncomfortable in its personal moments, so burdened with its author's male,

middle-class, childhood instruction in the shame of making scenes or showing vulnerability. No wonder such a person, even after decades of contrary
instruction, tends to hear accounts of personal experience in academic or
other public discourse as outbreaks of self-indulgence among the privileged,
or competitive displays of victimization, or unsporting claims on sympathy,
and in any case distractions from the urgent work at hand.

No, I do not think the personal vein is bled dry or politically irrelevant.
But let me add two thoughts to the caveat embedded in my attempt to historicize it. The personal itself is not a stable category, any more than the
"real" in literary representation. Conventions of privacy change. Richard E.
Miller tells a nice anecdote of his Rutgers seminar for beginning teachers of
composition. By request, he included a session on coming out as gay or lesbian in class, a topic not just taboo but unimaginable, thirty years ago. Ex-
cited discussion, revelation, story upon story, until one TA came out to the
seminar as a *Christian* and revealed her fear of doing that in her comp section. Consternation and silence. Miller comments that "what gets seen as
merely personal and better left unsaid in the academy has shifted over time
and across locations."[23] Globalization and the crisis of the university have
brought coming-out stories by graduate TAs, adjuncts and other casualties
of the new order, linked to organizing struggles on university campuses and
in organizations like MLA. Are there other realms of what used to be "better
left unsaid" to be explored now, by way of building new memberships and
collectivities?

Second, it is easy to understand how the word "objective" sprouted cynical quotation marks, how "abstract" and "impersonal" became pejoratives,
how "formal," "linear," and "adversarial" came under censure.[24] No plea, here,
for a return to the blindly self-assured, contestatory, male academic conventions of 1965. But the inheritors of sixties movements have real enemies who
can't be conjured away by forswearing the adversarial style. We need (maybe
more than ever) new knowledge of this difficult world in order to try changing it; that knowledge will have to be in part abstract because real relations
are not evident on the surface of things; and we can't get there without
working through the impossible ideal of objectivity. (Would "fairness" and
"open-mindedness" be more acceptable terms?) The knowledge we need
must be personal, too, but will not accord epistemological privilege to personal experience. Joan Scott: "When experience is taken as the origin of
knowledge, the vision of the individual subject . . . becomes the bedrock of

evidence on which explanation is built," and "the constructed nature of experience" becomes invisible, along with the "given ideological systems" in which experience offers itself as pristine and natural.[25] For all that, the personal turn has I think been more beneficial than not. It is in any case irreversible. I hope we can keep alive in it the social and the political, from which it has historically been inseparable, and without which it is at best incomplete and isolating.

A CONVERSATION
BETWEEN RICHARD OHMANN
AND JOHN TRIMBUR

◆

The remaining two sections of this book are edited transcripts of interviews from the early 1990s. I include them to show how I understood the historical pressures that bore in on my own work and on the profession at the end of the Reagan–G. H. W. Bush years. Also, I hope the interviews complement the more formal excavation of my career in the previous chapter. John Trimbur, of Worcester Polytechnic Institute, conducted the first interview on September 11, 1992, at the Center for the Humanities at Wesleyan University. I appreciated his informed and sympathetic yet critical interest.

JT: Dick, I've read back through your work recently, and one thing I'm struck by is the voice that comes through in your writing. There's an immediacy and directness that seem unaffected by the current poststructuralist mannerisms and quite unlike a good deal of writing coming from the academic Left today. I'm curious about your own practice as a writer. How do you see the politics of your prose?

RO: Thank you for the compliment. Your question might have been turned around in the other direction: how come you aren't able to write in the accepted language of the academy? There is some truth in that. A small part of the answer is I have not earned the use of poststructuralist language. That's partly a matter of choice, partly just a matter of life being too short. I'm interested in some strands of poststructuralism, especially Foucault. But, as you know, my main register is a kind of Gramscian

Marxism, combined with certain feminisms, so I'm not tempted to compete with the Derrideans for high-stepping it. But of course Marxism and feminism have jargons of their own, and I try not to depend on them except as they express needed ideas that are alien to common idiom.

The politics of it is pretty obvious—to work against specialization and to adapt a common language. I find that it's usually quite possible to do that. Certainly one of the reasons is that I've taught about history and power and Marxism, more or less directly, so that I'm used to talking and writing to students, as you know from the ways I teach courses. Partly my writing comes out of my teaching practice.

Looking back farther, looking for the genesis of this way of trying to do it, I would say an important moment was when I was still working on my degree and studied philosophy for a while at Oxford. This was the high moment of the ordinary-language philosophers at Oxford. It wasn't so much that I read their writing and decided it was the way to write as that there was a certain style of debate that took place in classes and seminars. Philosophers would be slicing away at any unnecessary complexity. Occam's razor was the instrument of choice in that kind of discourse. And there was also a kind of intense though friendly combativeness in debate, energetic and more fun than standing behind the walls of academic neutrality.

But the main moment surely was the 1960s—as with so much else, when people in the movement were challenging various kinds of authority and discourse that had no implied subject and that came from some place outside of particular historical circumstance. I suppose a general principle was to carry on a ruthless critique of all things existing and to enter contestational politics into the very niches of daily professional life. Part of the task was to say that the emperor had no clothes and to say it plainly.

JT: Let me follow that up. One critique of the New Left is that the principles operative at the time amount to a kind of commonsense radicalism and the perspective that once we expose the system for what it is, all reasonable persons will do the right thing. This critique holds, by contrast, that in order to subvert the languages of power, you need a new critical language. I'm not persuaded by the critique, but let me ask—to what extent is there any validity to that critique of the common sense of the New Left?

RO: In the first place, you might or might not agree that for people like us who were coming into active politics at that time, without experience in the Old Left, the late 1960s felt like a thrilling explosion of common sense—a deeper, more radical common sense. The authoritative voices, after all, had been claiming to speak out in the name of common sense. Scrutinized from a radical perspective, their kind of common sense seemed like crackpot realism, or whatever C. Wright Mills's phrase is. The analysis put forward at the time by people who seemed intellectually adventuresome and exciting was an overthrow of a certain kind of common sense.

To take the question from a slightly different angle, my own trajectory was first to get really angry about a lot of things and try to find ways to be active and then eventually to reflect on what we had been doing, to begin theorizing and abstracting beyond the heat of the moment. Somewhere around 1969 or 1970, I ran into a few people in meetings who used terms like "ruling class" or "dialectic." There was an infiltration of fairly traditional Marxist ideas into New Left movements. Ideas put in that form seemed exciting and persuasive, and gradually, around 1971 or 1972, I tried to make good on one of the huge gaps in my education by learning about Marxism. My route was not through the classics primarily, certainly not through the century of encrustations, commentary, and exegesis that had built up around the classics, but mainly through Anglo-American Marxists associated with the New Left, radical political economists like Bowles and Gintis or the *New Left Review* people, who were in the movement but were academics regenerating Marxism. It was through that new formation of Marxism that I gradually backed into Marx, Engels, and to a lesser extent Lenin. I think that meant that although I was now drawing on that tradition, I was not committed in any way to the Old Left's hagiography or endless disputes about what Marx really meant. In a sense I was fortunate to be able to adopt and adapt some of the theoretical tradition in a way that came, in the first place, out of political activism and, in the second place, from other people in a similar milieu who were trying to theorize activist politics.

I absolutely am pro-theoretical. I don't think we can get anywhere without theory. You know the kind of theory I've affiliated myself with, and I have no reluctance to draw on the kinds of vocabulary and concepts that are necessary to critique. I see nothing wrong with people like us doing some writing to other people like us in a language we've built up with some labor over some time, using it as a shorthand. There's a kind of solidarity in doing that, as long as the "we" here is a politically constructed we and not just we the profession.

The issue that always arises, though, is how do we stop talking just to ourselves, how do we get out there and attract more and other people, a wider public? I don't think the main problem is we can't write like human beings. I think the main problem is that the United States has a very familiar form of free speech and free press, which means that I can say whatever I want to an audience of three hundred—and I don't want to derogate that kind of work—but the audience of millions is simply not available to us, and that's not a matter of censorship. (It was simpler in the Soviet Union because there everybody understood the terms of censorship.) All the counterhegemonic scholarship on Central America, on the Middle East, on the class structure of the United States is out there, published and available, in journals you and I can read, and it tends to stay there until some crisis brings it into a wider arena. So I don't think it's just a matter of the way we write. A lot of what I read, such as the NACLA (North American Congress on Latin America) reports, is cleanly written and direct, and there's no reason why such sentences couldn't appear in the *New York Times*. There are other reasons, however, why they don't appear.

When people do get media hearings, as in the case of political correctness, it tends to be in the celebrity format. *McNeil-Lehrer Report* or *Firing Line* will bring Catharine Stimpson on to stand up to Lynne Cheney and battle it out for ten minutes. That's the way, partly because of journalistic routines and conventions, that the media frame these issues. If somehow we get constituted as one of the sides that has to be heard from—which rarely happens—it happens in this way. I'm glad Stanley Fish or Catharine Stimpson is present, on those rare occasions, but the reason they appear is not that they write clearly and other people don't, but because of the need to fill up a certain television format with people who can stand as celebrities and who can answer to the demand for equal time. When somebody from our profession, such as Camille Paglia, does get more widely read—as opposed to seen on TV—it usually means that she has managed to popularize certain questions.

JT: The equal time, pro/con format of *Firing Line* and other programs also situates the speaker in an individual relationship to the public. One of the things you argue in your critique of Russell Jacoby's *The Last Intellectuals* in "Graduate Students, Professionals, Intellectuals" is that intellectuals never really speak directly to the public but always in mediated ways through institutions, organizations, forms of media, and so on. This suggests to me that the issue isn't how we write but whether we have been able to create spheres in which that writing can have a different weight, a different purpose. You cite the women's movement as an instance. Do you see other popular spheres for radical intellectuals?

RO: In spite of my pessimism at this moment, the progressive movements are out there and established and fighting in a way that's incomparably more potent than in, say, the early 1960s. The Central American support groups, the African and Middle East groups, tenants organizations, housing organizations, environmental groups, antiracist and antimilitary groups—they're all there. I realize they are not adding up to a revolution, but they are deeply a part of our political culture now. Intellectuals work in those movements and draw from them, and there's a kind of feedback. Of course, naturally, I think the main arenas are within our own institutions and our own teaching.

JT: Let's talk about *English in America*. One reading of the book, and one that would locate it in its times—the late 1960s and early 1970s—is that it is a pessimistic book. One way to read the book is as an exposé of power and of the connections between teaching writing and the formation of a professional-managerial class under meritocratic auspices. In this sense the book might be seen as part of a venerable American tradition of muckraking. It's not unlike, say, Upton Sinclair's writings on higher education. To what extent would you accept that criticism?

RO: I think absolutely the book is subject to that criticism. I think—to put it in the most extreme way—that what comes through is a kind of revolutionary paralysis. There's a place where I say that you've got to have socialist revolution, that you can't just change the schools. Although I don't think the texture of the whole book feels that way, nonetheless it would be easy to come away—and it would be my fault if readers did—with the idea that we can't change anything until we change everything. And that's partly because I was pursuing some old habits of totalization, of trying to encompass everything in a huge picture because I wanted to point the finger at illegitimate power in the center of things. The irony is that through the years I was writing the book, I was involved in social change activities in the arena of the classroom, the university, and the MLA, and the fact is that many of the essays I pulled together in *English in America* were written as contributions to those struggles. There's no question at all that the book should be criticized and was criticized by the Left, as well as the Center and the Right. I remember a review in *Science and Society* that accused me of petit-bourgeois pessimism.

JT: What's striking about a lot of your work since *English in America* is that you foreground very prominently the notion of contradiction. It's easy to do an exposé of power, but what I think you go on to do after *English in America* is to show the contradictions within the professional-managerial class [PMC] and how they might open a space for agency that seems cut off in a lot of left and Foucauldian analyses. I'm curious about this sense of contradiction as a gesture toward an orthodox Marxism, and I wonder about the history of your thinking, and when and how it seemed to you that the notion of contradiction is an important tool.

RO: It didn't just dawn on me. We were living those contradictions all along. At the 1968 MLA, for example, some of these contradictions played themselves out explosively. It was wonderful to see and be part of those cross-currents as the stiff old professional organization was suddenly a place where antiwar and feminist resolutions were being passed, where you could see PMC rebels being tugged in two ways—trying to claim the eternal authority of the MLA as the sponsor of our activism and at the same time to attack it. There was a great confusion, but there were also clarifications emerging that continued in the New University Conference and radical caucuses in the professions, not only academic but also the Medical Committee for Human Rights and elsewhere. People began to understand their contradictory positions as professionals and to develop them, which no doubt helped the Ehrenreichs theorize as they did in their article.[1]

JT: Let me ask about the unwritten "Chapter 6 ½" in *English in America,* where you call for an empirical study of how social class is reproduced through writing courses. The research program you suggest could have been pursued in rhetoric and composition. My question is multilayered. One is, to what extent do you think your proposal has been pursued? The second is, to what extent has such a research program been preempted and depoliticized by social constructionist currents in rhetoric and composition?

RO: I think you're right, that the program has to some extent been carried out, in a depoliticized way: probably not in response to my call in 1976, but if people had responded to my call, that's probably how they would have done it, because there is something deficient about the call. Essentially, there is no idea of class and class reproduction connected to the idea of professional and academic reproduction. What I like, reading back, is that there is a neat sketch of what I would later call the hegemonic process, in which there are all kinds of overlayers and crosscurrents operating to reproduce power rather than simply hand it down. But I think I was falling into the professional deformity myself, thinking that our work is more than it is or more important in isolation than it could possibly be, thinking that what students learn in the fifty minutes they spend three times a week in our classrooms could be of titanic importance and somehow we could change the world by changing that experience. It's the opposite of the revolutionary paralysis I talked about before.

JT: It's really a version of the literacy myth—a left version of the literacy myth.

RO: Yes. Several times in recent years I've found myself bemused in settings where people are discussing contestatory pedagogy and actually reworking ideas that burst to the surface in the 1960s. I found myself in the position of saying—or wanting to say—the single most important thing that students learn does not come from the classroom but from whatever economic background or trajectory brought them to college. For this reason, students at Wesleyan, for example, learn something very different from Freirean pedagogy than would students at Middlesex Community College.

JT: The way you cast your response about current radical and contestatory pedagogies as a rediscovery of the 1960s suggests that there was a hiatus in between. That's very much my experience of the profession, that with the rise of Reaganism there was a hiatus, not only of political activity but of political consciousness that seemed to parallel the rise in the professional status of rhetoric and composition, the proliferation of journals, the hiring for endowed chairs and of senior professors. To put the question as bluntly as I can, do you think rhetoric and composition took a political dive in the 1980s, and if so why and how?

RO: That's an interesting and hard question. Of course, part of my experience through the 1980s was one of continuity. I stopped being editor of *College English* in 1978, but we were still getting articles of the 1960s sort right through that period. In 1975, some of the remnants of the MLA Radical Caucus started the magazine *Radical Teacher* in which this political culture maintained itself and maybe even developed itself. So where I was, there was a kind of continuity that makes me less able to respond to your questions.

I think you're right: there was a king of a dive, but it wasn't as if everything was cut off. I think of the literacy crisis of 1975 and 1976 and the back-to-basics movement. On the other hand, writing teachers' efforts to professionalize themselves probably took place in that context, and a profession in the making will seize on whatever impetus and opportunity there are. That moment of "Johnny Can't Write" and "back to the basics" probably had somewhat of a depoliticizing effect on how writing teachers were seizing on opportunities to secure more legitimacy and more full-time jobs and simply to get paid better than starvation wages for doing this work so many people do under conditions of extreme exploitation. The professionalizing itself inevitably has to create something that looks like a body of knowledge, some sort of theory at the center. You have to acquire it to gain admittance or otherwise it isn't going to be a profession. It seems to be disinterested and neutral.

I think it's partly a combination of the logic of professionalism itself along with the way educational issues were put on the national agenda at that time, and a recoil against 1960s activism in various ways.[2] Through the Carter administration you could see that being played out. In reference to foreign policy, the so-called Vietnam syndrome actually worked a bit. We didn't intervene in Angola, for instance. But by the end of his four years, Carter had allowed the process of subverting the Nicaraguan revolution to begin, and there was a recovery, unfortunately, from the bewilderment and confusion of mainstream elites over the Vietnam experience and the other 1960s movements. The Right began regrouping and eventually did so very successfully.

JT: Let's go back to the current cultural Left. I'm struck by your sense of continuity—and *Radical Teacher* is exemplary in that respect. I sense currently a fissure or gap between politically committed radical teachers and theorists on the academic left, with mutual suspicions back and forth. I wonder if this is your perception and what, if anything, can be done about it.

RO: There's been a fissure for a long time. To go back to movements in MLA around 1970 or so, some of the people who had been involved in the MLA uprising seized the opportunity to get on the MLA program in a big way and organized a forum on Marxist criticism. There was a certain amount of dispute and tension because the people now linked to *Radical Teacher*—relatively spontaneous activists—said this was buying into the traditional format of MLA and that you're going to have celebrities up there and boring papers and nothing is going to happen as a result of it. Other people said we can't just go around putting posters on walls and disrupting. We have to form a stable and growing body of intellectual work, and we can do it within this institution. We were both right. Both groups are right. But there was a rift and it continued for a while, putting a distance between the Radical Caucus and the Marxist Literary Group in MLA. I don't think that's a real bad one anymore.

As long as we're talking about people who are leftists and are committed to democratic social change, that embraces a lot of people. It embraces me, and it embraces Fred Jameson. Last year when I asked him about some critique of his work in terms of its being too abstract, too highly theorized, and too divorced from movements, Jameson said he thought there could be some kind of division of labor, and I agree. Jameson himself, since I pulled his name out of the hat, has been absolutely reliable whenever some kind of crisis came up and people needed to take a stand. But do I think we would be better off if Fred had spent all his time supporting strikes of the secretaries' union instead of writing? No, I don't. Within the Left, there can be a certain division of labor.

What's a little more galling to me is that a bunch of people who have been identified as tenured radicals or the academic Left don't do anything but write books and build careers. It becomes possible for the villainous pundits and power brokers on the right to make fun of academic radicalism as just a lot of hot air and fancy language. And there's some justification. Whenever I read those things, I think, wait a minute, they're not talking about me. You can read through Roger Kimball's book *Tenured Radicals*, and you won't find the names of any academic activists. He's not talking about Chomsky; he's not talking about Said except to the extent Said writes theory; he's not talking about Said and the Palestine Na-

tional Council and that kind of work. Maybe we should consider it fortunate that they've decided to turn their attack on people who discuss
canon busting in a very remote kind of language instead of turning it on
people like Chomsky.

To come back to your question about a possible hiatus in the 1980s and
a certain discontinuity, I certainly agree this has hurt the Left. But I think
one would have to be impressed by a widening of political awareness
within and around composition teaching and studies. Your book is one
pretty concrete expression.[3] I've run into a lot of interest in that book.
The panel that you were on and that I chaired at [the 1991] meeting of the
4Cs [Conference on College Composition and Communication], with
presentations by James A. Berlin, Linda Brodkey, and Lester Faigley—
entirely a left panel, and it was obvious from the program that's what it
would be—filled the room with at least 150 and there were another 150
trying to get in. From what I could gather that was the event of the day at
CCCC. But if I'm allowed to ask you a question—is this really happening
now or are these just a few blips in the trajectory?

JT: I've tried to account for the growing political mood, but when I wrote
"Cultural Studies and Teaching Writing" in 1988, I was more optimistic. It
was before the political correctness backlash, for one thing. I thought rising professional expectations certainly were one important factor that led
to a growing self-confidence that made people more willing to speak.
Nineteen eighty-eight was the twentieth anniversary of 1968, and I think
it was more than symbolic that people were reexamining what had happened since then and were increasingly fed up with Reaganism. I think
Reagan's higher-education people—William Bennett, Diane Ravitch, and
so on—politicized the curriculum in such a way that people had to respond. And I think there was a shift within critical theory away from what
I'd call pure or severe textualism. My colleagues who are unreconstructed
old historicists used to complain eight or nine years ago about deconstruction at MLA but now they're complaining about race, class, and gender. I think they are marking a change from textuality to cultural materialism. So I think all these things brewed together.

RO: But there's something about it that didn't turn out to be just a reaction
to Reaganism. There must have been a gathering of forces for a longer
time. The authority, in a loose sense, that you, Berlin, Brodkey, and
Faigley come to hold can't have been just a reflex against Reaganism.

You've been saying interesting things and people want to hear about them. I still get invited by graduate student associations to speak under the by now false impression that I know something about writing instruction. There is something of a progressive political culture, and of course feminism is an absolutely major component of it—or maybe we're a component of feminism—that's been gathering. It's not just a matter of people saying, "Oh my God, we've got to save ourselves from Reagan and Bush." In your opinion, just to finish this line of thought, am I overly optimistic about the rootedness of political contestation within the writing part of the profession?

JT: It is a current, and it's a current that's going to stay. I think, though, that it is more fragile than might appear at CCCC. If you look at the profession exclusively through its journals and conferences, you get a distorted picture of the study and teaching of writing and of the realities of classroom life across the United States. I worry about the attacks on political correctness. It's easy to see them as a backlash. But I worry they tap deeper anxieties and a kind of right-wing populist suspicion of experts and academics that Lynne Cheney has been one of the sharpest in talking about, in what seems a reasonable way, in terms of overspecialization and the gap between humanists and the public. There's a popular groundswell that the National Association of Scholars, among others, has been able to mobilize that will seek to politicize cultural issues in the 1992 election. I think that's part of the agenda.

RO: And they have succeeded very well in politicizing the NEA and the Mapplethorpe controversy. This is an interesting thing that's happening. I have no idea how political correctness is playing in Keokuk. I don't dismiss PC as merely a media spasm, though it certainly is that. There has been a long gradual effort on the part of the organized Right—the Heritage Foundation, for example—to find effective ways of waging cultural warfare, and they've gotten better at it. The NAS was a good organizing idea. There is a fluidly operating alliance of conservative academics, right-wing action intellectuals, and Reagan-Bush politicos that has to be contended with. I don't think that a reasonable response is to ignore it for another six months and assume it will go away. And PC may tap into a wider right-wing populism. But here again I go back to my thoughts about who are constituted in the media as tenured radicals. The attack on PC is an attack on a kind of left-wing populism which isn't established well and deeply in very many places but some universities and colleges have built up a tradition.

At the same time, there is a culture here at Wesleyan and other places that has induced a good deal of tension about what kind of language you use to refer to people of color, women, or homosexuals, or about people who are "vertically challenged" or "follically challenged." That kind of PC is something that I would like to be attacking myself. That is to say, I think it implies a kind of identity politics and a politics of gesture, of feeling good, that is superficial and fragmented. As long as you're fighting it out on the terrain of what is polite speech and allowable speech, there is no totalizing vision possible and therefore no general strategy. In the present context, I wouldn't want to write an article in the *New York Times* magazine, even if I could get into the *New York Times* magazine. It would be an attack on this kind of identity politics but I'd rather attack the other side. It's frustrating because there's a broader kind of progressive politics in and around the academy whose existence isn't even acknowledged by the way the argument about PC has taken shape.

JT: Can you characterize those politics?

RO: A general vision of a better society and how we might go about building it are somehow outside the margins of the current discussion. At the extreme of PC attitudes is the thought, probably never actually subscribed to by anybody but there as a horizon, that if we all only used the right terms about one another, social problems would go away.

JT: In the past year, I found myself in a similar position when talking to radical teachers about the goals of pedagogy. Occasionally someone would propose that the goal of a writing classroom is for students to admit they're implicated in the system. I see this as a politics of guilt and self-laceration. So I said how are you going to project a vision of social reconstruction, and they said that's Marxism and then pulled out Baudrillard and the problems of productivist ideology. I felt for the first time a kind of generation gap between what I'd call my own neo-Marxism and a kind of post-Marxism that is under the auspices of poststructuralism and the critique of totality that has given up a vision of reforming society. I found this distressing when I thought the point of socialism is to overcome scarcity.

RO: Right, and for people to be more or less equal and get on to a better life . . . .

JT: I've become interested in how to address that audience without giving comfort to the Right. How can you, say, talk about the limits of speech codes and identity politics without telling Dinesh D'Souza-style horror stories? That's a conflict within the Left I think needs to be thought through.

RO: I certainly do myself. Gerry Graff is organizing Teachers for a Democratic Culture as explicitly a counterpart to the NAS in order to expose some of the lies of the Right, to recast issues of free speech and controversy, and to restore some sanity to the discussion of race and gender and sexuality in the universities. I think it's important to do it on that level. More important for the longer run is for us to rethink what's going on in the world. Some of the basic terms we've used to think about history have changed and dissolved. What's the Third World if there's no Second World? Are we seeing a quite decisive but temporary victory of Thatcherism and Reaganism, or is it more fluid? Will the regrouping of the formerly Soviet societies run into insuperable difficulties in trying to be capitalist and retain parts of the social contract they had before? Will they somehow get the better things or the worse things from each system? Is there a "new world order" ideology—no longer a cold war ideology—that will cover up and justify the really horrendous conditions in much of what used to be the Third World, so that groups in power now in the Western countries will be able to pursue their project of further class separation and concealment of the consequences by shoving them off into the Third World or the ghettos? How should we conceive of a liberatory project in that context? It's an intellectual task that of course you can't address by getting four or five heavies to spend a summer in the woods and figure it all out, but we need to carry it on by talking to each other and to our students in the classroom.

JT: One more question about PC. I want to get at another motive we haven't talked about that's suggested in your work—that there's a right-wing mobilization in part in response to a crisis in meritocracy and the anxieties among the middle classes about increased competition for college admissions, credentials, and jobs. When SAT scores no longer do the work they once did so self-evidently, when they are under scrutiny by Educational Testing Service itself, when colleges aren't weighting them as much—an arena is opened up that provides spaces for leftists who want to provide wider access to higher education. One thing I'd like to see more discussion of within universities is selectivity in admissions, something the academic Left hasn't talked much about since the late 1960s and early 1970s.

RO: Well, it's complicated by the budget crisis. I don't know exactly why so many private universities and colleges are in trouble. Every time I talk to a colleague or acquaintance at another institution it turns out they're as bad off, or worse, than we are. The possibilities for more open admissions simply do not exist, for financial reasons. We'll be lucky if we hang on to what we've got. We've made a lot of cuts at Wesleyan, and I'd be surprised if they didn't affect our ability to increase openness in admissions. In the meanwhile in the public institutions, the fiscal crisis of the state is in firm sway. It's partly a matter of Reagan-Bush politics and partly a matter of forces that were already building years ago. I'd like to be cheerful about the possibility of the Left's once more bringing forth the vision of open admissions, but we're beleaguered on all sides. The crisis in the savings and loans and banks and insurance companies—all of these things are a direct consequence of right-wing economic policy, and they're going to circle around to what can be done in education. I think more in terms of angry defensive action, finger-pointing, blame-assigning, and consciousness-raising now than I do of the possibilities opening up for the provision of free education for all.

JT: How do we respond as faculty in private schools to the end of need-blind admissions? What do leftists say to administration and students?

RO: Six or seven years ago, our board of trustees formally abandoned the commitment to need-blind admissions. They said need-blind admissions is very important to us and we want to keep doing the best we can, but we simply cannot guarantee it from here on because we could be bankrupted if certain things eventuate. Now I believe it's the case that every year since they made this decision we in fact have been able to follow the need-blind policy. But it's under threat here, not because of institutional willingness but because of money. And I'm sure that's true elsewhere. The Justice Department hasn't helped by bringing an antitrust suit against schools like Wesleyan.[4] One of the few relatively good things expensive elite colleges have done or started doing in the sixties was to maintain at least the illusion of equal opportunity. But now there's been a bit of movement perceptible among private colleges in the direction of giving merit-based instead of need-based scholarships, and the Justice Department will make that far more likely than it was before.

JT: One more line of inquiry. It seems in the late 1970s and early 1980s that you turn in your published work toward an analysis of mass culture. Is that about right chronologically? I'm interested in the genesis of that work. It anticipates so much of what's going on in CCCC and what a cultural studies approach to teaching writing might be.

RO: The quick answer, like the answer to so many of your questions, is that in the beginning was the sixties. One of the understandings that emerged in the 1960s is that power isn't just a matter of bad people in high office and running corporations. It is partly engineered consent, though that phrase is highly problematic. The politics of communication is just as important as, and inseparable from, the politics of fighting in the streets and at the polls. I got interested in the media as an urgent practical matter. I started thinking about contemporary U.S. mass culture in the early to mid-1970s. In one course I developed a way of teaching about fiction as part of the culture industry that I later wrote up in the article "The Shaping of a Canon: U.S. Fiction, 1960–1975."[5] A little later (in 1977) I started teaching a course called "Bread and Circuses" that was devoted to media analysis. So this turn in my professional life came first out of an attempt to teach things that seemed politically pointed. Then, as almost always, teaching led to writing.

JT: I'm curious about your sense of how the term "popular" is used in cultural studies by people like John Fiske, Lawrence Grossberg, and Janice Radway. As I understand it, they are trying to see the popular as a practice rather than as a genre, and this view considerably complicates the traditional models of communication. In their work, reception is not simply an effect of what is sent out, and content analysis by the expert is inadequate unless you do ethnographies of actual readers and viewers, fans, et cetera. Like them, you resist a theory of manipulation, but it seems like you've opted for a kind of historical, political economic analysis of the media rather than one I'd call ethnographic.

RO: That may be partly just a temporal accident. The study I'm pursuing about mass culture in the 1890s is all about dead people, so you can't interview them. Then there's a terminological tangle one works through the best one can. As your examples of Fiske and Grossberg implied, there's a difference in the way terms such as "mass" and "popular" are used in Britain and in the United States. For some reason, "popular" became entrenched to describe many of the same things I mean by "mass." The stipulative definition I offer in the article "On Teaching Mass Culture"[6] is a useful one—it's handy because there are differences between things that are produced for millions by a few culture specialists and things that are generated more broadly and maybe by implication more democratically. That's just one distinction among many. I don't think you can deduce an exclusive set of categories.

But the question you raise is a more interesting one. To what extent is the popular infused with the mass and vice versa? Michael Denning wrote an article recently called "The End of Mass Culture,"[7] where he says mass culture is everywhere, it's the air you breathe, and there's no point in distinguishing it any longer from high culture. That's a distinction you can't get any more mileage out of. I disagree with him, but it's well argued and an interesting idea. But as to the politics of reception, it's important. We ought to think more about it. It's hard to do. It's made more difficult by the historical fact that in this country the communications discipline, which is pretty old and huge, is, unlike in Britain, separate from cultural studies. A meeting of the ICA [International Communications Association] in Boston a couple of years ago did have panels on Stuart Hall, but that's fairly recent. There are major graduate programs that have done massive "effect studies" in a different tradition, not ethnographic, though they use focus groups. The genesis of such studies has much to do with helping the people who sell and advertise and make culture learn how to do it to their best advantage.

JT: Your work on mass culture raises the issue of what that last "C," communication, is doing in CCCC. We know where it came from—the general semantics movement of the late 1940s—but it's there and your work especially has highlighted it. I think there's a returning interest and more reading of journals in communication by rhetoric and composition people and by literature people as well.

RO: I don't know how to negotiate it, but maybe that fourth C in CCCC might lead to some effort to think about possible regroupings that would bring together people in the communication discipline and people in writing and language and cultural studies. But I would make the very unoriginal point that some explorations of reception and the popular in search of resistance and contestation are pretty far-fetched, suggesting that whatever Elvis's fans do is inevitably an act of resistance.

15

ENGLISH IN AMERICA REVISITED

RICHARD OHMANN TALKS WITH

JEFFREY WILLIAMS

◆

Jeffrey Williams, editor of minnesota review *and now in the English Department at the University of Missouri, conducted this interview on December 22, 1993, at the Center for the Humanities at Wesleyan University. I appreciated his wide-ranging and well-informed questions.*

JW: The question I want to start with is about *English in America,*[1] which strikes me as having been ahead of its time in dealing with issues like institutionalization and professionalization that are very current now. What was the field like when you wrote it?

RO: I remember when I came to think that I was writing a book, rather than just the stray article, and knew that I wanted to write about the institutions of English, I looked around to find out what the historians and the sociologists had said about [academic] departments, and I was astonished to find that they had very little to say at all. There was literature on professionalism that was some help, especially by an older scholar named Everett Hughes, but the sociologists were remarkably silent about departments, the institutions in which they themselves and the rest of us work. So I felt that I was making the analysis up as I went along, clearing the brush, and I'm sure that the path was erratic, but it was a kind of a path. I don't claim credit for the later explosion of interest in professionalization in the academy, but I think that what I did in *English in America,* along with work that was under way simultaneously by Burton Bledstein and by Magali Sarfatti Larson, really opened up a field of inquiry and exhibited a certain political urgency in doing so. So I'm satisfied about that, though I have not read parts of *English in America* during the intervening eighteen years, and I'm sure that there are parts that I would find very embarrassing now if I read them again.[2] But some parts of it seem to have set some energies going for people in our field or in other fields—the section on composition and the sections on departments especially.

JW: Michael Sprinker [Williams's mentor at State University of New York at Stony Brook] once told me that it changed the way he looked at the profession and in some ways brought him to Marxism.

RO: Really? You said it was a work that was slightly ahead of its time, but in another way, it was entirely part of its moment, which was really a few years before it came out. That was the time when a whole bunch of people in the United States were engaging in a ruthless critique of all things existing, to use one of my favorite phrases, and when it seemed as if every day when you went to a meeting, new knowledge and thought opened up. It was very exciting. There's no possibility that *English in America* could have turned into what it was without the Radical Caucus of the Modern Language Association, without the New University Conference, and the people in literary and cultural studies who had small meetings within the bigger NUC meetings and astonished ourselves mutually with the way we were looking again at the work we did for a living. In short, my ideas came out of the politics of that time and the efforts of mostly younger intellectuals. I was the one, as it turned out, that specialized in departments and the institutions of writing instruction, but the book itself, as can be said of almost all books, is best thought of as a kind of collective project, or the result of a collective project of that time. It was unthinkable without the Movement, as we used to call it.

JW: What do you think of the current concern with these issues?

RO: I hope that there is more and more of it. I value very much things that people like Evan Watkins and Bruce Robbins and Jim Berlin have done. They've gone, in some ways, well beyond what I did, and it seems to me that there are also a lot of historical studies of the discipline and institutions, especially of writing. People like Robert Connors have been grounding and correcting the kinds of conjectures I made in serious research.

JW: How did you come to do this kind of work, to be interested in the things you deal with in *English in America*?

RO: I was increasingly discontent and uneasy with what we were doing in our own rush toward fuller professionalization and specialization in the early sixties, and I was angry about race and militarism and class in our country, and those two strands fused for me. I turned back to look at our work in light of the critiques that were being staged of American power around the world and of domestic racism, and then a little bit later, male supremacy; so those two feelings came together because I needed to know why I was doing the things I did and what they were contributing to, or how they were critical of, the uses of power in the country. I never thought I was writing a book. In fact, I've never in my career set out to write a book and written it. The ones I've set out to write, I haven't written. The ones I've written, I did not intend to write.

JW: Really? What were you planning on writing next?

RO: [A book on linguistics and style.] But I found myself talking and writing about [political and disciplinary] questions and eventually I began to see that these could be part of an overview of our profession. And some time around 1974 I decided that I would turn that into the book. In the material you sent me, you asked a question about writing style, and I think that one of the ways I came to the kind of—we'll say "conversational"— style I now try to use is that so much of that writing was addressed to particular moments, crises, occasions, and it came out of a ferment of, well, anger, among other things. I wanted to write with a certain energy, as if there were real people there reading it.

JW: What's the connection with *College English*? You were editor for a time; could you fill in that background? It seems relevant to this question of writing style, since it reaches a larger and more general audience than most other journals except maybe *PMLA*.

RO: Oh, absolutely. It probably has about fifteen thousand readers. *College English* was very important to me. I feel it was more important to me, in a sense, than I was to it, though I am proud of what *College English* was during those years. It seems to me now that an editor would have had to be an idiot at that time not to produce an interesting journal—partly because of the ferment that I talked about earlier, and partly because things just poured in. We got articles from Oregon or Arkansas or from a person you'd never heard of that gave the "Gee whiz, Marge, look at this" effect, as an editor of the *National Inquirer* once put it. It was exciting. Don Gray, who was the next editor of *CE*, told me once that he had looked back over a number of the issues during my editorship and thought material like that just wasn't coming in any more. Of course, we [W. B. Coley, the associate editor, and I] did do some soliciting and farmed out some edited issues so that we were active in cultural production. But also, we were learning a lot and having our eyes opened. Most of the writing had a certain intensity—not all of it in the conversational voice—but with energies that were not conventionally academic, so I'm sure I learned something from the writing that came in to *College English* at that time, too.

JW: How did you come to be affiliated with it? Was it the interest in teaching?

RO: Well, when I was a graduate student and a teaching fellow at Harvard, there were two or three journals around the staff room, the place where the TAs hung out, and one of them was *College English*. I realized then, in the late fifties, that in each issue there was usually something that I was interested in, maybe that I could use in my own embryonic teaching efforts, and that it was different from *PMLA* and *JEGP* [*Journal of English and Germanic Philology*] and so on, and I kind of liked it. So I went to a couple of NCTE meetings, but I was more active in MLA before 1966. *College English* is the journal of the college section of the National Council of Teachers of English; the College Section Committee picks its editor. They opened up a competition in 1964 when Jim Miller at the University of Chicago was about to end his term, and they asked me if I wanted to apply. I put in an application and got the job. And then history took it up. I had a prospectus in *College English* some time during 1965, and it was, I think, much more oriented toward theorizing everything, theorizing literature, the profession, language, and so on, than it was towards political intervention.

JW: Some of your early stuff—some of the citations I've seen—deals with linguistics.

RO: Yes. I did two bodies of work early on. One had to do with stylistics and was grounded especially in transformational grammar, and the other had to do with pragmatics and was grounded in speech act theory, and there was some overlap between the two. I still retain an interest in speech act theory, though I don't practice it very extensively anymore. So those were my interests, and by the time I became editor of *College English*, I was disturbed, as I mentioned earlier, by the seeming juggernaut of professional expansion and the kind of irrationality of some of the practices that were developing—for instance, too many books to read and books read only by eight people—which became, if anything, more extreme. But events took their course, and *College English* turned out very differently from what I envisioned.

I mentioned that there were guest-edited issues, some of them especially important, including one of the first issues of feminist criticism and critique, about 1970.

JW: Who edited it?

RO: Elaine Hedges and Susan McAllester. And there was one that Ira Shor and Dick Wasson edited on Marxist criticism, which was one of the first such issues to come out [in the United States]. Another was an issue in 1974 edited by Louie Crew and Rictor Norton called "The Homosexual Imagination," which was the first issue of a scholarly or professional journal ever on that subject.

JW: Long before Eve Sedgwick . . .

RO: Long before Eve Sedgwick. That was the only time that the people to whom I theoretically reported—the College Section Committee—raised objections to anything I was doing in *College English*. They didn't mind the Marxists, the anarchists, the feminists, and so on, but it deeply upset them that the homosexuals were now in *College English*. But they didn't try to fire me.

JW: Really? There was grumbling?

RO: Oh yes. Some people did not want that issue to be there. And now it's twenty years later, and I'm going to chair a session at 4 C's [Conference on College Composition and Communication] this spring that celebrates the twentieth anniversary of "The Homosexual Imagination," which is an indication of how things can turn around.

JW: Speaking of changes in the profession, how would you update *English in America* now? Obviously, you talk about some of the same things in *Politics of Letters* and some articles I've seen, but what would be one angle you would take now to update it? Any afterthoughts on it?

RO: Well, there would be no simple way to update that book, except by looking back critically upon it and attempting some kind of dialectical interaction with it. There are parts of it that, if it were to be reprinted, would probably just have to be scrapped. But even in some of those portions of it—the last three chapters, for example, where I made distant and conjectural forays into issues of knowledge and power—even those parts were generative for me—things having to do with technology and the environment and the challenges to the biosphere, the particular way that our society had and to an extent still has of generating and deploying knowledge that serves capital and profit. It's just that I wasn't very well equipped to write about those things at that time.

JW: I was wondering when I first read it, because it seems implicitly Marxist in that you work out, for the most part, how English education is an ideological state apparatus.

RO: That was not available to me as a Marxist critique then. That is, I did not know Althusser, and I hardly knew the Marxist classics. I knew at that time some writing by radical political economists and other radical groups within the U.S. academic professions. Just at the time that *English in America* came out, I was working with study groups, with faculty members and students, to learn about Marxism. The kinds of language and concepts that were available to me then had to do with power elites and the power structure and the technostructure, things of that sort. I mean, it turned out, of course, that Marxism tremendously enriched and deepened for me those sorts of perceptions and arguments, but it really joined in afterward. There was another part of that question.

JW: Yes, how would you update it? There are different factors on the scene now, obviously, and there are different contours of multinational capitalism that have been played out.

RO: I couldn't, without rebuilding the entire architecture of the book, in the light of what happened later. Incidentally, within two or three years of publishing *English in America,* I had read some things that would have made a big difference had I known them at the time. Braverman's *Labor and Monopoly Capital* especially was a crucial text for me in rethinking the subject of work. There was probably nothing more important for me than Braverman in deciding that I was willing to try to be a Marxist. But then, on top of that, of course there have been major changes in the positioning and structure of the professional managerial class.

JW: Which wasn't even a phrase at that point.

RO: No, that wasn't available to me. Anyway, there were new structures and processes, and there was also new writing about that class, which would have helped if I had had it available. Nonetheless, *English in America* is tentative and hesitant and in some ways rather crude about the way that a certain section of the PMC [professional-managerial class], mainly people who teach English, work for capital. There's little there beyond saying we teach students to be obedient and punctual and so on.

jw: Neat manners and handling memos . . .

ro: Right. Those things are really more about how the PMC reproduces itself than they are about how we discipline the proletariat; those things have been theorized better, and I would want to talk about that. I definitely want to talk about the evolution of late capitalism, post-Fordist capitalism, with the help of people like David Harvey, whose book *The Condition of Postmodernity*, when I finally got to it a year and a half ago, helped me much in thinking about these matters. I sometimes write now about the regime of flexible accumulation and the development of highly mobile forms of capital, credit, and so on, intensely innovative production, with technology, and especially the creative uses of flexible pools of labor all around the world, as characterizing the situation we find ourselves in now. It's remarkable the extent to which, as I've written in an article called "English after the USSR," you could understand some of the things that have been happening in the academic work force, English especially, as homologous to more general developments from Fordism to the regime of flexible accumulation. We were a little laboratory for the use of mobile, exploited, part-time, flex-time labor.

jw: All under the optimistic auspices of giving people more opportunities.

ro: Absolutely. There's no law that forbids you to teach eight courses a semester at seventeen hundred dollars a course at eight different colleges.

jw: I have a former student who is getting his Ph.D. at the University of Maryland and he teaches three different courses at two local colleges, which I think is horrible. I mean, the profession has abandoned him.

ro: It's terrible. Jim Slevin wrote an article about this in *The Politics of Writing Instruction*,[3] which lays out the dismal facts, and proposes professional remedies—not exactly unionization, but banding together to fight administrations to end this scandal. I don't think that's easy to do. I don't think it's possible to do without a much more integrated, national, politically savvy organization of academics. The attractions of this kind of work policy to administrations are simply too overwhelming. I've been serving as a consultant to one of the State University of New York colleges for the last three years, and between my first visit there and my second visit there, the seven or eight full-time, non-tenure-track faculty members, who had benefits and decent salaries and who were doing most of the composition work, had disappeared entirely, to be replaced by a group of part-time adjuncts at a salary something like the one that I mentioned above. I'm talking about a very remote place in upstate New York where they've been able to find a phalanx of adjuncts at those salaries to come in and teach. I spoke about this with the dean on my last visit there, and he said that even now this college was not up to the benchmark for the SUNY system, meaning that it didn't have as many adjuncts in relation to tenure-track faculty as the average for the entire system; therefore, it had to do more of such hiring. These are budget-driven decisions, and the ethics of them can easily be adjusted—tempered—by the observation that there are people out there who are willing to do this work. But it's a very serious obstacle to organizing professionally and politically because we do have these increasingly divided groups. Anyhow, it was dumb of me in *English in America* not to have paid attention to the job crisis which already existed. In fact, the job crisis in English burst upon us in 1969 at the MLA convention in Denver.

JW: It was my understanding that it was much later, in 1975 or so. You mentioned, in a piece that I just saw in *College English*, "Graduate Students, Professionals, Intellectuals" [essay 5 in this book], that the situation you came out of was a lot different because jobs were so plentiful.

RO: They were plentiful up through 1968, and then our field participated in the tectonic plate shifts that Harvey describes in his book. That is, all those changes that you can mark from about 1970 included, as a very, very minor part, the job crisis in the humanities, especially in English. The 1969 MLA convention was supposed to have been held in Chicago, but because of what happened at the Democratic Convention in 1968, a number of organizations were boycotting Chicago; MLA was persuaded to do that and went to Denver instead. The Radical Caucus people went out there expecting to carry on inquiry and provocation and disruption in the same ways that we had in 1968 in New York, and to an extent, we did. But suddenly, on the first day of the convention, there was a new organization called the Job-Seekers Caucus. Graduate students who were finishing their Ph.D.'s and had no historical reason to expect that there wouldn't be jobs, found that there were no job interviews. A lot of jobs had dried up—a situation that has continued for the intervening twenty-four years with small oscillations one way or another.

So that was definitely out there in professional space to be charted. I can't remember whether I even alluded to it in *English in America*, but the general critique that I staged was one of an affluent profession, able to take advantage of a historical conjuncture to strengthen its own position. That was true for the tenure-track and tenured people, but meanwhile the peripheral army of the unemployed was being recruited right then in a very big way. I would want to talk about that in an updated edition. I might also mention another consequence for our field: the college in the SUNY system that I alluded to earlier has essentially no one in the English department, except for the very recent hires, who came there after about 1970. In 1970, after expanding for fifteen years from an old normal school into a rather large college, the money began to run out. They participated in the job crisis that began in the sixties, so there were no more additional positions. Most of the people who were hired then got tenure between 1970 and 1975. That, in itself, is a minor problem for English departments all over the country: too many of my generation are occupying the tenured jobs.

JW: I realize that it's a complicated set of factors, but what is the political stake of that pool of unemployed? I mean, is it some sort of deliberate emaciation of intellectuals, or just a function of the job market and post-Fordism?

RO: That's such a complicated question; let me just say that there are contradictory forces at work here. One is that because the jobs are so few and the stakes are so high for graduate students and untenured faculty members, there are some pressures to do whatever it is that needs to be done in your particular institution, and that may be a repressive influence, but at the very same time, the little victories of the last twenty-five years are nonetheless victories, and intellectual work of the sort that you and I do now can also claim its own rewards. That is, you can get tenure for being a feminist, a queer theorist, or a Marxist, so I don't think that there's a simple way that the two-class system in our profession is going to bear on intellectual work.

But it's such a hard question to think about politically. You asked me in the questions you sent what chances there are for political work in the academy; it's hard to think about that as a labor question. I know that's only part of what you meant, but it seems to me that this sort of dual labor system, which has been developing and strengthening for twenty years or more, is basically in all sectors and all economies. It's worldwide, and the break-up of so-called actually existing socialism is just going to mean further possibilities for maquiladora schemes, and the farming out of labor processes, and places where people are very poor in what used to be the Second World, as well as what used to be the Third World, and of course many parts of the United States of America. So you can't look at your unfortunate younger colleagues who are adjuncts and exploited graduate students and think of the chances for improving their and all our lives without thinking about the people who are assembling electronic devices in Mexico and the Philippines and so on, about the new knowledge markets of various sorts that have developed all over the world. It's a challenge that far exceeds my powers of analysis, but I am convinced this can't be solved within English as a profession.

JW: What do you think about the prospects for the new university and for the corporatization of the university?

RO: Here again, this is an important subject, and it's one that's beyond my grasp at the moment.[4] David Noble, who wrote *America by Design* and some other really important books, is suggesting that the universities essentially are getting out of the education business now.

JW: And what are they in now?

RO: Well, contracting more and more. An anthropologist at Berkeley told me that about 75 percent of the University of California's budget is money that does not come from the state of California.

JW: It's from grants and contracts?

RO: Grants, contracts, federal money, tuition. There are also ways in which knowledge and learning are being packaged and sold entirely outside the university system, so that universities will have to compete with things like IBM, Whittle Communications, Channel One. Companies are spending more and more on education of their own people, I guess I should say training, that is, retooling employees with the kinds of knowledge that they will need as new technologies get in place. And then the states and municipalities and probably even countries compete to attract capital, increasingly, by offering a pretrained workforce to companies that will move in. South Carolina did this with BMW—I talk about these things in "English after the USSR." Universities cannot take for granted anymore, really, that they are the main purveyors of knowledge, theoretical or useful, to our society or to the world. Public schools are going to be competing more and more with these other agencies, and I think that the ideal of the university, which was always belied by circumstances but was nonetheless not a bad ideal, will have a harder time flying as an ideology and certainly as a practice in the future.

You asked, and I think rightly so, what the universities were doing before, and you mentioned class reproduction. Yes, they were always doing class reproduction.

JW: Although most people just didn't go to the universities before. I think in [Gerald] Graff's book, *Professing Literature*, there's a statistic that only something like 2 percent of the population went to university in, say, 1900 to 1920.

RO: A little earlier. The PMC established and expanded its class position in connection with the growth of the university—two things that are inseparable—and our class helped make the universities invaluable to the entire economic system. Now, universities will still certainly be in the business of class reproduction.

JW: On the other hand, one could see it as providing more possibilities for working-class people to go to a university and be trained for bourgeois life.

RO: That happened a lot in the postwar period, and there are millions of students in community colleges and in state colleges now and in the elite colleges who are the first in their families to go to college. The hegemonic process works in part because some of those people do in fact achieve their ambitions and their parents' ambitions. The ideology of equal opportunity would not be so durable an ideology unless there were some truth in it. I think the truth is going to diminish and that the promises being implicitly made to working-class students, that if they work hard in education, they will be able to climb above their parents, are increasingly false promises. This too is part of the division of the world's workforce into core workers and peripheral and flex-time workers. I think that more and more of those working-class students who go to our colleges will find themselves driven toward very job-specific training. And it's also getting harder and harder for them to go to college at all. I don't know the specifics on this, but I bet that more are choosing other ways of moving into the job market now than just a few years ago.

JW: Right, there's been a severe reduction in financial-aid programs and things like that.

RO: Reduction of financial aid, the increases in cost of public and private institutions, the cutbacks in universities which are making many students take six years to complete the B.A., partly because the courses that they need to get through their majors aren't there at the right time, partly because they have to keep dropping out to work. It's getting tougher.

JW: There's a sweatshirt at my school that says on the back, "ECU, the best five or six years of your life."

RO: There you go. I don't think the universities will play quite the role, either, in preserving the porosity of the class structure as they have in the past or sustaining the ideology of equal opportunity as they have. But, on the other hand, they of course will go on, at least for a while, playing several important roles: one is to reproduce the professional managerial class and the bourgeoisie. Even with the exorbitant cost of education at places like Wesleyan, they still, knock on wood, have plenty of applicants who want to come here and are qualified to do it. The colleges and the universities that survive the squeeze of the last decade and the first half of this decade, I think, will still be in a strong position to keep reproducing those two classes. Even with the move toward training, it looks to me as if cultural capital will continue to be valuable, and that students whose parents have money will continue to want to go to places like this, and many students who don't have money will continue to want to try to get financial aid to go to places like this.

JW: It seems to me that there is a greater hierarchization of universities now. You don't hear the rhetoric that you used to, that the state universities, say a Stony Brook, compete with places like Harvard or Yale.

RO: I think that polarization is going on, though one must remember that the private institutions, with a few exceptions, are also under duress right now, and have experienced some cutbacks and speed-ups, that I think impair the quality of education, but your point is right.

JW: I wanted to ask you about your work with *Radical Teacher*. You publish fairly frequently there, and I know that you're an active member of the group around it. So, what's your connection with it? What does the group do?

RO: *Radical Teacher*, well, we call it a socialist/feminist news journal, and that's accurate except for the inappropriateness of the term "news journal" for a magazine that appears irregularly. It came out of the Radical Caucus in the Modern Language Association after five or six years, when Radical Caucus was quite active inside MLA politics and intellectual activities.

JW: About when was that?

RO: That was 1975. I think a particular concern of the people who started the magazine was that there was a risk that the move towards High Theory, including high Marxism, might deny teaching the critical scrutiny that it needed. Somebody needed to be looking at teaching as its ówn political activity or arena, and that was our particular aim—to think about the politics of teaching itself, pedagogy along with the politics of institutions and professions and the politics of knowledge. The magazine has always had a kind of a pragmatic urgency about it—that you meet your classes three times a week and things go on there, those things are important, and there are ways to do them more or less effectively.

JW: It seems to me that the focus on teaching distinguishes your work from other well-known Marxist theorists, and it also implicitly answers the question what is to be done. And the style that you write in—maybe we can talk about this in a few minutes—uses more ordinary language, in the way Orwell prescribes in "Politics and the English Language," than most theorists.

RO: There have been times in the last thirty-five years when Radical Caucus people have stood in some antagonism to Marxist literary criticism because of these kinds of issues: how theoretical they are going to be and how practical they are going to be and to what extent those two things are in some sort of jarring relationship to each other. But I don't want to leave the impression that I align myself with "what do we do Monday morning" in opposition to theory, and I have strong theoretical interests of my own.

JW: There's an essay in *Politics of Letters*—I think it's called "Teaching as Theoretical Practice"—where you talk about a course and cite a handout that you pass out. You talk very specifically about ideology and Marxist theory, as well as how they bear on the works of literature in the course.

RO: Exactly. I've mentioned some theorists today that have been important to me, and I'd certainly add Fred Jameson to that list. Fred said to me once when we were talking about this that he had always assumed there would be a certain division of labor on these matters, and I agreed. I don't want to align myself with the . . .

JW: The antitheory crowd?

RO: Right, or the pragmatic get-out-in-the-streets-and-put-up-the-barricades kind of people over against the theorists. That antagonism is sometimes real enough and worth sharpening, but I don't believe that we all have to be one sort or the other.

JW: That's sometimes the knee-jerk response. How do you find Jameson useful?

RO: Well, in so many ways. I want and need the drive toward both master narratives and utopian visions. When I read him, I often find that I labor pretty hard and I've read two or three pages without much payoff, and then the light bulb comes on. You know, I think that if you get one idea every three pages, that's a reward for the effort. The first chapter of *The Political Unconscious* is very important in thinking about some of the things we've talked of earlier today as well as some of the writing I'm doing myself. The article that Fred did on Third World literature as allegory is a valuable provocation, probably 80 percent wrong, as Aijaz Ahmad and others have argued, but still, he has to say those things in order for those debates to take place. Or, of course, "The Cultural Logic of Late Capitalism," of which I had a serious criticism—but he put those things out and initiated debates. He's done that time and again over the years, and he is willing to be wrong. I think that's great.

What I get from him are fresh and productive ideas. If you look back on something that you read or were fond of that you wrote fifteen years ago, you wouldn't want to say, "Well, I really settled that argument," so much as to say, "Well, I can see I was wrong in a lot of ways, but you know, I joined in and intervened in the process of critique, and that article or that book can now be thrown in the dustbin of history and I won't feel sorry about it at all." One of the little conventions of our profession that is personally irritating to me, though I probably do it to others, is the use of the present tense—"Ohmann says," "Jameson says"—and it's something that you wrote in 1975. Well, I don't say that now, you know. I said that, and it was sort of right and sort of wrong, and we've moved way beyond it.

JW: To take up the question of style, it seems to me that criticism has circled back from High Theory—Jameson, for instance—to more publicly accessible criticism—as in Michael Bérubé's work. I see this change in writing as salutary in some ways, although I'm skeptical of it too. Anyway, what do you think of it as far as your writing is concerned, and also about it as a general trend?

RO: Well, you have to think very seriously about a bunch of issues when you raise this question. One is about who reads, and that sounds obvious, but there are contradictory forces here, too. The entire professional-managerial class and many other working-class people are now positioned to read and be interested in serious but accessible and energetic writings about a variety of subjects, and that's a huge audience. On the other hand, it's an audience that doesn't, in fact, read a whole lot. Probably less in the United States than any of the other advanced countries. And although the [*Village*] *Voice* plays a dynamic part in the intellectual life of our metropolis, it's important to remember that just writing reader-friendly prose will not mean your work gets read in McDonald's or at factories at lunch time, and so on. And if anybody's serious about that, then they've got to turn to other media; even to reach some of the more general print channels for us is not all that easy. One of the essays in *Politics of Letters*—the one on television and the sterilization of politics— came out of an effort on my part to try to push through the professional borders. I gave that, initially, as an improvised lecture the morning after election day, 1976. I had a class then, and I watched the evening news the night before, and I got some notes together and talked about it with a class of people who would have watched it, and then I gave it as a talk someplace later. I tried it out on the *Atlantic*. Then I sent it to *Mother Jones*, but they didn't want it either. They wanted more journalistic writing. They didn't want to hear about hegemony. It's not a great piece, but I'm telling this story just to suggest that writing in a lucid and lively way is not necessarily going to get you into *TV Guide*, though Barbara Ehrenreich has been in *TV Guide*.

JW: Jameson certainly doesn't write that way.

RO: No, I wish that he wrote a little more accessibly. Anyway, what I would insist on is that questions of writing never be detached from questions of social relations. You won't get very far about public voices and broad audiences and accessible writing without thinking very precisely about who writes, who reads, at what sites, under what circumstances, when there are times that perhaps intellectuals can answer a need beyond our own circle. It's more a question of being able and ready to write in such a way or to talk or make videos in such a way when circumstances present themselves.

JW: I see what you mean. Even a hero like Orwell was speaking to a limited public. In the *College English* piece that I mentioned before, you talk about how critical thought spills over from the university. How does that spilling go on?

RO: Well, many people in universities are involved in organizations and activities that are not university-based, so they carry ideas with them and come into some kind of contact with people who are not at universities—that's obvious, but of course the spilling does go in both directions, like a tidal flow.

JW: I like the analogy. One question I wanted to ask you, apropos your *minnesota review* essay on PC, where you say that "we're feminists; we're socialists; some of us are Leninists, not all of us; some of us. . . ." That's a line I try to remember when people ask me what exactly I am. It seems to me that you have a sense of coalition on the left, and you're certainly not doctrinaire, so how do you see the Left?

RO: Um, coalitions . . . they can be very important to rebuilding left politics in the United States. The self-conception of the Left needs to be flexible, and I think we need to be open to thrusts and ventures in various directions, all the way from the New Party to whatever vanguard party starts up next, but you won't find me joining the vanguard party. In some ways, it's rather grand to be talking about the Left as if with a capital "L" and to be agonizing over which strategic turn would be just the right one for this moment. And it's clearly a moment of disarray, of regrouping, I hope, rethinking, reflecting on what did happen, the end of socialism and why, trying to understand what is salvageable from that historical project, if anything. I think we ought to have more of an open-mindedness and candor and admission of ignorance of a lot of these things. The world is not in great shape; certainly the Left is not in great shape. I've seen some good theory about the things we discussed earlier in this interview—the movement past Fordism—but I don't think I've seen very many political practices out there that respond to that. I don't have very much to suggest of my own here. I wouldn't mind if we all said, "All right, let's stop talking about socialism, and let's talk about democracy and equality."

JW: Kind of what Rorty would do . . .

RO: I wouldn't do it that way, but if it would somehow make a difference to fly the banners of equality, including gender equality, racial equality, equality of persons of all sorts, and the banner of democracy, which, needless to say, has never been tried any place in the world, then sure, I would say let's do it. I don't think it's going to work that way. I think we have to continue a critique of the bourgeois ideals, the enlightenment ideals of equality and democracy, even while defending them. Half of the world's population, a billion and a half, earn one dollar a day or less now, and that is comparable to situations in Europe two hundred years ago, but of course far, far, far worse because at that time, so much was outside the market economy. In other words, the world's people are probably worse off now than they have been any time in the history of the whole human race, and a lot of people like you and me are better off than anybody but kings and princes two hundred years ago. There always is crisis, but it seems to me, toward the end of the twentieth century, the crisis is pretty grave and it's global, and it not only covers starvation and epidemics, but the destruction of species and threats to air and water and earth. And without being too dramatic or apocalyptic about this, these questions should always be somewhere in the margins of political arguments of all sorts, even arguments about how we teach in our classrooms. We shouldn't be carrying on arguments about organizing or pedagogies of composition without keeping in mind that we are in a very strange and very threatening historical time.

JW: As a closing question, I wanted to ask what you're working on. You had mentioned that you're finishing up a book. And I'm also curious to find out which books you haven't finished or had wished you had done, that you mentioned before.

RO: Well, I never wrote the one on stylistics. I was going to settle for good the question of form and content, but unfortunately the world will have to wait for my reincarnation to solve the problem of form and content. And then I was going to do a book on the culture industries, which was going to take off from some of the things that are in *Politics of Letters*, and I was going to theorize mass culture, or popular culture, in the Gramscian mode. That book will never get written either, thank heaven. That would have been a terrible book! What I am doing now is something that I intended to be just one chapter of or essay in that never-to-be-written book, on the genesis of the mass-circulation magazine and the advertising industry. That carried me away and turned me in a different direction. Once the institutions and practices of a national mass culture are established, the situation is quite different from the moment when they are being created. Just for example, there are thousands of studies that say advertising in general doesn't make very much difference—that you have to do it if your company is efficient and have to do it to sell your product, but that it doesn't really make very much difference in total demand or in the demand for particular products. But at one time there was no image-filled, complexly interpellating, nationally circulated advertising, and when that all happened within a decade or so, it made a hell of a difference. Dozens of products like Ivory Soap built major corporations at the time when advertising became a major force. So I'm trying to understand how, in a moment of rapid change in the United States in the 1890s, processes that later have become routine were inaugurated. What were the conditions of possibility for those processes then? Who were the multiple agents who, seeking aims of their own, managed an unintentional collaboration among themselves and with the bourgeoisie so that the hegemonic process was redrawn and redirected on a different plane from where it had been before? I hope to make a contribution to thinking about hegemony, as well as about culture and cultural process.

JW: Where are you at with it?

RO: Well, it's close to the end. When I had to stop writing last summer, I was in the middle of a penultimate chapter, so probably another summer's work to do or more. It's probably about 550 pages of manuscript. This has gotten to be a kind of fascination and maybe an obsession—I never thought that I would be writing 30 pages on changes in the conception and use of the parlor in the late nineteenth century. There are all kinds of little byways I've been carried into, and I've learned a lot. We'll see if I can put it together as part of a master narrative or not.[5]

Is that work important enough to be done? Yes, I do think that cultural studies—the kind I like!—is important, and its potential for reorganizing some of the intellectual work in the academy—making it more political as well as seriously interdisciplinary—is great. The chances of that not happening are also great because of the imperatives and dynamics we all know about: professionalism and many of the exigencies of university finances now, the things that we talked about earlier today. So I consider the future of cultural studies an open question. In the past, the question of pedagogy has been woefully underconsidered in cultural studies, but when something new comes along most of the payoff is in the teaching.

Anyway, those are directions; I want to finish this book and then I'm not sure what I want to do next personally. I think I've got three choices. Like in poker, you've always got three choices: call, raise, or fold. And I

may, after a considerable amount of time off after I finish this job [direct-
ing Wesleyan's humanities center], I may teach full-time in the English
department; I may teach half-time for a while, or I may just stop altogether and do more writing.

JW: One other question: my interest has been to spell out the current scene
and piece it together. What do you see on it? What do you see that's
interesting?

RO: Well, we've mentioned a number of the names already, and I would want
to add social constructionists of various sorts and feminists. Joan Scott's
work, I think, is important, and there is also a stack of books that I want
to read when I get my sabbatical. But I'm really not looking for sharp
turns or new directions in theory. I think a lot of people have been interested over the last thirty-five years in reviving Marxism, putting it
into conversation with feminism and gender theory, but also adding
much to them about the unnaturalness of everything that there is. I guess
I don't look for any new paradigms or theory to come along now. Maybe
in a sense I don't want one—I'm too old for one. Aside from the people
we've mentioned, it's probably obvious that I learn a lot from historians.
There's stuff by Stuart Blumin about the evolution of the middle class in
the nineteenth century in the United States that's factually lavish and astonishing and theoretically strong. And it seems to me that some historians who have earned their credentials by getting into the archives and
building specific arguments are also interested in cultural theory, and
some of those people are helpful to me, so I'm turning your question
away from the direction of theory, to history.

NOTES

INTRODUCTION

1. Louis Menand, "The Marketplace of Ideas," American Council of Learned Societies Occasional Paper 49 (New York: ACLS, 2001).

2. David W. Breneman, "For Colleges, This Is Not Just Another Recession," *Chronicle of Higher Education*, June 14, 2002.

1 ENGLISH AND THE COLD WAR

1. I say "English" for simplicity. The range of my discussion will sometimes widen to include other literary studies, foreign-language instruction, American studies, occasionally the humanities in general. I hope these expansions and contractions of scope will not confuse.

2. William H. Epstein, "Counter-Intelligence: Cold-War Criticism and Eighteenth-Century Studies," *English Literary History* 57 (1990).

3. See Robin W. Winks, *Cloak and Gown, 1939–1961: Scholars in the Secret War* (New York: William Morrow, 1987), 495–97.

4. If scholars belong to "any movement, organization, group which does their thinking for them . . . they get no help from us. Without qualification, we know that this condition of un-freedom of mind includes all those who have membership in the Communist Party" (*Reports of the Secretary and the Treasurer* [New York: Guggenheim Foundation, 1951 and 1952], 15). Thanks to G. Thomas Tanselle of the John Simon Guggenheim Memorial Foundation for sending me these reports.

5. Who were "we"? I am drawing on memories of my graduate school cohort and teachers at Harvard through most of the 1950s and my colleagues at Wesleyan in the early 1960s, as well as of scholarly and professional talk at meetings and in journals. My contemporaries who apprenticed in other venues will have to judge how well my memories match theirs.

6. I quote my *English in America: A Radical View of the Profession* (New York: Oxford University Press, 1976; reprint, with new introduction, Middletown, Conn.: Wesleyan University Press, 1996), 75. The phrases quoted from Cleanth Brooks are from his *The Well Wrought Urn: Studies in the Structure of Poetry* (New York: Harcourt, Brace & World, n.d); the quotations from I. A. Richards are from his *Principles of Literary Criticism* (New York: Harcourt, Brace & World, n.d.). Page references of quotations are given in brackets in the text. Throughout this section on New Criticism, I paraphrase my argument of twenty years ago.

7. Ohmann, *English in America*, 76.

8. Women didn't figure much in the making or propagation of these ideas, but it may be worth noting that actual women were beginning to enter the profession; they made up about one-fifth of each new graduate class at Harvard/Radcliffe. By contrast, there were virtually no women coming into science, the harder social sciences, law, medicine, business. Their presence in English, along with that of gay men (of whom there was a lively subculture at Harvard, some all but "out") and indeed that of many Jews, may have contributed subliminally to our sense of apartness from business and government elites.

9. Ellen Schrecker, *No Ivory Tower: McCarthyism and the Universities* (New York: Oxford University Press, 1986).

10. Ibid., 267–68.

11. Ibid., 188–89.

12. Ibid., 189–90.

13. See Ohmann, *English in America*, 45–47.

14. Schrecker, *No Ivory Tower*, 189.

15. See essay 2 for a fuller development of this idea. Force always backs up hegemony, if only as a threat held in reserve. The work of police and intelligence agencies went quietly forward after Senator McCarthy's downfall.

16. I take the phrase "conservative restoration" from the subtitle of Ira Shor's *Culture Wars: School and Society in the Conservative Restoration, 1969–1984* (Boston: Routledge & Kegan Paul, 1986), an excellent account, which has helped me organize my thoughts on this subject.

17. See my essay "The Strange Case of Our Vanishing Literacy," in Richard Ohmann, *Politics of Letters* (Middletown, Conn.: Wesleyan University Press, 1987), 230–35.

18. This story is told in splendid if revolting detail by Ellen Messer-Davidow, "Manufacturing the Attack on Liberalized Higher Education," *Social Text* (fall 1993).

2   ENGLISH AFTER THE USSR

1. Raymond Williams, *Marxism and Literature* (Oxford: Oxford University Press, 1977), 112–13.

2. David Harvey, *The Condition of Postmodernity: An Inquiry into the Origins of Cultural Change* (Cambridge: Basil Blackwell, 1989).

3. Nancy Folbre, "The Bottom Line: Business to the Rescue?" *Nation,* September 21, 1992, 281–82.

4. Jonathan Kozol, *Savage Inequalities* (New York: Crown, 1991).

5. Evan Watkins, *Work Time: English Departments and the Circulation of Cultural Value* (Stanford: Stanford University Press, 1989), 83.

3 SOME CHANGES ACROSS THIRTY-FIVE YEARS

1. Many German and Austrian Jews, fleeing Hitler, settled in the far Upper West Side neighborhood of Manhattan. Louis Kampf, whose family was among them, became president of the MLA after its 1968 uprising.

2. William Bennett and Lynne Cheney chaired the National Endowment for the Humanities and held other high posts during the Reagan and G. H. W. Bush years. Bennett later wrote the best-selling *Book of Virtues.* Cheney (married to the current U.S. vice president) has worked at right-wing foundations and written for the op-ed page of the *Wall Street Journal.* Her having twice attacked me there has in no way influenced the fair-minded assessment of her ideas that I offer in the following paragraph.

3. Louis Kampf and Paul Lauter, eds., *The Politics of Literature* (New York: Pantheon, 1972).

4 TEACHING HISTORICALLY

1. The ad is reproduced on p. 176 of Maria-Regina Kecht, ed., *Pedagogy Is Politics,* and on p. 205 of my *Selling Culture: Magazines, Markets, and Class at the Turn of the Century* (New York: Verso, 1996).

2. A few pages of this essay appeared under the title "Teaching for a Critical and Historical Sense" in the *Gallatin Review* 7 (winter 1987–88). Since I wrote this essay, we have had to suspend the course because of staffing shortages and have compressed some of its contents into the second half of English 201, the close reading course. We made this decision without much debate; hence I cannot say why, in a pinch, close reading seemed more basic or elemental than historical reading.

3. Jane Austen, *Emma,* vol. 2, chap. 7.

4. Lionel Trilling, "*Emma* and the Legend of Jane Austen," in *Beyond Culture* (New York: Harcourt Brace Jovanovich, 1965), 46, 40, 42.

5. Austen, *Emma,* vol. 1, chap. 4.

6. E. J. Hobsbawm and George Rudé, *Captain Swing* (New York: Norton, 1975).

7. E. J. Hobsbawm, *Industry and Empire: From 1750 to the Present Day* (Harmondsworth: Penguin, 1969).

8. Trilling, "Emma and the Legend," 55.

9. Raymond Williams, "Three around Farnham," in *The Country and the City* (New York: Oxford University Press, 1973), 117.

10. David Aers, "Community and Morality: Towards Reading Jane Austen," in *Romanticism and Ideology: Studies in English Writing 1765–1830,* ed. David Aers, Jonathan Cook, and David Punter (London: Routledge and Kegan Paul, 1981), 120.

11. Williams, "Three around Farnham," 115.

12. D. W. Harding, "Regulated Hatred: An Aspect of the Work of Jane Austen," *Scrutiny* 8 (1940): 347.

13. Austen, *Emma*, vol. 3, chap. 6.

14. Perry Anderson, *In the Tracks of Historical Materialism* (Chicago: University of Chicago Press, 1984), 48.

15. Ibid., 40, 45.

16. Jonathan Culler, *On Deconstruction: Theory and Criticism after Structuralism* (Ithaca: Cornell University Press, 1982), 130.

17. S. P. Mohanty, "Radical Teaching, Radical Theory: The Ambiguous Politics of Meaning," in *Theory in the Classroom*, ed. Cary Nelson (Urbana: University of Illinois Press, 1986), 155.

18. Vincent B. Leitch, "Deconstruction and Pedagogy," in Nelson, *Theory in the Classroom*, 54.

19. Mohanty, "Radical Teaching," 156.

20. Jean-Paul Sartre, *What Is Literature?* trans. Bernard Frechtman (New York: Washington Square Press, 1966), 20.

5 GRADUATE STUDENTS, PROFESSIONALS, INTELLECTUALS

1. Russell Jacoby, *The Last Intellectuals: American Culture in the Age of Academe* (New York: Basic Books, 1987), 8.

2. Magali Sarfatti Larson, *The Rise of Professionalism: A Sociological Analysis* (Berkeley: University of California Press, 1977), 14–15.

3. E. D. Hirsch, *Cultural Literacy: What Every American Needs to Know* (Boston: Houghton, 1987), xii.

4. Noam Chomsky, *American Power and the New Mandarins* (New York: Pantheon Books, 1969), 324–25.

6 POLITICS AND COMMITMENT IN WRITING INSTRUCTION

1. For a thorough analysis, see Magali Sarfatti Larson, *The Rise of Professionalism: A Sociological Analysis* (Berkeley: University of California Press, 1977).

2. Richard Ohmann, *English in America: A Radical View of the Profession* (New York: Oxford University Press, 1976; reprint, with new introduction, Middletown, Conn.: Wesleyan University Press, 1996).

3. Larson, *The Rise of Professionalism*, 25.

4. A. W. Coats, "The Educational Revolution and the Professionalization of American Economics," in *Breaking the Academic Mold: Economists and American Higher Learning in the Nineteenth Century*, ed. William J. Barber (Middletown, Conn.: Wesleyan University Press, 1988), 358.

5. Ibid., 371.

6. John C. Gerber, "The Conference on College Composition and Communication," *College Composition and Communication* 1 (1950): 12.

7. Virginia M. Burke, "The Composition-Rhetoric Pyramid," *College Composition and Communication* 16 (1965).

8. For example, John Graves, "On the Desirable Reluctance of Trumpets," *College Composition and Communication* 14 (1963).

9. Ernece B. Kelly, "Murder of the American Dream," *College Composition and Communication* 19 (1968).

10. Edward P. J. Corbett, "The Rhetoric of the Open Hand and the Rhetoric of the Closed Fist," *College Composition and Communication* 20 (1969).

11. In her paper "Discourse and Politics: New Agendas for Composition," given at the general session of the Thomas R. Watson Conference on Rhetoric and Composition, University of Louisville, 1996, where I gave the talk that was the basis for this essay.

7 WHAT'S HAPPENING TO THE UNIVERSITY AND THE PROFESSIONS? CAN HISTORY TELL?

1. Goldie Blumenstyk, "Companies in the 'Education Industry' Get Optimistic Revenue Predictions," *Chronicle of Higher Education,* June 28, 2002, A27.

2. I take the concept and the term from Barbara and John Ehrenreich's "The Professional-Managerial Class," in *Between Labor and Capital,* ed. Pat Walker (Boston, Mass.: South End Press, 1979), 5–45. I work with it extensively in my *Selling Culture: Magazines, Markets, and Class at the Turn of the Century* (London: Verso, 1996), some of whose analysis is encapsulated later in this essay.

3. These terms evoke different standpoints and theories but name the same phenomenon, a perhaps encouraging sign that analysts who disagree about much agree on some main features of twentieth-century capitalism. I favor "corporate capitalism" and, for brevity, "Fordism," though the latter implies a beginning date around 1920, instead of 1900 or so, which is what I have in mind.

4. I have presented versions of this argument in talks at the State University of New York at Buffalo, University of New Hampshire, University of Wisconsin–Milwaukee, Temple University, Trinity College, and elsewhere. Thanks to questioners and commenters there and to Rich Daniels, Barbara Foley, Louis Kampf, William Roseberry, and others who offered useful criticism and suggestions.

5. Ehrenreich and Ehrenreich, in Walker, *Between Labor and Capital,* 12. Their essay includes a compact survey of earlier views on the question. The rest of the book comprises essays by various hands proposing to qualify or refute the PMC thesis, along with the Ehrenreichs' rejoinder.

6. As the Ehrenreichs themselves insisted, their political aim was to understand that defection and its limits. This part of their analysis is pertinent to the situation and agency of the PMC today.

7. The next few pages summarize and extrapolate from the argument of *Selling Culture.* In essay 11, I encapsulate another part of that argument.

8. John Frow, *Cultural Studies and Cultural Value* (Oxford: Clarendon Press,

1995), 91. Frow's chapter "Class and Cultural Capital" is an especially clear and helpful exploration of the ideas I work with here, using slightly different terms.

9. I take the term "regime of flexible accumulation," from David Harvey, *The Condition of Postmodernity: An Enquiry into the Origins of Cultural Change* (Cambridge, Mass.: Blackwell, 1990). He spells out this narrative of recent times in part 2 of his book, "The Political-Economic Transformation of Late Twentieth-Century Capitalism," and especially in chap. 9, "From Fordism to Flexible Accumulation." Also see essays 2 and 12 in this volume, for fuller accounts.

10. The same scenario unfolded in Thatcherite Britain, and, with less publicity, in Canada, where the decline since 1980 has been more abrupt: government support dropped from 60 percent of all costs to 40 percent.

11. Andrew Brownstein, "Tuitions Rise Sharply, and This Time Public Colleges Lead the Way," *Chronicle of Higher Education,* November 2, 2000, A52. This was before a recession brought on deep fiscal crisis in most states.

12. See, among many other accounts, "Why Is Tuition Going through the Roof," *University Business* (April 1999), reporting a study by the Institute for Higher Education Policy; Brownstein, "Tuitions Rise Sharply"; Jacques Steinberg, "State Colleges, Feeling Pinch, Cut Costs and Raise Tuitions," *New York Times,* September 7, 2001; Yilu Zhao, "As College Endowments Slip, Tuition Increases Fill the Void," *New York Times,* February 22, 2002.

13. The budget problems derive to some extent from a great increase, over decades, in the portion of total expenditures going to administration itself. But that's another story.

14. Kit Lively, "U. of Florida's 'Bank' Rewards Colleges that Meet Key Goals," *Chronicle of Higher Education,* February 26, 1999, A35. From this point in the essay onward, I refer to specific practices and institutions. I warn the reader that the half-life of news in this arena is very short. Universities are trying out and then modifying or scrapping arrangements almost as fast as the agile corporations they emulate, and certainly faster than the elapsed time between my reading about these practices and the publication of my analysis.

15. Anne Brockhoff, "Building a Culture of Quality," *University Business* (July/August 2001): 55.

16. "Common Sense," interview with Carol Twigg, *University Business* (December 2000/January 2001): 26.

17. Florence Olsen, "Fed Up with Delays, a President Pushes to Outsource Technology Operations," *Chronicle of Higher Education* (February 15, 2002), A41–42.

18. Susan Carr, "Another Web Company Eyes Academe, This One Offering Tutoring Assistance," *Chronicle of Higher Education,* December 3, 1999, A45.

19. For a balanced and sympathetic account, see "The New U: A Tough Market Is Reshaping Colleges," *Business Week,* December 22, 1997.

20. Martin van der Werf, "A Vice-President from the Business World Brings a New Bottom Line to Penn," *Chronicle of Higher Education,* September 3, 1999, A72.

21. Peter Schmidt, Jeffrey Selingo, and Sara Hebel, "As Legislators Convene, Colleges Push Their Spending Priorities," *Chronicle of Higher Education,* January 7, 2000, A43; Christy Hoppe, "Texas University Tries to Set Test Standard for Higher Ed," *Boston Globe,* August 19, 2001. A number of other states have initiated similar efforts.

22. Writing on this subject is abundant. Well-known discussions from which I have profited include David F. Noble, *Digital Diploma Mills: The Automation of Higher Education* (New York: Monthly Review Press, 2002), a gathering of Noble's Internet and journal articles on this subject; Lawrence C. Soley, *Leasing the Ivory Tower: The Corporate Takeover of Academia* (Boston: South End Press, 1995); Sheila Slaughter and Larry Leslie, *Academic Capitalism: Politics, Policies, and the Entrepreneurial University* (Baltimore: Johns Hopkins University Press, 1997); Masao Miyoshi, "Ivory Tower in Escrow," *Boundary 2* (spring 2000); Eyal Press and Jennifer Washburn, "The Kept University," *Atlantic Monthly* (March 2000); Bill Readings, *The University in Ruins* (Cambridge, Mass.: Harvard University Press, 1996). Most of these authors are academic professionals (indeed, humanists), and their titles convey the anger and feeling of betrayal that drive much commentary. Emotionally, I'm with them. But in this essay I would like to achieve a certain distance. The university is changing in response to large historical pressures whose genesis and direction may come clearer if studied dispassionately.

23. Martin van der Werf and Goldie Blumenstyk, "A Fertile Place to Breed Businesses," *Chronicle of Higher Education,* March 2, 2001, A28; Scott Carlson, "A 1,000-Acre Incubator for Research and Business," *Chronicle of Higher Education,* April 14, 2000, A49. Note that these projects take universities a good deal farther into business than they go by simply selling research.

24. Goldie Blumenstyk, "Turning Patent Royalties into a Sure Thing," *Chronicle of Higher Education,* October 5, 2001, A26.

25. Martin van der Werf, "As Coke and Pepsi Do Battle on Campuses, Colleges Find a Fountain of New Revenue," *Chronicle of Higher Education,* October 15, 1999, A41.

26. Ron Feemster, "Selling Eyeballs," *University Business* (September 1999): 43.

27. Goldie Blumenstyk, "Some Students Think 'Smart' Identification Cards Go Too Far," *Chronicle of Higher Education,* September 10, 1999, A39.

28. Welch Suggs, "Novel Corporate Deal Will Finance New Basketball Arena for U. of Maryland," *Chronicle of Higher Education,* January 14, 2000, A54.

29. Dan Carnevale, "Survey Finds 72% Rise in Number of Distance-Education Programs," *Chronicle of Higher Education,* January 7, 2000, A57; Eyal Press and Jennifer Washburn, "Digital Diplomas," *Mother Jones* (January/February 2001): 34. I have read much higher estimates of the number of courses on the Internet.

30. Florence Olsen, "'Virtual' Institutions Challenge Accreditors to Devise New Ways of Measuring Quality," *Chronicle of Higher Education,* August 6, 2000, A29.

31. Sarah Carr, "Union Publishes Guide Citing High Cost of Distance Education, *Chronicle of Higher Education*, May 11, 2001, A39.

32. Katherine S. Mangan, "Expectations Evaporate for Online MBA Programs," *Chronicle of Higher Education*, October 5, 2001, A31; Eric Pfeffinger, "Kentucky's Virtual Dynamo," *University Business* (November 2000); Jeffrey R. Young, "Dispatches from Distance Education," *Chronicle of Higher Education*, March 3, 2000, A41.

33. Ben Gose, "Surge in Continuing Education Brings Profits for Universities," *Chronicle of Higher Education*, February 19, 1999, A51.

34. Editors of *University Business*, "Certificates: Credentials of Choice," and James Martin and James E. Samels, "Launching a New Certificate Program," *University Business* (November 2001): 49; see also Gose, "Surge in Continuing Education."

35. Peter Schmidt, "States Set a Course for Higher-Education Systems," *Chronicle of Higher Education*, June 30, 2000, A28.

36. Ethan Bronner, "College Freshmen Aiming for High Marks in Income," *New York Times*, January 12, 1998, A14.

37. Goldie Blumenstyk, "Knowledge Is 'a Form of Venture Capital' for a Top Columbia Administrator," *Chronicle of Higher Education*, February 9, 2001, A20, A21; Karen Arenson, "Columbia Sets Pace in Profiting off Research," *New York Times*, August 2, 2000, B1, B6. I have drawn on articles too numerous to mention for additional information about UNext and Fathom.

38. James Traub, "Drive-Thru U.," *New Yorker*, October 20 and 27, 1997; Mark Fischetti, John Anderson, Malena Watrous, Jason Tanz, and Peter Gwynne, "Education? The University of Phoenix Is Just around the Corner" *University Business* (March/April 1998); Jeffrey Selingo, "Aiming for a New Audience, U. of Phoenix Tries Again in New Jersey," *Chronicle of Higher Education*, November 21, 2001, A23; Goldie Blumenstyk, "How For-Profit Institutions Chase Community-College Students," *Chronicle of Higher Education*, December 8, 2000, A30. I have given estimates and blurred figures because this company is growing fast.

39. Lisa Kartus, "Gaining by Degrees," *University Business* (February 2000); Goldie Blumenstyk, "Turning a Profit by Turning Out Professionals," *Chronicle of Higher Education*, January 7, 2000, A46.

40. Margaret Littman, "Kaplan's New Test," *University Business* (September 1999): 32–34; Goldie Blumenstyk, "Kaplan Moves beyond Test Preparation with Purchases of For-Profit Colleges," *Chronicle of Higher Education*, February 15, 2000, A36–37.

41. Anne Marie Borrego, "A Wave of Consolidation Hits For-Profit Higher Education," *Chronicle of Higher Education*, August 10, 2001, A42–43.

42. Jeanne C. Meister, "The Brave New World of Corporate Education," *Chronicle of Higher Education*, February 9, 2001, B10–11; "What's New at the Corporate U?" *University Business* (September 2000): 13–14.

43. Allison Lehr, "The World Campus," *University Business* (June 2000): 27; Julia Hinde, "Made in Australia," *University Business* (November 2000): 31, 35.

44. Bill Readings, *The University in Ruins* (Cambridge, Mass.: Harvard University Press, 1996).

45. See for a good discussion, John Palattella, "May the Course Be with You," *Lingua Franca* (March 2001).

46. Steven Greenhouse, "Angered by H.M.O.'s Treatment, More Doctors Are Joining Unions, *New York Times*, February 4, 1999, A1, A25; Katherine S. Mangan, "Academic Medicine Becomes a Target for Labor Organizing," *Chronicle of Higher Education*, August 6, 1999, A14.

47. Andrew Hacker, *Money: Who Has How Much and Why* (New York: Scribner, 1997), chap. 7.

48. Elliott A. Krause, *The Death of the Guilds: Professions, States, and the Advance of Capitalism, 1930 to the Present* (New Haven: Yale University Press, 1996).

49. Gary John Previts and Barbara Dubis Merino, *A History of Accountancy in the United States: The Cultural Significance of Accounting* (Columbus: Ohio State University Press, 1998), 348, 352. For these paragraphs I have also drawn upon Paul J. Miranti Jr., *Accountancy Comes of Age: The Development of an American Profession, 1886–1940* (Chapel Hill: University of North Carolina Press, 1990); and Gerard Hanlon, *The Commercialisation of Accountancy: Flexible Accumulation and the Transformation of the Service Class* (New York: St. Martin's, 1994).

50. Jill Andresky Fraser, *White-Collar Sweatshop: The Deterioration of Work and Its Rewards in Corporate America* (New York: Norton, 2001), 100–101.

51. Richard Marens, "Life after the Organization Man," *Left Business Observer*, December 31, 1998, 2.

52. Ibid.

53. I hear on the radio that several dozen philosophy Ph.D.'s are now in business as therapists. Wittgenstein, who thought of philosophical dilemmas as "mental cramps," might be pleased.

8 TEACHING LITERACY FOR CITIZENSHIP

1. A powerful recent reminder that some would like the university to underwrite national culture was the November 2001 report of the American Council of Trustees and Alumni, "Defending Civilization." It cited over a hundred post–September 11 statements by university people for weak or absent patriotism and blamed this *trahison des clercs* on the university's abandonment of a core curriculum explaining the values of our founding fathers and of Western civilization. Such a curriculum, the report said, was America's "first line of defense."

2. A professor of rhetoric at Minnesota wrote in 1895 that, where students who were otherwise promising could not speak without Scandinavian accents or write without foreign idioms, "the fundamental work of the University must be a struggle for correctness." From William M. Payne, ed., *English in American*

Universities (Boston: Heath, 1895), 96. Quoted in my *English in America: A Radical View of the Profession* (New York: Oxford University Press, 1976; reprint, with new introduction, Middletown, Conn.: Wesleyan University Press, 1996), 249.

3. T. H. Marshall, "Citizenship and Social Class"; this 1949 lecture series was published in *Class, Citizenship, and Social Development: Essays by T. H. Marshall* (Garden City, N.Y.: Doubleday, 1964). The quotation is from p. 84. I am paraphrasing in this paragraph from my "Thick Citizenship and Textual Relations," *Citizenship Studies* 3.2 (1999).

4. Or, if not for more equality, for a higher level of "adequacy," regardless of equity. Suits demanding that states provide resources to bring poor schools up to a level that will "equip students for their roles as citizens and enable them to succeed economically and personally" have succeeded in a number of states (Peter Schrag, "Defining Adequacy Up," *Nation*, March 12, 2001, 18). In 2001, a decision in New York used similar language, mandating education for "productive citizenship" and "civic engagement," and holding that the state's system of financing schools denied such education to many children in New York City (ibid., 19). The principle, more and more widely accepted, that states have such responsibilities in small part explains their recent intrusiveness in curriculum and assessment.

5. Geoffrey White, *Campus Inc.: Corporate Power in the Ivory Tower* (Amherst, N.Y.: Prometheus Books, 2000).

6. Bill Readings, *The University in Ruins* (Cambridge, Mass.: Harvard University Press, 1996).

7. Daniel Green, "Abandoning the Ruins," *College English* 63.3 (January 2001): 280.

8. Martin van der Werf and Goldie Blumenstyk, "A Fertile Place to Breed Businesses: Campus-Based Incubators Try to Help Entrepreneurs Bring Brainstorms to Market," *Chronicle of Higher Education*, March 2, 2001, A28–A29.

9 HISTORICAL REFLECTIONS ON ACCOUNTABILITY

1. Joel W. Meyerson and William F. Massy, eds., *Measuring Institutional Performance in Higher Education* (Princeton: Peterson's, 1994).

2. *University Business* is a magazine founded by the publisher of *Lingua Franca* and sent free to 34,000 college and university administrators—itself a sign and a facilitator of marketization and accountability.

3. "Regime of flexible accumulation" is David Harvey's phrase, in *The Condition of Postmodernity: An Enquiry into the Origins of Cultural Change* (Oxford: Basil Blackwell, 1989); his analysis has strongly influenced my own.

4. Thanks to Cynthia L. Spell of the Reference Department at the University of Massachusetts library for finding this out.

5. Leon M. Lessinger, *Every Kid a Winner: Accountability in Education* (Palo Alto: Science Research Associates, 1970).

6. In 1971, for instance, the Educational Testing Service sponsored the "Con-

ference on Educational Accountability," and Ralph Nader organized one on "corporate accountability." That phrase continued to sound in liberal and left circles, but the official discourse of accountability was irreversibly about schooling, not about holding the powerful to account.

7. Frank J. Sciara and Richard K. Jantz, eds., *Accountability in American Education* (Boston: Allyn & Bacon), 1, 3.

8. Terrel H. Bell, "The New Look of Federal Aid to Education," in Sciara and Jantz, *Accountability in American Education*, 41–47.

9. T. R. McConnell, "Accountability and Autonomy," in Sciara and Jantz, *Accountability in American Education*, 200.

10. Ira Shor, *Culture Wars: School and Society in the Conservative Restoration, 1969–1984* (Boston: Routledge and Kegan Paul, 1986).

11. Bill Readings, in *The University in Ruins* (Cambridge, Mass.: Harvard University Press, 1996), 233, among other places.

12. See for instance, "The New U: A Tough Market is Reshaping Colleges," *Business Week*, December 22, 1997, 96–102.

13. The quotation is attributed to Jack Gordon, in *Training* (November 1998). It continues: "And that market is about to explode in the same way, except that the time frame will be collapsed. What took 40 years in health care will take only 10 in education."

14. See Elliott A. Krause, *Death of the Guilds: Professions, States, and the Advance of Capitalism, 1930 to the Present* (New Haven: Yale University Press, 1996).

15. See Paul Lauter, "'Political Correctness' and the Attack on American Colleges," *Radical Teacher* 44 (winter 1993), for an early and excellent account.

16. For an interesting survey from the corporate point of view, see "The New U: A Tough Market Is Reshaping Colleges," *Business Week*, December 22, 1997.

17. Thanks to David Downing for pointing out this connection to me.

10 ACADEMIC FREEDOM, 2000 AND AFTER

1. Including, to the cheers of this retired faculty member, the president of Wesleyan University, Douglas Bennet.

2. An ample survey from this point of view is *Zealotry and Academic Freedom: A Legal and Historical Perspective*, by Neil Hamilton (New Brunswick: Transaction, 1995). Hamilton's appendices include some of the most important AAUP statements, including the ones from which I quote in this essay.

3. The *Chronicle*, like any paper, has unstated principles of selectivity and importance. I use it for convenience, and because it is ideologically centrist—that is, about equidistant from me and Herb London.

4. Daphne Patai, "Speak Freely, Professor—Within the Speech Code," *Chronicle of Higher Education*, June 99, 2000, B8–B9.

5. Ellen Schrecker, *No Ivory Tower: McCarthyism and the Universities* (New York: Oxford University Press, 1986)

6. Louis Menand, ed., *The Future of Academic Freedom* (Chicago: University

of Chicago Press, 1996). The AAUP sponsored this useful book as an intervention in the PC controversy.

7. Stanley Fish, *There's No Such Thing As Free Speech and It's a Good Thing, Too* (New York: Oxford University Press, 1994), 102. He applies the argument to academic freedom in his essay " Academic Freedom: When Sauce for the Goose Isn't Sauce for the Gander," *Chronicle of Higher Education,* November 26, 1999.

8. See my *Selling Culture: Magazines, Markets, and Class at the Turn of the Century* (London: Verso, 1996), for much more on this subject.

9. Thomas L. Haskell, "Justifying the Rights of Academic Freedom in the Era of 'Power/Knowledge,'" in Menand, *The Future of Academic Freedom,* 57.

10. That is, every group of workers with professional recognition has achieved at least partial control of and independence in its practices of research and communication. This achievement was more difficult for professionals working for salaries than for those, like physicians, who worked mainly for themselves.

11. I joined the effort: see my *English in America: A Radical Critique of the Profession* (New York: Oxford University Press, 1976; reprint, with new introduction, Middletown, Conn.: Wesleyan University Press, 1996).

12. William Greider, *One World, Ready or Not: The Manic Logic of Global Capitalism* (New York: Simon & Schuster, 1997); Robert Brenner, *New Left Review* 229: *The Economics of Global Turbulence* (May/June 1998).

13. When the Medical College of Pennsylvania (MCP) and the Hahnemann University Medical School merged in 1994, "MCP" became part of the institution's name.

11 BOOK AND MAGAZINE PUBLISHING THROUGH THE PERIOD OF CORPORATE REVOLUTION

1. My account of it is in Richard Ohmann, *Selling Culture: Magazines, Markets, and Class at the Turn of the Century* (London: Verso, 1996).

2. Newspaper publishing went through a similar but more uneven change at about the same time.

3. Gerald R. Wolfe, *The House of Appleton* (Metuchen, N.J.: Scarecrow Press, 1981), 27–30.

4. Ibid., 175–76. On Scribner, see Donald Sheehan, *This Was Publishing: A Chronicle of the Book Trade in the Gilded Age* (Bloomington: Indiana University Press, 1952), 42–43. For Houghton Mifflin's experience, see Ellen B. Ballou, *The Building of the House: Houghton Mifflin's Formative Years* (Boston: Houghton Mifflin, 1970), 366. Mifflin's letter was to F. Hopkinson Smith in 1896, quoted in Ballou, ibid., 429. For Scudder's and Perry's views and for other information on Houghton Mifflin and the *Atlantic,* see Ballou, ibid., 295, 425, 433, 444, 467.

5. Quoted from the *Riverside Bulletin,* September 1, 1873, in Ballou, *Building of the House,* 350. On the *Atlantic* as prestigious money-loser, see Ballou, ibid., 452–53. On *Scribner's* in the nineties, see Roger Burlingame, *Of Making Many*

Books: A Hundred Years of Reading, Writing and Publishing [an informal history of Charles Scribner's Sons] (New York: Charles Scribner's Sons, 1946), 43.

6. Much of this information is from John Tebbel, *A History of Book Publishing in the United States*, vol. 2: *The Expansion of an Industry, 1865–1919* (New York: Bowker, 1975).

7. See Peter Lyon, *Success Story: The Life and Times of S. S. McClure* (Deland, Fla.: Everett Edwards, 1967), pt. 2: "The Syndicate—1884–1893," 51–110.

8. See Sheehan, *This Was Publishing*, 190–95.

9. Janice Radway, *A Feeling for Books: The Book-of-the-Month Club, Literary Taste, and Middle-Class Desire* (Chapel Hill: University of North Carolina Press, 1997), 135.

10. I abbreviate these ideas (and take the phrase "gentlemanly exchange") from Christopher P. Wilson, "The Rhetoric of Consumption: Mass-Market Magazines and the Demise of the Gentle Reader, 1880–1920," in *The Culture of Consumption: Critical Essays in American History, 1880–1980*, ed. Richard Wightman Fox and T. J. Jackson Lears (New York: Pantheon, 1983).

11. Eugene Exman, *The House of Harper: One Hundred and Fifty Years of Publishing* (New York: Harper & Row, 1967), 180. For other information in this paragraph see Tebbel, *History of Book Publishing*, 47, 149, and Ballou, *Building of the House*, 419, 445.

12. The standard work on this process is Alfred D. Chandler Jr., *The Visible Hand: The Managerial Revolution in American Business* (Cambridge, Mass.: Harvard University Press, 1977). See my *Selling Culture* for many details and references.

13. Sheehan, *This Was Publishing*, 21–22.

14. Ibid., 224–37.

15. Ballou, *Building of the House*, 425–27. I rely for the picture drawn in this paragraph chiefly on Sheehan's chapter "The Assault on the Consumer" and on Tebbel, *History of Book Publishing*, 150–70. The data are soft, at best.

16. Tebbel, *History of Book Publishing*, 153.

17. Sheehan, *This Was Publishing*, 19–23.

12 EPOCHAL CHANGE: PRINT CULTURE AND ECONOMICS

1. Thomas Whiteside, *The Blockbuster Complex: Conglomerates, Show Business, and Book Publishing* (Middletown, Conn.: Wesleyan University Press, 1981), 1.

2. Quoted by Whiteside, ibid., from the *New York Times*, April 9, 1978, 130.

3. Gerald Stanley Lee, *The Lost Art of Reading* (New York: G. P. Putnam's Sons, 1907), 18, 20. The book was originally published in 1902.

4. Christopher P. Wilson, "The Rhetoric of Consumption: Mass-Market Magazines and the Demise of the Gentle Reader, 1880–1920," in *The Culture of Consumption: Critical Essays in American History, 1880–1980*, ed. Richard Wightman Fox and T. J. Jackson Lears (New York: Pantheon, 1983).

5. Richard Ohmann, *Selling Culture: Magazines, Markets, and Class at the Turn of the Century* (New York: Verso, 1996).

6. Book publishing as a whole includes college and K–12 textbooks, scholarly monographs, and several other conventional categories. This essay focuses on trade books, along with closely related mass-market paperbacks, mail order books, and book club offerings. These have in common a direct appeal to readers as unaffiliated individuals; they are consumer goods. By contrast, professional, scholarly, and textbooks are marketed in connection with schooling or work, and for textbooks in particular, the end user (the student) does not choose which books to buy. The books I hold in view amount to about half the total market.

7. Karen Raugust, quoted by M. P. Dunleavy in "License to Publish," *Publishers Weekly*, February 6, 1995, 127.

8. Whiteside, *The Blockbuster Complex*, 87–88.

9. I have drawn a good deal of such information from Albert N. Greco, *The Book Publishing Industry* (Boston: Allyn & Bacon, 1997). See pp. 46–49 for a survey of mergers from 1960 to 1995.

10. Lewis A. Coser, Charles Kadushin, and Walter W. Powell, *Books: The Culture and Commerce of Publishing* (New York: Basic Books, 1982), 26.

11. Greco, *Book Publishing Industry*, 58; "The Media Nation: Publishing" [chart], *Nation*, March 17, 1997, 24; Robert W. McChesney, "The Global Media Giants: The Nine Firms That Dominate the World," *Extra!* November/December 1997, 13. Now the merger with AOL makes this an Internet power, as well.

12. Greco, *Book Publishing Industry*, 58.

13. Ibid., 224.

14. Among the works that have shaped my outlook are David Harvey, *The Condition of Postmodernity: An Enquiry into the Origins of Cultural Change* (Cambridge, Mass.: Blackwell, 1989), and Robert Brenner, "Uneven Development and the Long Downturn: The Advanced Capitalist Economies from Boom to Stagnation, 1950–1998," *New Left Review* 229: *The Economics of Global Turbulence* (May/June 1998).

15. I am aware that my focus slides back and forth between U.S. capitalism and world capitalism. The global system entered a time of crisis around 1970, but because the crisis owed in part to conflicts among capitalist powers, it was variously realized in those countries. My main subject is its expression in the United States.

16. Steven L. Goldman, Roger N. Nagel, Kenneth Preiss, *Agile Competitors and Virtual Organizations: Strategies for Enriching the Customer* (New York: Van Nostrand Reinhold, 1995), 17.

17. The best survey I know is Joseph Turow, *Breaking Up America: Advertisers and the New Media World* (Chicago: University of Chicago Press, 1997).

18. Goldman et al., *Agile Competitors and Virtual Organizations*, 11–12.

19. Richard J. Barnet and Ronald E. Muller, *Global Reach: The Power of the Multinational Corporations* (New York: Simon & Schuster, 1974).

20. William Greider, *One World, Ready or Not: The Manic Logic of Global Capitalism* (New York: Simon & Schuster, 1997).

21. See essays 7–10 in this volume.

22. Ian Willison, "The History of the Book in Twentieth-Century Britain and America: Perspective and Evidence," *Preceedings of the American Antiquarian Society* 102 (1992): 355.

23. Greco, *Book Publishing Industry*, 54.

24. Jim Milliot, "Newcomb Looking to Instill New Corporate Culture at Simon and Schuster," *Publishers Weekly*, January 9, 1995, 18–19.

25. McChesney, "Global Media Giants," 15.

26. Ibid., 16.

27. *Publishers Weekly*, January 16, 1995, 312.

28. Whiteside, *The Blockbuster Complex*, 71.

29. Harvey, *The Condition of Postmodernity*, 160.

30. For a while it looked as if publishers would forgo instant books about the Oklahoma City bombing, in unaccustomed deference to grief and loss. Then Random House, followed by Ballantine, announced plans for books that would pay tribute to the dead or the heroic living, with part or all of the profits going to relief and charity (*Publishers Weekly*, May 15, 1995, 16).

31. Though many conglomerates do not own magazines, and a few magazine companies own nothing else: see the charts in Charles P. Daly, Patrick Henry, and Ellen Ryder, *The Magazine Publishing Industry* (Boston: Allyn & Bacon, 1997), 22–23.

32. Interview with Ira Herbert, in *Making and Selling Culture*, ed. Richard Ohmann (Hanover, N.H.: Wesleyan University Press, 1996); I owe this observation to Gage Averill, whose essay, "Global Imaginings," appeared in the same volume.

33. I make this argument in the previous essay.

34. Jason Epstein's "The Rattle of Pebbles" (*New York Review of Books*, April 27, 2000, 55–59) and "The Coming Revolution" (*New York Review of Books*, November 2, 2000, 4–5) are sections of a book in progress.

35. Dawson Church put out a similar vision, including the idea of book machines on the model of ATMs, that print and spit out the book you want and charge it to your credit card: "Information for Sale," *Publishers Weekly*, May 29, 1995, 39–41.

13 THE PERSONAL AS HISTORY

1. Here's a symptomatic story: one paper was a third-person account, modeled on Henry Adams, of "the boy's" first walk into Harvard yard. Hal Martin

thought it was wonderful, and wanted to submit it to the alumni magazine (which did in fact print it). I had given it a B+, and asked Hal if he thought that a little ungenerous. Yes, he said. I changed the grade to A. Did Arthur Pett— the student's name, if memory serves—benefit from my exquisitely high standards? A graduate student colleague of mine, when asked why a grade was so low, would say: "For a B, you have to write as well as I do; for an A, as well as Hemingway." Western civilization was safe in our hands.

2. Mentor and friend, Hal saw better than I what I could do, and launched my career.

3. No one spoke these lessons to me and my graduate student cohort; they were in the air we breathed. Yet in time I did actually take vows of scholarship, administered with great seriousness to inductees into Harvard's Society of Fellows, by such as W. V. Quine, Wassily Leontiev, and my dissertation director Harry Levin. For example: "You will practice the virtues, and avoid the snares, of the scholar. You will be courteous to your elders, who have explored to the point from which you may advance and helpful to your juniors, who will progress farther by reason of your labors. Your aim will be knowledge and wisdom, not the reflected glamour of fame. You will not accept credit that is due to another or harbor jealousy of an explorer who is more fortunate. You will seek not a near but a distant objective, and you will not be satisfied with what you may have done. All that you may achieve or discover you will regard as a fragment of a larger pattern of the truth, which from their separate approaches every true scholar is striving to descry." A high vocation, a heady moment.

4. What a missed opportunity for discussion of literature and belief, of my and the students' relations to the texts we were reading and the culture we were studying.

5. To have done so at the time would have been all but unthinkable, in a context such as the present one. I remember a few personal essays about teaching; for instance, Theodore Roethke's marvelous "Last Class" (*College English*, 18.8 [May 1957]). But see: reminiscence was a prerogative of poets and novelists.

6. In the process I became more explicitly the interpreter, as well as teller, of my tale. It's hard for the "personal turn" to displace lifelong habits of academic authority.

7. And have done: see my "English and the Cold War," in Noam Chomsky et al., *The Cold War and the University* (New York: New Press, 1997), and in this volume.

8. When I obtained it in the mid-1970s, under the Freedom of Information Act, I was surprised to find how many tax dollars the FBI had squandered clipping my letters to the *Middletown Press* and to Wesleyan's student newspaper, and also miffed that its agents had sized me up as a sincere but harmless protester, not a dangerous enemy of the state.

9. A friend stopped me on the street: his first-grade kid came home from school with the news that I was likely to go to jail. I had tried to explain what I

was doing to *my* first-grade kid, and she had disclosed her version of the story in "show and tell."

10. Translation: academic vice president. Since our president more or less vacated the premises that year, I and the other vice president found ourselves in charge, though hardly in control.

11. Objections from readers of *College English* were plentiful, and I dutifully printed those that came in as letters. A few members of NCTE called for my ouster. But in the twelve years of my editorship, those in the NCTE to whom I was directly responsible grumbled aloud to me just once: not about unpatriotic or Marxist or feminist sallies in the journal, but about a 1974 special issue on "The Homosexual Imagination." Interesting.

12. And for a parental leave policy, the one idea too much before its time to be enacted.

13. I supported the dean. He went on to become president of a small state university, then of two large ones. I returned to teaching as fast as I was able.

14. The discussion spilled out into journals, as well, particularly in English. My own commitments are perhaps enough to explain the proliferation of articles in *College English* that reexamined pedagogy under the sign of the political, but the same interest invaded the pages of *College Composition and Communication*, whose editor (William Irmscher) espoused politics very different from mine.

15. David Bleich, *Know and Tell: A Writing Pedagogy of Disclosure, Genre, and Membership* (Portsmouth, N.H.: Boynton/Cook, 1998), esp. 13–19.

16. Ibid., 16.

17. For instance, the student-led course "Towards a Socialist America," which reproduced itself at Wesleyan through shifts in political climate, official opposition, a softening of purpose and of title, over twenty years. See Eric Arneson, David Ebb, Stephen Rome, Stephen Ward, "A Student Initiated Course in Socialism," *Radical Teacher* 9 (September 1978). The course was accorded a surprising honor when Lynne Cheney attacked its catalog description (ignorantly) on the editorial page of the *Wall Street Journal*, March 14, 1996.

18. See "Teaching as Theoretical Practice," chap. 8 of my *Politics of Letters* (Middletown, Conn.: Wesleyan University Press, 1987).

19. See Louis Kampf and Paul Lauter, eds., *The Politics of Literature* (New York: Pantheon, 1972), for such an effort, in which I played a small part.

20. *Selling Culture: Magazines, Markets, and Class at the Turn of the Century* (New York: Verso, 1996), my most learned work, germinated in a course I taught on American mass culture (with invaluable help from undergraduate TAs) in the late seventies, and gained momentum from several other courses that I devised along the way—courses very far from my early training and interests.

21. Yes, I doled out the grades; no escape from that. Two strategies eased the contradictions. First, I made grading a subject of explicit discussion, often in the context of power and social reproduction as these topics came up in the course. Second, in comments on papers I excused myself from the task of ex-

plaining the grades I had given. I credited students with having taken seriously an intellectual challenge and written something they stood behind, not just having tried to please me in an academic exercise. (This working premise was of course not always correct.) I framed my comments as responses to their ideas, often critical but not according to some paradigm of A-ness or C+-ness to which I had privileged access. If they wanted to know why I had assigned the grade I had, and how to get a better one, they could come and talk with me about that. Few did. And I came to take intellectual as well as teacherly pleasure in reading sets of papers.

22. Even so, I can hear the muse chiding: look at what you've left out—family, friends, health, sex, disaster, guilt, pleasure, everything *really* personal. True. By comparison with, say, Jane Gallop (whom I admire), I'm a timid hand at this.

23. Richard E. Miller, "The Nervous System," *College English,* 58.3 (March 1996): 280.

24. For a lexicon inflected this way, see, e.g., Diane P. Freedman, Olivia Frey, and Frances Murphy Zauhar, eds., *The Intimate Critique; Autobiographical Literary Criticism* (Durham, N.C.: Duke University Press, 1993), especially the introduction and the essays by Frey and Jane Tompkins. I agree with them but want to save some of what they object to, in both intellectual and political work.

25. Joan W. Scott, "The Evidence of Experience," *Critical Inquiry,* 17.4 (summer 1991): 777–78.

14 A CONVERSATION BETWEEN RICHARD OHMANN
AND JOHN TRIMBUR

1. Barbara Ehrenreich and John Ehrenreich, "The Professional-Managerial Class," in *Between Labor and Capital,* ed. Pat Walker (Boston: South End Press, 1979).

2. See essay 6, "Professionalizing Politics," for a more orderly answer to Trimbur's excellent questions.

3. The colleges were accused of sharing information about applicants and their scholarship needs; they agreed to abandon that practice.

4. Richard Bullock and John Trimbur, eds., *The Politics of Writing Instruction: Postsecondary* (Portsmouth, N.H.: Boynton/Cook, 1991).

5. Richard Ohmann, "The Shaping of a Canon: U.S. Fiction, 1960–1975," in my *Politics of Letters* (Middletown, Conn.: Wesleyan University Press, 1987).

6. Richard Ohmann, "On Teaching Mass Culture," in *Politics of Letters.*

7. Michael Denning, "The End of Mass Culture," in *Modernity and Mass Culture,* ed. James Naremore and Patrick Brantlinger (Bloomington: Indiana University Press, 1991).

15 ENGLISH IN AMERICA REVISITED

1. *English in America: A Radical View of the Profession* (New York: Oxford University Press, 1976; reprint, with new introduction, Wesleyan University Press, 1996).

2. Soon after this interview I did read the whole book again, to write a retrospective on it for a reissue by Wesleyan University Press, 1996.

3. James F. Slevin, "Depoliticizing and Politicizing Composition Studies," in *The Politics of Writing Instruction,* ed. Richard Bullock and John Trimbur (Portsmouth, N.H.: Boynton/Cook, 1991).

4. Maybe it still is beyond my grasp in 2002, but see my effort to grasp it in chapter 7.

5. It came out in 1996: *Selling Culture: Magazines, Markets, and Class at the Turn of the Century* (London: Verso).

PERMISSIONS

"English and the Cold War" first appeared in Noam Chomsky et al., *The Cold War and the University: Toward an Intellectual History of the Postwar Years* (New York: New Press); © 1997 by New Press; reprinted by permission of The New Press.

"English after the USSR" first appeared in *Radical Teacher* 44 (1993), and was reprinted in *After Political Correctness*, ed. Christopher Newfield and Ronald Strickland (Boulder, Colo.: Westview Press, 1995). Reprinted here by permission of the Center for Critical Education.

"Some Changes, across Thirty-Five Years" first appeared as "What Happened?" in *Radical Teacher* 53 (1998); reprinted by permission of the Center for Critical Education.

"Teaching Historically" first appeared in *Pedagogy Is Politics: Literary Theory and Critical Teaching*, ed. Maria-Regina Kecht (Urbana: University of Illinois Press, 1992); reprinted by permission of the University of Illinois Press.

"Graduate Students, Professionals, Intellectuals" first appeared in *College English* 52.3 (March 1990) and was reprinted in *Cross-Talk in Comp Theory*, ed. Victor Villanueva Jr. (Urbana, Ill.: NCTE, 1997). Copyright 1990 by the National Council of Teachers of English. Reprinted with permission.

"Politics and Commitment in Writing Instruction" first appearerd as "Professionalizing Politics," in *History, Reflection, and Narrative: The Professionalization of Composition*, ed. Mary Rosner, Beth Boehm, and Debra Journet (Stamford, Conn.: Ablex, 1999); reprinted by permission of Ablex Publishing Corporation.

"Teaching Literacy for Citizenship" first appeared as "Citizenship and Literacy Work: Thoughts without a Conclusion," in an issue of the online journal *Workplace* 4.1 (June 2001) on composition as management science. It is forthcoming in *Composition as Management Science: Literacy Work in the Managed University*, ed. Marc Bousquet, Leo Parascondola, and Anthony Scott (Carbondale: Southern Illinois Press, 2003).

"Historical Reflections on Accountability" first appeared in *Radical Teacher* 57 (fall 1999) and, simultaneously, in a condensed version, in *Academe* (January–February 2000). The present version, further expanded, and titled "Accountability and the Conditions for Curricular Change," appeared in *Beyond English Inc.: Curricular Reform in a Global Economy*, ed. David B. Downing, Claude Mark Hurlbert, and Paula Mathier

(Portsmouth, N.H.: Boynton/Cook, 2002). Reprinted here by permission of the Center for Critical Education.

"Academic Freedom, 2000 and After" first appeared in *Radical Teacher* 62 (winter 2001–2002) and is reprinted by permission of the Center for Critical Education.

"Book and Magazine Publishing through the Period of Corporate Revolution" is forthcoming (as "Books and Magazines") in *A History of the Book in America*, vol. 4: *Print in Motion: The Expansion of Publishing and Reading in the United States, 1880-1945*, ed. Carl F. Kaestle and Janice Radway. It is reprinted here with the permission of Cambridge University Press.

"Epochal Change: Print Culture and Economics" was the eighteenth annual James Russell Wiggins Lecture at the American Antiquarian Society. It first appeared as vol. 110, pt. 2 of the *Proceedings of the American Antiquarian Society* (October 2000). Reprinted courtesy of the American Antiquarian Society.

"The Personal As History" first appeared in *Personal Effects: The Social Character of Scholarly Writing*, ed. Deborah H. Holdstein and David Bleich (Logan: Utah State University Press, 2001). Reprinted by permission of Utah State University Press.

"A Conversation between Richard Ohmann and John Trimbur" first appeared in *PRE/TEXT* (spring/summer 1992). Reprinted by permission of Victor Vitanza.

"English in America Revisited: Richard Ohmann Talks with Jeffrey Williams" first appeared in *minnesota review* 45–46 (1995–1996).

Most of these texts have been slightly edited for their appearance in this book.

INDEX

ABOUT THE AUTHOR

Richard Ohmann taught English at
Wesleyan University for thirty-five years.
From 1989 to 1995 he directed the
Center for the Humanities there.
He edited *College English* from 1966 to 1978
and has been on the board of
Radical Teacher since its founding
in 1975.